LC21

A DIGITAL STRATEGY FOR THE
LIBRARY OF CONGRESS

Committee on an Information Technology Strategy
for the Library of Congress

Computer Science and Telecommunications Board

Commission on Physical Sciences, Mathematics, and Applications

National Research Council

NATIONAL ACADEMY PRESS
Washington, D.C.

NOTICE: The project that is the subject of this report was approved by the Govern-ing Board of the National Research Council, whose members are drawn from the councils of the National Academy of Sciences, the National Academy of Engineer-ing, and the Institute of Medicine. The members of the committee responsible for the report were chosen for their special competences and with regard for appro-priate balance.

Support for this project was provided by the Library of Congress under contract No. C-LC98046. Any opinions, findings, conclusions, or recommendations ex-pressed in this material are those of the authors and do not necessarily reflect the views of the sponsor.

Library of Congress Card Number 00-111489
International Standard Book Number 0-309-07144-5

Additional copies of this report are available from:

National Academy Press
2101 Constitution Ave., NW
Box 285
Washington, DC 20055
800-624-6242
202-334-3313 (in the Washington metropolitan area)
http://www.nap.edu

THE NATIONAL ACADEMIES

National Academy of Sciences
National Academy of Engineering
Institute of Medicine
National Research Council

The **National Academy of Sciences** is a private, nonprofit, self-perpetuating society of distinguished scholars engaged in scientific and engineering research, dedicated to the furtherance of science and technology and to their use for the general welfare. Upon the authority of the charter granted to it by the Congress in 1863, the Academy has a mandate that requires it to advise the federal government on scientific and technical matters. Dr. Bruce M. Alberts is president of the National Academy of Sciences.

The **National Academy of Engineering** was established in 1964, under the charter of the National Academy of Sciences, as a parallel organization of outstanding engineers. It is autonomous in its administration and in the selection of its members, sharing with the National Academy of Sciences the responsibility for advising the federal government. The National Academy of Engineering also sponsors engineering programs aimed at meeting national needs, encourages education and research, and recognizes the superior achievements of engineers. Dr. William A. Wulf is president of the National Academy of Engineering.

The **Institute of Medicine** was established in 1970 by the National Academy of Sciences to secure the services of eminent members of appropriate professions in the examination of policy matters pertaining to the health of the public. The Institute acts under the responsibility given to the National Academy of Sciences by its congressional charter to be an adviser to the federal government and, upon its own initiative, to identify issues of medical care, research, and education. Dr. Kenneth I. Shine is president of the Institute of Medicine.

The **National Research Council** was organized by the National Academy of Sciences in 1916 to associate the broad community of science and technology with the Academy's purposes of furthering knowledge and advising the federal government. Functioning in accordance with general policies determined by the Academy, the Council has become the principal operating agency of both the National Academy of Sciences and the National Academy of Engineering in providing services to the government, the public, and the scientific and engineering communities. The Council is administered jointly by both Academies and the Institute of Medicine. Dr. Bruce M. Alberts and Dr. William A. Wulf are chairman and vice chairman, respectively, of the National Research Council.

COMMITTEE ON AN INFORMATION TECHNOLOGY STRATEGY FOR THE LIBRARY OF CONGRESS

JAMES J. O'DONNELL, University of Pennsylvania, *Chair*
JAMES BLACKABY, Mystic Seaport Museum
ROSS E. BROWN, Analog Devices, Inc.
GINNIE COOPER, Multnomah County Library
DALE FLECKER, Harvard University
NANCY FRISHBERG, New Media Centers
JAMES GRAY, Microsoft Corporation
MARGARET HEDSTROM, University of Michigan
CARL LAGOZE, Cornell University
LAWRENCE H. LANDWEBER, University of Wisconsin, Madison
DAVID M. LEVY, University of Washington
ANN OKERSON, Yale University
DOUG ROWAN, interLane Media
JEROME H. SALTZER, Massachusetts Institute of Technology
HOWARD TURTLE, Cogitech Group
MARY ELLEN ZURKO, Iris Associates

Staff

ALAN S. INOUYE, Study Director and Senior Program Officer
SUZANNE OSSA, Senior Project Assistant
DAVID PADGHAM, Research Assistant

vii

PREFACE

The Library of Congress (LC) is a living and vital library and at the same time an icon. It is easier to be a library than to be an icon, but it is no easy thing to be a library amid the turmoil of the digital revolution. As icon, LC has functioned at least since 1945 as the benchmark for what capabilities new information technology might bring to the communication of information. Every technology is spoken of as one that can store or transmit or search "the entire Library of Congress" in square inches of disk space or minutes or seconds of processing time. Though even LC falls far short of containing every book ever written, its record of extraordinary comprehensiveness and reach has captured the popular imagination as has no other library since ancient Alexandria's.

Inevitably, reality falls short of what the icon seems to promise. The Library of Congress is a relatively small federal government agency of about 4,000 employees, with all the challenges of focus and service quality that impose themselves upon an organization that depends on taxpayer funding and civil service policies and procedures. The physical management of a collection of objects of almost limitless variety, size, shape, material, and fragility—objects that are repeatedly sought out, used, abused, disarranged, and rearranged—has always taxed human ability to index, tag, and control.

This report arises from the Library's own sense of its vulnerability and uncertainty at the dawn of the information age and attempts to respond closely to the institution's own sense of its mission. Accordingly, the Librarian of Congress asked the Computer Science and Telecommuni-

---

BOX P.1
Statement of Task

• Identify strategic directions for the application of information technology within the Library of Congress into the next decade.
• Assess the structure and system needs for LC to pursue its stated missions, including the adequacy of plans for modernizing and integrating those systems and the institutional and management structure for implementing the modernization.
• Examine systems and structures across the main components of LC and for its major programs.
• Identify opportunities for interaction between LC and other digital library initiatives, for the integration of electronic collections with existing analog materials, and for the preservation of library collections using digital technologies.

---

cations Board (CSTB) of the National Research Council (NRC) to conduct a study to provide strategic advice concerning the information technology path that LC should traverse over the coming decade. The statement of task is given in Box P.1.[1]

COMMITTEE COMPOSITION AND PROCESS

The study committee convened by CSTB included experts in digital libraries, databases, networks, computer security, metadata and information retrieval, digital documents and collections, digital archiving and preservation, academic and public libraries, museums, electronic publishing, information technology management, and human resources (see Appendix A for biographies of committee members). The committee did its work through its own expert deliberations and by soliciting input from a number of experts (see Appendix B for a list of briefers to the committee and Appendix C for a list of letters received). The committee met first in February 1999 and four times subsequently in plenary session and obtained extensive input when subcommittees visited the Library and other

---

[1]*LC21: A Digital Strategy for the Library of Congress* builds on a number of CSTB reports. The issues of digital copyright and public access to digital information addressed in *The Digital Dilemma: Intellectual Property in the Information Age* (Washington, D.C.: National Academy Press, 2000) are, not surprisingly, central to this report. Previous CSTB work in reviewing systems modernization at other federal agencies also informs the committee's work: see *Elements of Systems Modernization for the Social Security Administration* (Washington, D.C.: National Academy Press, 1991) and *Continued Review of the Tax Systems Modernization of the Internal Revenue Service: Final Report* (National Academy Press, 1996).

sites between March 1999 and May 2000. The typical LC site visit involved several members of the committee, the study director, and staff members of the Library. Library staff were informed that their remarks would be held in confidence. Additional information came from reviewing the published literature, monitoring selected listservs, and obtaining informal input from members of the library community and the information industries. During the editorial phase of the study, facts were checked for accuracy with either authoritative published sources or subject experts.

The observer affects the system observed. One cannot study an organization for more than a year and expect to have absolutely no impact on it during that time. Because the committee was asking for testimony from particular people or was asking certain questions, some of the issues of concern to it became apparent to LC staff. The committee has a strong sense that the internal conversation in LC over the months of its study has already benefited as a result of the issues and concerns the committee has raised. Thus, in addition to this final report, another outcome (in the committee's view, a desirable one) seems to have been to encourage LC staff to think about the opportunities and challenges presented by the digital revolution.

The committee focused its efforts on the present and future of information systems and technologies that are intimately tied to the mission of the Library—namely, to the acquisition, processing, management, storage, and preservation of library materials and to making those materials available to users. The Library, like other organizations, has information systems that support the administrative aspects of the organization, such as accounting, financial planning and budgeting, and human resources management; for want of time, the committee did not study those information systems in any detail.

The committee did not construe its charge as calling for an information technology report of the sort that any reputable consulting firm could provide. Rather, the committee accepted the Library's encouragement to pool its own wide-ranging expertise in considering how information technology could affect the Library's mission and core processes during the new decade. The strategic perspective taken looks first at how information technology could transform the acquisition, collection, preservation, and accessibility of digital materials and then addresses questions relating to information technology infrastructure.

Although the report refers to a number of companies, products, and services by name, such reference does not constitute an endorsement by the committee or the National Academies. The committee did not evaluate any product or service in sufficient detail to allow such an endorsement.

ACKNOWLEDGMENTS

The committee would like to acknowledge James Billington for his leadership in requesting this study; it takes no small amount of courage to voluntarily invite a panel of national experts to examine closely one's organization. We appreciate his guidance and support as well as that of Donald Scott and Jo Ann Jenkins. The day-to-day support for this study rested with Virginia Sorkin, who worked diligently to ensure that the committee had the access it needed to documents and LC staff; Ms. Sorkin's efforts played an important role in supporting the timely completion of this report. Many other LC staff members provided invaluable assistance to the committee through their testimony—whether in public plenary session or in private small meetings (see Appendix B for a list of all LC staff who made presentations to the committee).

Throughout the course of this study, a number of individuals not connected with the Library also contributed their expertise to the committee's deliberations. The committee is grateful to those who agreed to provide testimony at its plenary meetings and site visits (see, again, Appendix B).

The committee appreciates the thoughtful comments received from the reviewers of this report and the efforts of the NRC review coordinator. The comments were instrumental in helping the committee to sharpen and improve this report.

Finally, the committee would like to acknowledge the staff of the National Research Council for their work. Alan Inouye served as study director with overall staff responsibility for the conduct of the study and the development of this final report. Without his breadth of understanding, keen sense for the salient detail, and highly effective management, this report would have been either a far poorer one or entirely nonexistent. He was assisted first by David Padgham and later by Suzanne Ossa. The committee would like to acknowledge the important role played by William Wulf, Jane Bortnick Griffith, and Marjory Blumenthal in launching this study. Jane Bortnick Griffith also provided invaluable advice to the committee throughout the study. The committee acknowledges the important contribution of NRC editors Liz Fikre and Susan Maurizi. Editorial and research assistance was provided by consultants Laura Ost and Kim Briggs and NRC librarian Jim Igoe. The committee thanks Charles Starliper and David Padgham for providing comments on report drafts. Janet Briscoe and D.C. Drake of the CSTB and Claudette Baylor-Fleming, Theresa Fisher, and Sharon Seaward of the NRC's Space Studies Board also contributed to the preparation of the final report.

James J. O'Donnell, *Chair*
Committee on an Information Technology
Strategy for the Library of Congress

ACKNOWLEDGMENT OF REVIEWERS

This report has been reviewed in draft form by individuals chosen for their diverse perspectives and technical expertise, in accordance with procedures approved by the NRC's Report Review Committee. The purpose of this independent review is to provide candid and critical comments that will assist the institution in making its published report as sound as possible and to ensure that the report meets institutional standards for objectivity, evidence, and responsiveness to the study charge. The review comments and draft manuscript remain confidential to protect the integrity of the deliberative process. We wish to thank the following individuals for their review of this report:

Christine L. Borgman, University of California, Los Angeles,
Stephen D. Crocker, Steve Crocker Associates,
Alan J. Demers, Cornell University,
David Ely, NXT Corporation,
Edward A. Fox, Virginia Polytechnic Institute and State University,
Laura N. Gasaway, University of North Carolina, Chapel Hill,
John P. Glaser, Partners Health Care System,
Morton D. Goldberg, Cowen, Liebowitz & Latman, P.C.,
Betsy Humphreys, National Library of Medicine,
Karen Hunter, Elsevier Science, Inc.,
Carole Huxley, New York State Education Department,
Brewster Kahle, Internet Archive,
Clifford Lynch, Coalition for Networked Information,

Deanna Marcum, Council on Library and Information Resources,
Charles McClure, Florida State University,
Jerry Mechling, Harvard University,
Candace Morgan, Fort Vancouver Regional Library,
Richard Nolan, Harvard University,
Jan Pedersen, Opengrid Corporation,
Kent A. Smith, National Library of Medicine,
Sarah E. Thomas, Cornell University,
Robert Wedgeworth, University of Illinois at Urbana-Champaign, and
Grayson Winterling, Rooney Group International.

Although the reviewers listed above have provided many constructive comments and suggestions, they were not asked to endorse the conclusions or recommendations nor did they see the final draft of the report before its release. The review of this report was overseen by Roy Schwitters, University of Texas, Austin, appointed by the Commission on Physical Sciences, Mathematics, and Applications, who was responsible for making certain that an independent examination of this report was carried out in accordance with institutional procedures and that all review comments were carefully considered. Responsibility for the final content of this report rests entirely with the authoring committee and the institution.

CONTENTS

Executive Summary

OVERVIEW

No stereotype of libraries as quiet, uneventful places could survive the 1990s. Whatever stability and predictability libraries once had as ordered storehouses of the treasures of the printed word were shattered by the digital revolution. The intellectual function of libraries—to acquire, arrange, and make accessible the creative work of humankind—is being transformed by the explosion in the production and dissemination of information in digital form, especially over global networks.

The transformation in principle awaits realization in fact. Libraries in the last decade have begun to sweep in mountains of new forms of information and have been remarkably innovative in presenting and linking it with their existing collections. But no clear new paradigm has emerged, even as the old one is shaken. Will the distinctive features of the Western library survive? Will preserved information continue to be widely and freely available in public libraries? Will the great research libraries continue to be the point of entry to the information universe for their select bands of users? Will the integration of digital with print information succeed, or will print suffer a damaging loss of prestige in the general rush to exploit the possibilities of the Internet? Will new integrators and organizers of knowledge emerge, perhaps from the commercial sector, bypassing libraries and finding ways that succeed in putting information directly in users' hands? No individual or committee knows the answers to those questions, but librarians must guide their institutions with an

1

acute awareness that the questions will be answered decisively—perhaps within a very few years.

The Library of Congress has totemic value as the largest and most prestigious library collection in the world. Its nature and location mean that it is perhaps used less (considering the size of its collections) than many smaller libraries, but the value of the use to which it is put is very high. Unique materials from all over the world are found there. The size and scope of the collection make it an invaluable laboratory for scholarly researchers. Equally important, the value of the collection means that its preservation is a task of national and global urgency.

But the central mission of the Library remains to serve the Congress that gives it a name and a budget. That mission sets up one tension that the Library has learned to manage. The possibility of extending access to its materials more easily than ever to individuals who do not wish to travel to Capitol Hill sets up another. Should the Library focus more attention on a broader American public? Does it have a role to play in direct library service to K-12 schools? Can and should it make the materials in its collection easily accessible to individual readers of all ages at home or in the office?

The Committee on an Information Technology Strategy for the Library of Congress was convened by the Computer Science and Telecommunications Board (CSTB), which had been invited by the Library in 1998 to review the status of information technology planning and implementation in the Library with a view to helping it handle tensions like those just mentioned and helping it fulfill its missions. The committee's task was emphatically not to prescribe a mission for the Library—that is for Congress and the Library itself to do. But the committee has ranged widely through the Library and its services and facilities in a fascinating voyage of exploration and interpretation. This report offers the Library support and guidance, along with some strong cautions, at this pivotal time.

The committee is firm in its belief that the Library continues to play a vital role in documenting and preserving the history of American creativity and in building a collection with truly worldwide scope. But the Library cannot go on as before.

The committee fears greatly that the Library's function as a creature of Congress, within the federal bureaucracy, will make it unable to respond in a timely and effective way to the challenges that it faces. It sees signs that the Library is already losing the momentum and purchase required to make the next steep ascent. It is not so much that the Library is objectively behind other libraries in what it has done (although it is far from a leader in most areas) but that it is not thinking far enough ahead to enable it to act strategically and coherently.

At the heart of its recommendations is the committee's strong awareness of the role of digital information at the center of contemporary discourse. That role is a simple fact, unrelated to whatever e-zealots or bibliophiles might wish to be the case. For some important areas of human knowledge, the best new knowledge can be acquired exclusively in digital form. In other areas, digital presentation lags significantly—for the moment. For example, since the committee began its work in January 1999, the movement toward "books on demand" (that is, books stored in digital form and made available either digitally or on paper in single or a few copies, as required) has gathered surprising momentum. The broader cultural movement cannot be gainsaid.

The Library of Congress (LC), as recipient of mandatory deposit copies of works published in the United States, lags significantly in receiving and archiving the born-digital product of the nation. The several processes of copyright registration, deposit receipt, selection for the Library's collection, and entry into the Library collection remain focused on physical artifacts. The committee believes and recommends strongly that to create a truly functional contemporary Library, those processes should be adapted to accommodate both physical and digital artifacts. This means building a process that captures every form of the richness of human creativity—bound books on acid-free paper, ephemeral newspapers and journals, film and tape archives of the mass media of the twentieth century, newer forms of multimedia digital presentations on CD-ROM, and the multitudinous pages of the World Wide Web. The resultant process should capture the digital artifact, register and/or deposit it for the Copyright Office, pass it along to those who decide whether to include it in the Library, and allow it to be incorporated digitally in the collection, with the optimum flow-through of information for registration, cataloging, indexing, and preservation. Such a process would revolutionize access to information and the efficiency of its acquisition and preservation.

Can LC handle such tasks? The committee has reason for concern. This report details its concerns with the management and human resources processes (many of them imposed on the Library from outside) that make it respond slowly to challenge and change. The committee does not see, moreover, that the Library leadership has internalized and expressed a strategic vision or found the tools with which to implement any such vision well enough or fast enough.

The committee has praise for many of the Library's initiatives. For example, the National Digital Library Program has been a dramatic example of what can be done when there is innovative management and a clear goal. What the Library now needs to do is learn from that project and broaden and deepen its strategic awareness of how that project can help lead to the next generation of substantially more ambitious involvement with digital information.

The committee worries as well that the Library is not sufficiently involved in the wider international community of research and practice surrounding contemporary librarianship. It strongly urges that the Library be more open-minded and community-minded than it has been in the recent past. Involvement with that burgeoning and exciting body of thought and practice would have a powerful and transformational effect on the Library and its ability to perform its mission for future generations.

It is indicative of the Library's struggles in shifting to new forms of information that its technology infrastructure lags behind not only that of the commercial world but also that of ambitious, not-for-profit research libraries. The committee includes in this report specific recommendations for enhancing that infrastructure, particularly in the area of networks, databases, and information technology security.

The report ranges more widely than this summary can suggest and includes detailed recommendations on some aspects of the technology itself. But the committee is convinced that the heart of what it has learned and the heart of the Library's future are in the areas touched on above: (1) inventing a new form for acquiring and preserving materials that include digital information in all its forms, in particular information that is born digital; (2) opening itself to broader and deeper dialogue with the world of information professionals beyond its walls; (3) finding the management vision and will to make paradigmatic change happen in the organization; and (4) investing in the technology infrastructure required to support such change.

The alternative to progress along these lines is simple: the Library of Congress could become a book museum. It could house a collection of priceless materials less and less frequently consulted and less and less central to the concerns of the nation. But a library is not a book museum. A library's value lies in its vitality, in the way its collections grow, and in the way that growth is rewarded by the diverse and innovative uses to which its collections are put. The Library of Congress will, by the choices it makes now and in the next months and years, determine how much of that vitality will survive into the new millennium and how well it can avoid subsiding into diminished relevance.

FINDINGS AND RECOMMENDATIONS

This report ranges over many subjects, from managing human resources and developing collaborative arrangements to designing a digital preservation program and implementing computer security technologies. The mandate to provide the Library of Congress with both general direction and specific advice has led the committee to numerous findings and recommendations. This Executive Summary provides an outline of the report's conclusions and collects the findings and recommendations in one place. In doing so, however, it sacrifices an essential element—the richly textured context that is needed for full understanding. To read only this summary would gravely risk preferring tactics to strategy and quick fixes to hard institutional work.

Building Digital Collections

Collections and Access

While the Library of Congress and virtually all other libraries have well-developed policy statements to guide their acquisition of physical artifacts, analogous policy statements need to be fashioned for the digital content. No one institution, not even the Library of Congress, can hope to collect all or even a majority of all digital content. Thus, cooperative arrangements for distributed collections are not merely an option to consider but are essential for LC's future and need to be pursued more aggressively.

> **Recommendation: The Library should explicitly define the sets of digital resources for which it will assume long-term curatorial responsibility.**

> **Recommendation: For digital resources for which the Library does not assume long-term curatorial responsibility, the Library should work with other institutions to define appropriate levels of responsibility for preservation and access. Some materials that the Library acquires and makes available to its users may have only temporary value; other materials may be hosted on a Library site for more efficient access, with long-term archiving responsibilities accepted by another party.**

> **Recommendation: The Library should selectively adopt the portal model[1] for targeted program areas. By creating links from the Library's Web site, this approach would make available the ever-increasing body of research materials distributed across the Internet. The Library would be responsible for carefully selecting and arranging for access to licensed commercial resources for its users, but it would not house local copies of materials or assume responsibility for long-term preservation.**

---

[1]Portals serve as gateways to information. On the Web, Yahoo is an example of a portal.

Copyright Deposit

The Library is in a unique position to demand the deposit of many digital materials. The Library should put in place mechanisms to systematically address the infrastructure required for it to "collect" digital materials.

> **Finding:** The Library urgently requires a production-quality system for receiving and managing digital objects deposited with it and registered for copyright. Such a system will enable the Library to enforce the deposit requirement for born-digital materials.

> **Finding:** The new production system needs to integrate well with other Library systems; the new system should at the same time make it easier for providers of information to register and deposit their works.

> **Recommendation:** The Copyright Office should complete the statement of work for a production system in FY01, as planned, and as soon as possible (e.g., by the end of calendar year 2000). To achieve this goal, the resources and attention of Library-wide senior management should be directed to the Copyright Office, perhaps on a scale and with visibility comparable to those of the Integrated Library System implementation. The committee urges the Congress to support and fund the acquisition of a production system for receiving and managing digital objects.

> **Finding:** The Library's mechanisms and policies for the deposit of digital works currently favor printouts or tangible forms (such as CD-ROMs) over digital editions of digital works. This strategy is shortsighted because an increasing amount of born-digital information cannot be represented in tangible form and is much less useful if reduced to print or analog form. Tangible physical objects also require extensive physical handling for registration, cataloging, shelving, retrieval, and use.

> **Recommendation:** The Library should set new standards for the appropriate formats for digital materials acquired through copyright deposit, purchase, exchange, and donation and should review those standards annually. The concept of "best edition" must be revisited to remove the present bias in favor of

paper editions. Each class of materials should be considered separately, depending on its specific physical and digital properties, for current access and preservation purposes.[2] The complexity of these issues will increase as the digital environment evolves. Accordingly, the Library must have an ongoing capacity to monitor these issues closely and systematically and have sophisticated staff involved in the deliberations.

Licensed Resources

Copyright deposit is not the only means by which the Library can acquire digital materials for its collections. However, publishers may be reluctant to provide the Library with digital content without a specific agreement on how that content may be accessed. One experiment under way at the Library concerns the dissertations managed by ProQuest, whereby access is provided to users in LC buildings.

Recommendation: The ProQuest agreement serves as an interesting experiment in how the Library might handle digital collections. In such arrangements, the Library must pay particular attention to its legal rights and responsibilities in the event of default. It must establish and regularly test its capacity to accept and make available such collections, if it should be called on to do so.[3]

Recommendation: The committee believes that the Library is in a unique position to demand the deposit of some digital materials and to require agreements for shared custody or fail-safe preservation should the materials become unavailable; it should do so.

---

[2]See the discussion in Chapter 1 on the recent and dramatic rise of e-books. Consideration will have to be given in the very near future to the question of when the best edition of a popular new novel is the digital file from which both paper and electronic copies are derived.

[3]The committee has one worry about using the ProQuest agreement as a model, however. The Library chose in this case to deal with a commercial service provider to find ways to handle its "content." But there is no sign that LC recognized in undertaking the project that the academic community has a substantial interest in the way dissertations are managed. The committee urges that future arrangements take into account content as well as form and that LC seek to include stakeholders broadly in designing future arrangements for specific classes of information.

The World Wide Web

The Library should begin work immediately to define appropriate collecting policies for U.S. Web sites.

> **Recommendation:** The Library should aggressively pursue clarification of its right to collect copies of U.S.-based Web sites under the copyright deposit law. If questions about this right remain, then LC should seek legislation that changes the copyright law to ensure that it has this right. This right would not necessarily include the right for LC to provide unlimited access to the Web sites collected.

> **Recommendation:** The Library should conduct additional pilot projects to gain experience in harvesting and archiving U.S.-based Web sites. Such projects should be carried out in partnership with experts or organizations that have the requisite expertise.

> **Recommendation:** The Library should quickly translate the experience gained from pilot projects into appropriate collecting policies related to U.S. Web sites.

Infrastructure

To acquire, organize, serve, and preserve digital collections having the same breadth, depth, and value as its physical collections, the Library of Congress needs to develop systems, policies, procedures, and skilled staff equivalent to those in place for its physical collections.

> **Recommendation:** The Library should put in place mechanisms that systematically address the policies, procedures, and infrastructure required for it to collect diverse types of digital resources and to integrate them into its systems for description and cataloging, access, and preservation.

> **Recommendation:** Throughout the Library and particularly in Library Services, the acquisition and management of digital collections will require that the professional librarians have high levels of technological awareness and ability. The Library needs to undertake job redesign, training, and reorganization to achieve this goal.

Preserving a Digital Heritage

Digital Preservation as a Global Concern

Digital preservation raises issues that cannot be addressed fully within the walls of any one institution. The scale and scope of digital preservation demand cooperation among libraries and other information organizations. Engagement with electronic publishers and the research and development community is needed because many of the legal, economic, and technical issues surrounding digital preservation are unresolved. The involvement of the Congress will also be needed if the copyright law has to change to enable digital preservation.

Finding: Because of intellectual property law and the uncertainty of some publishers regarding the deposit of copies of digital works, institutions with long-term preservation responsibilities must seek and develop new means of ensuring continuing access to the valuable documentation of history, culture, and creativity. One possible approach is contractual agreements with rights holders who maintain digital information in off-site repositories, with provisions for deposit in a library or other institution should the publisher cease to maintain the information. Some publishers have agreed to provide perpetual access to their materials as one of the conditions of a license. The Library has initiated an experiment in reaching such an agreement with ProQuest. The committee believes that such arrangements need to be tested carefully and that other models need to be explored as well.

Recommendation: The Library should establish contractual arrangements (i.e., projects) in 2000 and 2001 with a pilot set of publishers and distributors of significant digital content, in order to conduct additional experimental programs for storing and maintaining digital information in off-site and on-site respositories.

Recommendation: For all fail-safe arrangements, the Library must regularly test the integrity of the materials and systems and its capacity to accept responsibility in a timely way. Such tests will demonstrate whether LC has the appropriate technical capability and whether the arrangements with publishers are realistic ones.

Finding: Many national libraries, university research libraries, national archives, bibliographic utilities, and organizations with large holdings of digital information are actively pursuing solutions to the problems of digital preservation. Although the Library of Congress might have been expected to provide leadership in this area as it once did in others, LC has at best played only a minimal role in these initiatives. As a consequence, it has little awareness of potential solutions that are emerging from joint research and development projects and has not contributed much to this important national and international problem for the library community.

Recommendation: Ensuring its leadership in digital preservation will require the Library to hire or develop relevant expertise. The Library should join and, where possible, lead or facilitate national and international research and development efforts in digital preservation. There are opportunities for the Library to learn from and contribute to such efforts in preserving born-digital information and converting certain types of information to digital form as a preservation strategy.

Recommendation: To make it a safe haven for preservation purposes, the Library should take an active role—including working with the Congress if necessary—in efforts to rework intellectual property restraints on copying and migration.

Actions by the Library of Congress

For many years, the Library has been a leader in the preservation of physical artifacts. By contrast, there has been little emphasis on digital preservation. Policies and practices for digital preservation need to be developed to accommodate the expected immense growth of digital materials in the Library's collections. Preservation issues need to be addressed in a coordinated way—that is, the copyright deposit of digital content, building of digital collections, design of the digital repository, and development of digital preservation capabilities need to be considered holistically.

Finding: The Library of Congress lacks an overarching strategy and long-range plan for digital preservation. (In recent years, it has also been without a permanent head for its Preservation Directorate.) Although the Library has preserved many of its own digital resources, including the full-text databases of the

THOMAS system, its own bibliographic databases, and the content, descriptive information, and retrieval capabilities of the National Digital Library Program, these efforts are not coordinated with each other or with efforts to address the larger problem of capturing and preserving born-digital content, nor is there any strategy, plan, or infrastructure to capture, manage, and preserve born-digital information that originates outside the Library.

Recommendation: The Library should immediately form a high-level planning group to coordinate digital preservation efforts and develop the policies, technical capacity, and expertise to preserve digital information. The hiring of someone who is knowledgeable about digital preservation as a new head of the Preservation Directorate must be given high priority.

Recommendation: The Library should put a digital preservation plan in place and implement it as soon as possible, taking into account life-cycle costs and minimizing the need for manual intervention. The Open Archival Information System (OAIS) reference model provides a useful framework for identifying the requirements for a digital archiving system. The initiative by the Council on Library and Information Resources that builds on the OAIS should also be consulted.

Organizing Intellectual Access to Digital Information: From Cataloging to Metadata

The Library of Congress has historically played and continues to play an essential role in coordinating the cataloging standards that have made cooperative cataloging possible. This coordination should continue, and LC should examine how its role could be extended and transformed in the Internet context. The past strategy of coordinating efforts primarily within the library community is no longer sufficient because now important new stakeholders such as Web search companies and online publishers are involved.

Finding: The Library of Congress is heavily involved in the creation and use of metadata and has long been a leader in the establishment of standards and practices. However, the metadata environment is evolving rapidly. This will have profound implications for libraries and other information providers generally and for the Library of Congress in particular. It is a responsibility of the Library, and indeed of the nation, to offer leadership here for the benefit of the national and worldwide communities of information providers and users.

Recommendation: The Library should treat the development of a richer but more complex metadata environment as a strategic issue, increasing dramatically its level of involvement and planning in this area, and it should be much more actively involved with the library and information community in advancing the evolution of metadata practices. This effort will require the dedication of resources, direct involvement by the Librarian in setting and adjusting expectations, and the strong commitment of a project leader assigned from the Executive Committee of the Library.

Recommendation: The Library should actively encourage and participate in efforts to develop tools for automatically creating metadata. These tools should be integrated in the cataloging work flow.

The Library of Congress and the World Beyond Its Walls

The Library of Congress as Convenor, Coordinator, Partner, Collaborator, and Leader

The committee observes that the Library of Congress has become increasingly insular during the past 10 years or so. At the same time, the library field has been changing radically, often impinging in areas that were not historically considered to be within its domain (just as other fields are impinging on library matters). Revolutionary changes in industries such as publishing, entertainment, and software and technological developments at universities and in government mean that outreach and engagement beyond Capitol Hill, at home and abroad, are more important than ever. The trend to insularity at LC must be halted and reversed immediately.

Finding: The current transition to digital content calls for extraordinary, unprecedented collaboration and coordination. In most aspects of its work, however, the Library of Congress functions too much in isolation from its clients and peers.

Recommendation: Each major unit of the Library should create an advisory council comprising members from the library, user, and service provider communities, including the private sector. The council for library services, for example, should include scholars, general readers, research librarians, public librarians, computer service providers, and publishers. Other units would benefit as well from consultation in this form. Different units of the Library will naturally lend themselves to different configurations of advisory council. Even the Congressional Research Service, which has the closest relationship with a defined community, would benefit from such an arrangement.

Finding: The Library has been too little visible on the national and international stages, particularly in the digital arena.

Recommendation: The Library needs to be more proactive in bringing together stakeholders as partners in digital publishing and digital library research and development (such as the Digital Libraries Initiative). Box 6.1 in Chapter 6 articulates some specific areas in which LC should take the initiative and/or play a leading role.

Recommendation: The Library of Congress needs to improve its relationships with the Online Computer Library Center and the Research Libraries Group to facilitate the collaborations that will need to take place. Regular executive meetings supplemented by ongoing staff contacts (e.g., a middle management working council) will be necessary to build cooperation.

Recommendation: The Library of Congress needs to develop a regular working relationship at the senior policy level with federal institutions such as the National Library of Medicine, the National Agricultural Library, the National Archives and Records Administration, and the Smithsonian Institution. Other federal agencies with related missions (such as the National Science Foundation and the Department of Education) might also be included.

Funding and Budgetary Issues

Many of the digital initiatives discussed in this report have additional direct costs, because they do not replace existing processes but instead add to the work of the Library. While the committee discussed possible sources for funding—including increases in the Library's congressional appropriation, gifts from industry or foundations, cost savings derived from reducing workload in certain areas of the Library, or revenue-producing initiatives—it does not make a specific recommendation regarding the source of funds, in part because it believes that such a recommendation is outside the scope of the study and in part because it lacks the expertise needed to make such a recommendation.

Finding: The Library of Congress is constrained in what it can do by its dependence on congressional funding as well as by other constraints on the ways in which its precious materials can be made better known and be more widely used by the world at large.

Recommendation: The Library of Congress should address the agendas that it is best positioned to address, especially those that are likely to be achieved with public funding. The committee points out two agendas in particular: (1) developing digital collections to address the needs of researchers and (2) facilitating progress on digital preservation and metadata.

Recommendation: Limitations on the Library's ability to generate revenue from its activities should be revisited and restrictions eased, where possible, in order to facilitate mutually beneficial relationships with outside entities. It is unlikely and undesirable that such activity would become a major source of funding—and the committee cannot emphasize too strongly that such revenues should never be taken as an excuse for limiting or reducing government funding for the core missions of the Library—but room must be made for experimentation and partnership.

Finding: Year-to-year operating funds and traditional capital funds will be inadequate sources of funding for new Library initiatives for the foreseeable future because the initiatives are not likely to result in significant cost savings and may well require increased funding—for instance, the National Digital Library Program adds costs and does not result in any savings, because the capabilities being developed are new and do not replace any existing processes.

Recommendation: Fund-raising successes with the National Digital Library Program and the Madison Council should be extended to give greater direct support for the Library's core strategy areas. Potential funders include traditional philanthropic givers, corporate partnerships, and newly established high-tech corporations (the "dot-coms") with an interest in the activities supported.

Management Issues

Recruitment

The Library shares with other federal government agencies the challenge of recruiting cutting-edge technical professionals, because it, too, has limited discretion with respect to compensation and hiring practices. There are also some Library-specific issues that compound the difficulties in hiring and promoting technical staff, namely, constraints stemming from the Cook case—a lawsuit that alleged discrimination in the Library's hiring and promotional practices.

> **Finding:** A nimble Library would be positioned to recruit the best and brightest and to keep up with changes in areas affecting its digital future (technology, library professionals).

> **Recommendation:** As Library employees retire, the automatic hiring of replacements with similar skills should be resisted. Retirements should instead be viewed as opportunities to hire staff with the qualifications in librarianship and technology needed to meet the digital challenge, and reengineering should be rewarded when senior management allocates staff positions to units.

> **Finding:** The National Digital Library Program has managed to attract an excellent and effective technical staff. The hiring of temporary "not to exceed" staff and contractors with special skills necessary for NDLP was accomplished rapidly.

> **Recommendation:** The idea of greater reliance on outsourcing and contract employees should be pursued. This initiative must be driven by senior LC management and led jointly by the Human Resources Services Directorate and the heads of the Library's major service units.

> **Recommendation:** Current staff of the National Digital Library Program should be aggressively recruited for retention and assimilation into the broader Library staff.

Professional Development and Organizational Learning

As a consequence of the digital revolution, the Library will need to change its core work processes in a fundamental way in the new decade. Commensurate changes in the capabilities of the staff and the structure of the institution will be needed. The Library must adopt policies and procedures that enable these changes.

Finding: **The long tenure of many LC employees means that new skills and ideas are less likely to come to the Library through new employees who bring them along from other employers or schools. Instead, innovation must be fostered by the development of existing staff. Thus, training for Library employees is even more important than for the employees of most private-sector organizations.**

Finding: **Employees of the Library who might be expected to want to develop their professional skills have few opportunities and receive little encouragement. As a result, they have little interest in or motivation for learning.**

Recommendation: **The Library needs to provide more training opportunities for staff. Professional development, outside technical training, and practice in using the training are all crucial. Congress should be asked to increase the Library's training budget by a significant amount. This increase should be more than an incremental one—it should be on the order of a doubling or tripling of this year's amount in the next budget submitted to the Congress (for FY02).**

Recommendation: **The Library must increase the number of junior- and senior-level staff involved in professional association activities. Such involvement can be a source of learning as well as of networking, which can lead to more effective recruitment. It must also increase its training and travel budget to encourage staffers to participate in and assume leadership roles within the Library and in the professional community.**

Finding: **Additional learning opportunities for LC staff could come through internships at other organizations and through linkages to professionals in every part of the Library. Opportunities for learning could also be created by rotating personnel out for temporary duty in congruent government agencies.**

Recommendation: Extending Library internships to both graduate and undergraduate students from professional schools and other academic institutions appears to have been successful and should be used more widely.

Recommendation: The Library of Congress leadership must encourage a culture of innovation and learning in the Library. Actively nurturing the development of staff to take on the next generation of responsibilities is a vital but neglected area of management in LC.

Recommendation: Teams of persons with unlike skills should be created, whereby those with more technical prowess are encouraged to help those with less. Such teams should be responsible for a real product or function and should have an identifiable audience or customer. The Whole-Book Pilot Program exemplifies an approach that should be adapted for other contexts.

Recommendation: A formal assessment and report of lessons learned from the Integrated Library System implementation should be prepared and completed by January 1, 2001, with an emphasis on findings that can guide future projects.

Recommendation: Human resources staff—both in the Human Resources Services Directorate and within the major service units—should become agents of change and business partners more rapidly than is foreseen in the HR21 plan.

Strategic Planning and Executive Management

The Library's ability to accomplish its fundamental mission is hampered by insufficient integration of strategic vision with an understanding of the nature, power, and impact of information technology. The question is not how to add or empower technical expertise, but how to suffuse the management and planning processes of the Library with a profound awareness of current and future technological developments.

Finding: Current decision making at the Library regarding information technology is neither transparent nor strategic. In particular, the lines distinguishing central responsibility from service unit responsibility are unclear.

Finding: Priority setting within the Information Technology Services Directorate is largely free from review by senior management.

Finding: The current level of attention to technical vision and strategy within the Library is not adequate, and the flow of information and ideas from the library community and the information technology sector at large into the Library needs to be enhanced.

Recommendation: The Library should establish an information technology vision, strategy, research, and planning (ITVSRP) group.

Recommendation: The Library should establish an external technical advisory board (TAB).

Recommendation: The Library should not appoint a chief information officer at this time.

Recommendation: The Library should create a limited number of visiting research positions in areas such as digital libraries and digital archiving and preservation.

Finding: The future of libraries and the future of information technology are inseparable.

Finding: The Planning, Management, and Evaluation Directorate might assist usefully with the process of strategic planning, but there remains a need for improved substantive input into the strategic planning process.

Finding: Before taking up their present appointments, the three senior-most members of Library-wide administration (the librarian, deputy librarian, and chief of staff) did not have particular expertise or experience in library administration or information technology.

Recommendation: The committee recommends appointment of a new deputy librarian (Strategic Initiatives) to supplement the strengths and capabilities of the three members of the Library-wide administration now in place.

Finding: Much of the workflow of the Library is manually based. There seems to be much opportunity for workflow automation. However, the approach should not be to use information technology to automate existing processes but rather to examine the processes themselves and rationalize them across unit boundaries before new information systems are designed and developed or acquired. The Whole-Book Cataloging Pilot Program of some years ago shows how such reengineering can be piloted in limited areas and then extended to a broader range of Library operations. The Copyright Office and the interface between it and Library Services is the first place that deserves attention.

Recommendation: The committee recommends that the Library publish, by January 1, 2001, its own review of this report and an outline of the agenda that the Library will pursue.

The Information Technology Infrastructure

Professional Development

As is true for the entire Library, the Information Technology Services (ITS) Directorate is underinvesting in professional development.

Finding: As the Library increasingly outsources its information technology tasks, it will continue to need a strong in-house information technology organization to perform some in-house development, training, support, and operations and to review and monitor these outside contracts as well as to provide technical feedback on proposed contracts.

Finding: The Library is underinvesting in the continuing education of its Information Technology Services Directorate staff in technical development and in new skills such as contract management.

Recommendation: The Library should budget much more of each technical staff member's time for continuing education and participation at professional conferences and should allocate more funds to cover travel and registration expenses.

Recommendation: A practice and a budget should be established to partner members of the Information Technology Services Directorate staff who are interested in exploring a particular new technology with staff in the service units or with outside institutions that are interested in working on a pilot project applicable to the Library's needs.

Managing the Information Technology Services Directorate

The ITS Directorate operates with relatively little accountability to the executive management of the Library and its major service units. The basic systems for oversight that are typical in a service organization need to be installed.

> **Finding:** The ITS Directorate lacks measurement and reporting systems and a cost-accounting system that would allow it and its clients to make trade-offs among implementation alternatives and to evaluate the quality of the ITS Directorate's service.

> **Recommendation:** Together, the Library's service organizations and its Information Technology Services Directorate should institute service-level agreements based on metrics of system availability, performance, and support requests. These metrics should be used to track ITS Directorate process improvements. Developing and implementing service-level agreements should be a high priority for the new deputy librarian (Strategic Initiatives) and the information technology vision, strategy, research, and planning group.

> **Recommendation:** Wherever possible, services provided by the Information Technology Services Directorate should be charged against the budgets of the client organization within the Library. This would allow comparing the costs and benefits of servicing from within the client organization, outsourcing to the ITS Directorate, or outsourcing outside the Library.

Hardware and Software

Many aspects of the technology at LC—computer and communications security, networks, and data storage—urgently need to be improved.

> **Finding:** E-mail is not yet universal in the Library.

Recommendation: Infrastructure should be deployed so that all Library employees have easy access to e-mail.

Finding: LC computer and information security competence and policies are seriously inadequate.

Recommendation: The Library should hire or contract with technical experts to examine the current situation and recommend a plan to secure LC information systems. Then, once a plan is in hand, the Library should implement it.

Finding: Although the Library has identified a disaster recovery strategy as a priority, Congress has decided not to fund the implementation of any such strategy.

Recommendation: Congress should provide the funding for a disaster recovery strategy and its implementation for the Library.

Finding: The Library's networking infrastructure needs urgent attention with respect to serving both current and future needs. The Library's current policy is to upgrade to fast Ethernet as needed, which is problematic (it is difficult to identify the need in an accurate and timely fashion). The ATM switch currently used as a backbone is poorly matched to the near-term needs of the Library. Network performance is measured on an ad hoc basis at best, so performance information is generally not available when it is really needed.

Recommendation: The Information Technology Services Directorate needs to upgrade all of the Library's local area networks to 100 megabit/second Ethernet on an as-soon-as-possible basis rather than on an as-needed basis. It also needs to replace the ATM switch with Ethernet switches of 1 gigabit or greater and institute continuous performance measurement of internal network usage and Internet access usage. The Congress should provide funding to support these upgrades.

Recommendation: The use of a network firewall as the sole means of segregating internal from external usage of LC systems needs to be augmented as soon as is feasible in favor of a "defense in depth" that incorporates defensive security on the individual computer systems of the Library.

Finding: The Library's storage pool goals of maintaining current, authoritative information very reliably and keeping track of older material are muddled. The current approach, which entails high-priced storage, makes it prohibitively expensive to put most of the Library online. The disaster recovery plan will nearly double the storage requirements.

Recommendation: The Library should establish disk-based storage for online data and for an online disaster recovery facility using low-cost commodity disks. The Library should also experiment with disk mirroring across a network to two or three distant sites that maintain replicas, for availability and reliability of archives, and use tapes exclusively to hold files that are rarely needed. Some of the resources being spent on installing a separate specialized storage area network for disk sharing should instead be spent on a general, high-performance network for those and other needs.

Finding: The implementation of a robust digital repository is needed to support the Library's major digital initiatives. The current rate of progress in implementing such a repository is not adequate.

Recommendation: The Library should place a higher priority on implementing an appropriate repository.

1

DIGITAL REVOLUTION, LIBRARY EVOLUTION

INTRODUCTION

Every reader of this report knows that the world of information is changing rapidly. Some readers might choose to emphasize the continuities between old and new and others the discontinuities, but all will agree that the change is rapid, powerful, and important. This chapter seeks to present a snapshot of the ferment, albeit with some inevitable blurring. The Library of Congress (LC) shares in the fate of libraries generally but has the size, distinction, and resources needed to help shape that fate. Accordingly, the evocation of context that follows suggests not only the forces affecting LC but also the roles LC might choose to play.

It is no easy thing in these times to conceptualize—or to manage—a library, large or small. Libraries are creatures of their societies' intellectual accomplishments. For centuries, at least as early as the founding of the library at Alexandria (circa 280 BC), readers in pursuit of knowledge have expected libraries to gather and make available to them a broad range of texts and artifacts. In every age, these creations have been conveyed by the media of the time: handmade tablets, leaves, scrolls, codices, and then, with the advent of printing, books and journals. The technology of printing enabled rapid production and copying and thereby wide dissemination of information and learning and led to the large-scale institutionalization and popularization of libraries. In the nineteenth and twentieth centuries, libraries—particularly public and academic libraries—achieved a fundamental, almost revered place in society. Libraries came to be identified not only with the collections they assiduously gathered but also with the wide and free access they gave readers pursuing personal, social, and public-minded goals. Libraries became the places where citizens of modest means could access books and other materials they could never afford to purchase. Libraries became, as well, places of learning and interaction for their readers. The special status of libraries is attested to by the fact that their communities support them with funding and other resources. As well, the copyright law of the United States recognized the role of libraries in serving and educating the public.[1]

By the 1990s, the development of computers and the networks and protocols that link them together (particularly the World Wide Web protocol developed by Tim Berners-Lee) and then the browsers that were needed to navigate this interconnected world had led to new ways of capturing intellectual creativity and distributing it widely and almost instantaneously to those who sought it. This revolution challenges the traditional role of libraries in contemporary and future society. The computer's transformation of our world and the upheavals it fosters rival or exceed those that grew out of the development of the printing press in the fifteenth century. It is worth taking a few moments to enumerate some of the recent changes that affect libraries and their service to users, even if we merely skim the peaks and omit much.[2] This chapter describes some aspects of the rapidly changing, new, untested, and exciting environment for libraries today. The leaders and managers of the libraries of the present must understand and master this environment if they are to find ways to continue to fulfill the purpose of libraries past and to carry out their mission.

CONTEXT

The Need for Cooperation Among Libraries

Libraries have always made information available. From the earliest days, they housed and facilitated access to information, through the selection, aggregation, organization, service, and ongoing care of their materi-

---

[1]In particular, Section 109 of the copyright law (contained in Title 17 of the United States Code), under the so-called first-sale doctrine, permits libraries to lend materials, even outside their premises, and Section 108 exempts certain reproductions and distributions of copyrighted works conducted by libraries under specific conditions.

[2]For recent discussions of the larger cultural issues, see *Future Libraries,* Howard R. Bloch and Carla Hesse, eds., (Berkeley, Calif.: University of California Press, 1995) or a special issue of the journal *Representations,* Spring 1993; also, see *Avatars of the Word: From Papyrus to Cyberspace,* by James J. O'Donnell (Cambridge, Mass.: Harvard University Press, 1998).

als, as a shared good. In the last half-century, forces such as the explosion of publishing, the rapid expansion of education at all levels, globalization, and ever-growing funding for many kinds of research have made us realize that no single library—not even the Library of Congress—can today collect and deliver comprehensively, if ever it could, the world's most important literature and information sources. For decades now, libraries have bonded into groups that work together to share information requested by their readers. Much, though not all, of this effort has concentrated on developing standards by which libraries describe and transfer information, such as the machine-readable cataloging (MARC) record and the variety of emerging approaches for organizing information that are discussed in Chapter 5.

Other strategies have focused on cooperative collection development programs within a group of libraries (for example, the creation in the 1930s of the Triangle research libraries' cooperative collection development program, which continues to be robust to this day[3]); the creation of highly cost-effective, computer-based, catalog-record-sharing cooperatives (the largest of them all, the Online Computer Library Center (OCLC), was set up in the late 1960s[4]); the conscious move toward having the catalogs of large research institutions serve from their readers' point of view as one catalog (the initiatives of the Committee on Institutional Cooperation (CIC) are notable in this respect, presenting to their readers in 12 institutions online catalogs and supporting services that aim to behave transparently as one collection[5]); the creation of statewide consortia to facilitate user-initiated interlibrary loans for traditional materials (Ohiolink, with more than 70 consortial library members, records more than half a million transactions every year at a cost of well below $10 each[6]); and the recent accelerated move of libraries to organize them-

---

[3]"Cooperative Collection Development at the Research Triangle University Libraries: A Model for the Nation," by Patricia Buck Dominguez and Luke Swindler, in *College & Research Libraries*, November 1993, pp. 470-496.

[4]See Chapters 2 and 5 for a discussion of OCLC.

[5]For a description of the CIC, visit its Web site at <http://www.cic.uiuc.edu>. For a narrative about the goals and visions of the CIC group of libraries, see "Consortial Leadership: Essential Elements for Success," a presentation by Barbara McFadden Allen for the Association of Research Libraries at its May 1997 membership meeting, available online at <http://www.arl.org/arl/proceedings/130/allen.html>. For more information, follow the links and footnotes in this presentation.

[6]Some articles that describe the Ohiolink interlibrary loan concept include "How the Virtual Library Transforms Interlibrary Loans—the OhioLINK Experience," by David F. Kohl, in *Interlending & Document Supply*, Vol. 26, No. 2, 1998, pp. 65-69, and "Resource Sharing in a Changing Ohio Environment," by David F. Kohl, in *Library Trends*, Winter 1997, pp. 435-437. Ohiolink's executive director, Tom Sanville, writes that its interlibrary loan (ILL) system is currently filling about 500,000 requests per year and is still growing (private e-mail correspondence, dated January 23, 2000).

selves into consortia that license electronic works from publishers and vendors, securing broad-based site licenses, often at advantageous costs, for dozens or hundreds of libraries of all types per license.[7]

The Rapid Rise of Information Resources in Electronic Formats

The past brought recognizable information formats such as books, journals, film, and other fixed media. Many electronic information resources, however, are brand-new creations that resemble traditional media less and less. They include the millions of Web pages and databases produced all over the world by individuals, companies, institutions, and government agencies. These creations represent a variety of information types, including descriptive materials, corporate reports, datasets, educational offerings, theses and dissertations (some universities now require dissertations to be submitted in electronic form[8]), and many more. But, along with these recognizable publication types are many new kinds of publications beyond anything anyone has ever imagined, in terms of size, scale, complexity, and function. These resources spring out of the energy and creativity of society's best minds in a ferment of excitement, and it is reasonable to expect that their variety and novelty will only increase. The committee heard about and reviewed numerous examples of current projects available in digital form that challenge traditional modes of publication, to say nothing of librarianship and collection practices.

For example, Corbis offers a huge collection of digital images derived from traditional photo archives, and the Survivors of the Shoah Visual History Foundation collects thousands of videotaped memoirs from Holocaust survivors and integrates them with related materials. Both projects (see Box 1.1) are marked by careful attempts on the part of the creating organizations to limit and focus distribution, in the one case to paying customers, in the other to institutions that will use the resource in a responsible and productive way. Microsoft's Terraserver project,[9] a collaboration with the U.S. Geological Survey, is a collection of satellite photos of many parts of the United States and selected parts of the rest of the world. The project, which is freely available and offers high-quality

---

[7]For a description of library consortia and their activities, particularly in the licensing arena, see the home page of the International Coalition of Library Consortia, available online at <http://www.library.yale.edu/consortia>.

[8]For descriptions of activity in the area of electronic dissertations, see <http://www.ndltd.org> and <http://www.theses.org>.

[9]The Microsoft Terraserver site with its satellite and aerial images provided by the U.S. Geological Survey is at <http://www.terraserver.microsoft.com>.

information, is an experiment in managing a very large database for public access. It is impossible to describe any of these projects in traditional terms that would allow comparing their collections to items now collected by libraries, nor is it easy to imagine how a given library would collect such items, although they are fully analogous to, and might well substitute for, library holdings (i.e., as in map rooms or special collections).

Even resources that seem to be more traditional, such as the research projects fostered by the Institute for Advanced Technology in the Humanities (IATH) at the University of Virginia,[10] challenge traditional expectations by virtue of their constant state of flux. The institute's Web site contains no single stable artifact to "collect"—it is very much a work in progress. *Arts and Letters Daily* (*A&LD*) is a Web site that goes one step further. In appearance, it is a daily "newspaper" whose content is cultural. But all that the editors provide is a front page with short descriptions and links to content found on hundreds of other freely available sites, many of them well-known resources in their own right. The repackaging accomplished by linking articles intelligently to a single site makes *A&LD* a hugely popular and highly useful site.[11] Is it possible to "collect" such a site if one can collect only the daily "front page"? If one can collect all the linked sites, can one reliably collect the work with all its links intact and stable? Long-established standard newspapers are avoiding links to material from other sources (for legal reasons, possibly); many of the newer newspapers and magazines, however, are filled with links to other sites. Preserving the news nowadays requires collecting not just the specific news source, but also the content of links to other Web spaces.[12]

---

[10]IATH's work is described on its Web site at <http://village.virginia.edu/>. IATH's goal is to explore and expand the potential of information technology as a tool for humanities research. To that end, it appoints fellows and provides them with consulting, technical support, applications programming, and networked publishing facilities. IATH also cultivates partnerships and participates in humanities computing initiatives with libraries, publishers, information technology companies, scholarly organizations, and others interested in the intersection of computers and cultural heritage.

[11]This synthesis of news (now a part of Jeffrey Kittay's *Lingua Franca* family of publications) from the fields of philosophy, aesthetics, literature, language, ideas, criticism, culture, history, music, art, trends, breakthroughs, disputes, and gossip is found at <http://www.aldaily.com/>.

[12]For example, <http://www.mediainfo.com> includes at the bottom of its daily headline page a set of links to stories on other sites. And <http://www.wired.com> provides that kind of link as well as numerous links within each of its own news stories to many other reports.

BOX 1.1
Digital Information, Networks, and the Creation of New Media

The growing importance of documents represented in nontraditional media is challenging the traditional notion of a library collection. How can a library collect, provide access to, and preserve materials that do not have an identifiable tangible form or whose representation depends on technology with a short useful life? Here are two examples of challenging nontraditional collections: the image collections held by Corbis, at <http://www.corbis.com>, and the multimedia collections developed by the Survivors of the Shoah Visual History Foundation, at <http://www.shoahfoundation.org>.

Corbis has assembled a collection of 65 million photographs and fine art images, 2.1 million of which have been digitized (40 terabytes) and are available online. The Corbis collection includes a wide variety of materials, ranging from news photo libraries (e.g., UPI) to stock photo and museum collections. The images in the Corbis collections are made available through professional service centers and directly to consumers over the Internet.

The Corbis collection faces two unique challenges. The first is its size. Most of the 65 million images are cataloged with varying levels of detail. The 2.1 million digitized images make up the largest commercial digital image collection in the world. The second challenge is the rapidly changing technology base. Images in the digitized collection have been captured with different scanning technologies, with such technology having improved markedly since Corbis began building the collections in 1989. At the same time, images are output using a wide variety of display devices ranging from relatively low-quality Web browsers to high-quality film for commercial uses. Thus, a variety of image representations need to be mapped to a wide range of supported output devices.

The Survivors of the Shoah Foundation was formed in 1994 to record firsthand accounts of the Holocaust. The foundation has conducted over 50,000 interviews; each interview consists of an unedited video transcript together with written background and descriptive information. The collection consists of more than 100,000 hours of video and a comprehensive catalog that captures background information and facilitates access to the collection. Interviews are conducted in the language with which the interview subject is most comfortable (32 languages to date) and

---

The nation is investing significant sums to advance research in scientific areas, investments that will bear fruit in many directions now little surmised. Both the Los Alamos National Laboratory's e-print archive[13]

---

[13]The LANL e-Print archive, now known as arXiv.org, was established in 1991. The service blossomed and expanded quickly (by February 1992) much beyond its original focus on high-energy physics. As of January 2000, arXiv.org contained 122,400 submissions. (See <http://arXiv.org/cgi-bin/show_monthly_submissions>.) Sixteen mirror sites operate around the world. Paul Ginsparg, the founder of the service, notes that he could still fit the current hardware under the hatch of his Honda (with plenty of room left over) and take it anywhere.

may incorporate photographs or other image information, which makes the collection not only large but also multilingual and multimedia.

The Shoah collection is to be used as an historical and sociological research tool and as a source of educational materials to promote tolerance and cultural understanding. Developing the infrastructure necessary to provide access to the collection has proved to be a challenge. The high-quality digitized video requires large (by today's standards) amounts of storage (180 terabytes) and a high rate of data transmission (3 megabits/sec/client); the design parameters look forward to a time soon when suitable storage (terabyte disk drives) and network technology (OC-3, 155 megabits/sec) will be commonplace and affordable. Shoah is particularly interesting because it is an open question whether the archive has been "published." Shoah chooses to make its resources available on a contractual basis in settings where it is assured of reasonable security and where the materials it provides will be handled in a way compatible with the goals of the foundation. These restrictions are understandable, but how ought the Library of Congress respond? Is this a publication to be demanded on copyright depository statute conditions?[1] Or is there to be a negotiation, assuring the foundation that LC is a responsible partner? There are no easy answers to these questions.

The Corbis and Shoah collections both contain important items of interest to researchers and other library patrons. Developing the organization, policy, and technology to provide materials of a similar nature to users is a challenge not only for LC but for other libraries as well. In fact, projects like these can serve as models for libraries to emulate as they begin to collect digital materials.

SOURCES: Corbis: "Corbis Images Build Market Momentum," *M2 Presswire*, October 15, 1998, and "Corbis Opens Its Art Collection," by Cameron Crouch, in *PC World Online*, November 17, 1999, both available at <http://www.corbis.com>. Shoah: "Multimedia Pedagogy for the New Millennium," by Rhonda Hammer and Douglas Kellner, in *Journal of Adolescent & Adult Literacy*, April 1999, available online at <http://www.shoah.org>.

[1] These conditions are discussed in Chapter 2.

and the Human Genome Database[14] are collective works that bring together new global communities based on special interests and have extraordinary power to advance and build scientific research. It is entirely reasonable to imagine that, particularly in scientific and technological

---

[14] The National Human Genome Database's home page is located at <http://www.nhgri.nih.gov/Policy_and_public_affairs/Communications/Publications/Maps_to_medicine/>. There one can read about the project and access information and data related to genome mapping from around the world.

fields, such initiatives offer only an inkling of what is to come.[15] As the committee was deliberating, initiatives such as PubMed Central (sponsored by the National Institutes of Health)[16] and the Department of Energy initiative PubSCIENCE[17] were set to be scaled up in the very near future.

Other resources are the electronic equivalents of printed information. The electronic mode makes it possible to deliver the information wherever the reader may be (for instance, to his or her computer in the home or workplace or, by wireless technology, to any place), to present information that cannot be captured in print (such as video attachments, tables that can be manipulated, and so on), and to facilitate use of the information through quality interfaces and search capabilities. Some of the speed with which this transformation is happening in the world publishing industry can be captured by briefly considering two well-established publishing formats—journals and books.

Online Electronic Journals

There is no truly reliable or single source of information on the growth of electronic journals. A careful study of the World Wide Web archives of the e-journal and magazine electronic announcement list NewJour[18] reveals that in 1989, fewer than 10 e-journals were available. They were created in basic ASCII (.txt) form and had to be distributed in small

---

[15]For example, the development of standards and technology for federating these e-print archives, such as that proposed by the Santa Fe Convention of the Open Archives Initiative, <http://www.openarchives.org>, offers the possibility of creating a global digital library of scholarly e-prints. Further information may be found in "The Santa Fe Convention of the Open Archives Initiative," by Herbert Van de Sompel and Carl Lagoze, in *D-Lib Magazine*, February 2000, available online at <http://www.dlib.org/dlib/february00/vandesompel-oai/02vandesompel-oai.html>.

[16]PubMedCentral is a creation of the National Institutes of Health. Its contents are intended to include both formal and informal articles in the fields of biomedical sciences for free access. It is located at <www.pubmedcentral.nih.gov>.

[17]The Department of Energy's (DOE's) Office of Science and the Government Printing Office (GPO) announced the development and public availability of PubSCIENCE as of October 1, 1999. GPO is sponsoring the free access through its GPO Access Web site. PubSCIENCE, developed by DOE's Office of Scientific and Technical Information, focuses on the physical sciences and other energy-related disciplines. It was modeled after the highly publicized PubMedCentral and is located at <http://pubsci.osti.gov/>.

[18]For the complete NewJour archive back to the start date of August 1993, see <http://gort.ucsd.edu/newjour>. Information about the NewJour announcement list, managed by James J. O'Donnell and Ann Okerson, with archives managed by James Jacobs at the University of California, San Diego Library, can also be found at this URL.

chunks, lest they crash the mailboxes of subscribers. Today, many large publishers around the world, both for-profit and not-for-profit, maintain Web sites that make available their full collections of print journals (with only limited back-file runs, so far) to subscribers. Given this penetration of new technologies into scholarly, scientific, and popular journal and magazine publication, a list such as NewJour will one day soon no longer be needed. In this decade (or even half-decade), most print magazines and journals will have a Web version, if they do not already have one (see Box 1.2). Furthermore, although for the moment it is convenient to think of print and Web versions as providing the same or identical information, the two styles are already beginning to pull apart and will only diverge

---

BOX 1.2
The Rapid Growth of Online Electronic Journals

Electronic journal publication is relatively new. There were no electronic journals 20 years ago and fewer than 10 in 1989. It is difficult to get an accurate count of journals currently published in electronic form. Two types of electronic journals can be distinguished: electronic versions of journals that are also published in paper form and electronic journals that are available only in electronic form. New-Jour (<www.gort.ucsd.edu/newjour>), a notification service that tracks electronic journals, listed 8,404 titles in February 2000 (up from 3,634 in mid-1997 and 6,900 in December 1998). Electronic versions of traditional journals are by far the most common, as many traditional publishers make their materials available in electronic form. Elsevier Science, at <http://www.elsevier.com>, for example, offers electronic versions of over 1,000 of its journals. In fact, Elsevier's full text was available to selected institutions by the mid-1990s through the University Licensing Program (TULIP), just as Springer's was available through Red Sage.[1] Many professional associations (e.g., the Association for Computing Machinery, at <http://www.acm.org>, and the American Mathematical Society, at <http://www.ams.org>) also offer electronic versions of their professional journals.

Efforts to digitize important retrospective journal collections have also been undertaken. JSTOR, at <http://www.jstor.org>, offers digitized versions of back files of 117 scholarly journals. JSTOR plans to expand its coverage and to add titles to its collections.

Scholarly journals published only in electronic form represent a small but growing body of material (*Journal of Artificial Intelligence Research*, at <http://www.cs.washington.edu/research/jair>, is an early example). A wide variety of electronic-only publications are associated with online discussion groups, newsletters, and other special interest groups.

---

[1]Information about TULIP may be found online at <http://www.elsevier.nl:80/homepage/about/resproj/tulip.shtml>; information about Red Sage may be found online at <http://www.ckm.ucsf.edu/projects/RedSage/>.

further. Not only will the same name ultimately denote collections of content that are in fact very different,[19] but some of the e-journals also will evolve into new genres. The prevailing vision is that this wealth of journal literature will be linked through indexing services and search engines and cross-linked internally online;[20] indeed, this vision is rapidly being realized. For as long as print versions continue to be published, tracking and collecting will be much more difficult.

The most significant problem for ubiquitous electronic access is that of long-term archivability and preservation, an issue that begs to be solved if publishers and libraries are not to maintain costly parallel print and electronic systems. So far, very few electronic journals (or any other resource) have had to survive on the Internet for even one decade. While some experts say that long-term sustainability is a trivial matter, studies suggest high costs and tremendous uncertainties.[21] Fundamental to these uncertainties is the matter of ownership, which libraries rarely have, given that electronic information produces no fixed artifact for libraries to possess and cherish (see the section "Digital Materials, Ownership Rights, and Libraries" below).

While rapid growth characterizes scholarly and research journals, the committee found similar or even faster growth in the even broader universe of all continuing publications that includes popular magazines and newspapers as well as annual reports, directories, series, and so on.

Books Finally Go Electronic

Standard periodical indexing and abstracting services (ranging from popular sources such as *Public Affairs Information Service* to highly research-oriented sources such as *Chemical Abstracts*) began to become available electronically in the 1970s through specialized vendors such as Dialog and BRS, whose proprietary systems required the mediation of expert searchers; by the mid-1990s, they were available through easy-to-use Web interfaces for any licensed subscriber. Thus it is no surprise that the

---

[19]Gerry McKiernan, of the Iowa State University Library, maintains a Web site of multimedia journals at <http://www.public.iastate.uedu/~CYBERSTACKS/M-Bed.htm>. See also, "Embedded Multimedia in Electronic Journals," by Gerry McKiernan, in *Multimedia Information and Technology*, Vol. 24, No. 4, 1999, pp. 338-343.

[20]The multipublisher initiative called CrossRef was announced in the fall of 1999 (<http://www.crossref.org>). Participation from numerous scholarly journal publishers is expected. A press release titled "Reference Linking Service to Aid Scientists Conducting Online Research," from Susan Spilka at John Wiley Publishers, New York, was posted to the liblicense-list (liblicense-l@lists.yale.edu: archive at <http://www.library.yale.edu/~llicense/ ListArchives/>) on November 16, 1999.

[21]See Chapter 4 for an extended discussion on digital preservation.

journal articles (which are relatively short and therefore easily distributed and used through present electronic technology) cited by these sources would become quickly available online (see the section "Online Electronic Journals," above). However, books—such as novels and scholarly monographs, for example—have seemed far less susceptible to electronic transformation. While some books are consulted in bits and bytes (for particular facts or small sections), many (the argument goes) need to be deliciously savored and contemplated from beginning to end, and an online screen is hostile to such prolonged congenial or intense reading. "You can't take it to bed or to the beach or onto the plane with you," is the oft-heard lament.

Accordingly, readers, publishers, and vendors have posed some chicken-and-egg questions: if we build a better e-book reading device or interface, will the critical mass of e-books—and attendant readers—materialize? Or do we first need a critical mass of e-books to bring the improved e-book devices and readers en masse? Maybe these questions are moot, for it seems, as one publisher said of his company's participation in the Barnes & Noble/Microsoft e-book alliance, that we might be able to skip the chicken and egg and go directly to the omelet.[22]

The vision now being articulated by many players in the book publishing industry and its partners (in printing, distribution, and software) is that the full text of all published books, at least from mainstream publishers, will exist on vast electronic information servers, there to be channeled to the output of the reader's choice: traditional print formats or digital formats (by accessing a local copy on a PC or portable device or by viewing a remote copy through the Web). That is, the authoritative source file of many books may soon be an electronic version that can generate various derivative versions.

The e-book may be on the verge of acceptance and success[23] because of the convergence of large computer servers, big network pipelines, rapid progress in developing e-book standards, and the increasing sophistication and utility of handheld book-reading devices, as well as business

---

[22]Steven M. Zeitchik in *Publishersweekly.com*, January 10, 2000, available online at <http://www.publishersweekly.com/articles/20000110_83924.asp>, quoting Dick Brass of Microsoft in "Microsoft, Bn.com in E-book Deal." The "omelet" is the widespread use of e-books.

[23]An instance that suggests acceptance is the release of Stephen King's short story "Riding the Bullet," which was made available for sale in downloadable electronic format on the Web only. Barnes & Noble officials reported that the story had the biggest opening day for any book on its Web site, regardless of the format of the book. See "Stephen King Rewrites E-book Biz" by Margaret Kane, in *ZDnet News*, March 16, 2000, available at <http://www.zdnet.com/zdnn/stories/news/0,4586,2469310,00.html>.

partnerships to take advantage of all this.[24] Like e-journals, e-books also have a history that goes back to the 1980s. In this arena, modern history can be said to have begun when two brothers opened the first Borders bookstore in Ann Arbor, near the University of Michigan, and invented the bookstore superstore chain that is by now commonplace. Until then, most bookstores were small, and unless they were subject-oriented, their stock comprised mostly popular literature with a smattering of less popular works.[25] With the opening of Borders, followed by dozens of offspring across the United States, the consumer of serious books knew that he or she could walk into a bookstore and find instant gratification. Thus, Borders began—but only began—to fill the role that hitherto had been met by the library. If you were to visit a superstore in the springtime and see the customers sitting on the floor of the travel section or surrounded by travel books in the cappuccino bar, with no intention of buying but taking careful notes, you might think you were in a well-appointed public library. The book superstore comes closer to the kind of service for readers that hitherto only libraries could aspire to and added some of the congenial atmosphere that libraries provide (comfortable reading spaces, for example). However, in the bookstore superstore, taking a book home requires an economic transaction, sometimes a substantial one.

In the mid-1990s, an entrepreneur making a car trip with his wife had a vision of "the world's largest bookstore," a virtual shop in which the discerning reader could obtain every book—or nearly every book—currently in print. Jeff Bezos, founder and CEO of Amazon.com, *Time Magazine*'s Person of the Year for 1999, achieved his dream: situating bookselling at the core of e-commerce and radicalizing the bookstore concept, to say nothing of notions of business success (Amazon.com, for all its millions of dollars in turnover, had yet to make a profit as of mid-2000[26]). Through the Web, the Amazon.com shopper fills a virtual shopping cart with the desired books, which are delivered a day or two or three later to the reader's address of choice. Through Amazon.com, large

---

[24]For additional information about e-books, see the home page of the Electronic Book Project of the National Institute of Standards and Technology, at <http://www.nist.gov/itl/div895/isis/projects/ebook/>.

[25]Several bookstores, such as Cody's in Berkeley, California, and Powell's in Portland, Oregon, have stocked a wide array of nonfiction and fiction literature for many years, but none of these bookstores was franchised or grew into a chain store.

[26]Amazon.com, Inc., reported a slightly smaller-than-expected operating loss for the first quarter of 2000, riding revenue growth that analysts say could finally make it profitable sometime next year, as reported in "Amazon.com Beats Analysts' Estimates," by Jim Carlton, in *Wall Street Journal*, April 27, 2000, p. A3.

collections of books have come one step nearer to their readers—and no library has played a part in this dramatic convergence of reader and book. In the case of the virtual superstore, the reader controls the atmosphere, which need not be as public as a library or bookshop and may be as comfortable as reading in a lounge chair wearing fuzzy slippers and a dressing gown.

Most significantly, the rise of the book superstore has implicitly changed the overall economics of access to books and information. Where once a good public library was the best and most accessible source of materials for many, if not most, communities, bookstores of similar size may be a few doors down the block, open longer hours, and with enough copies of popular titles to satisfy almost all comers. And, most libraries and physical bookstores are dwarfed by online bookstores.

These book superstores offer a remarkably wide range of library-like services—lectures, discussion groups, ready access to books, a sense of community. What they do not yet offer is information service—labor-intensive, provided by experts—but it is probably not wise to predict that they will not continue to expand their range. For now, it is most noticeably the information navigation functions of the library—the instruction in finding, filtering, and evaluating information from a welter of available sources—and its provision of historical depth that the bookstores make the least attempt to supplant. Borders began its career with claims about the literacy and helpfulness of its staff, all of whom had to pass a test to demonstrate their book lore as a condition of employment. Even so, the information desk at Borders or Barnes & Noble is not much like the reference desk in even a very small library. Despite this, the library is less than ever a primary supplier of access to new and current books. Libraries continue, however, to be strong in providing access to both older and more specialized material.

Another implication of the shift in the economy of information is that collecting and storing materials are arguably somewhat less the jobs of the library than before. The current emphasis is on services. Indeed, many public libraries have always had this bias, retaining from among older books only those of continuing interest to their readers, while clearing out shelf space for what a current generation demands. That service emphasis is accelerating and may be expected to accelerate further. Why? Although 50 years ago the public or college library may have been the only place to find a copy of Boswell's *Life of Johnson* or Dumas's *Man in the Iron Mask* and for this reason may have held on to several copies, now the work is readily available in physical and online superstores and so may begin to be omitted from some library collections. (To admit this publicly may get libraries into trouble, but the practice of deaccession is a routine one that probably will accelerate.)

In any case, the superstores and Amazon.com have by no means reached the end state of the publishing industry's book-to-reader vision, nor do libraries seem to have much of a role in that next vision either. If, some ponder, the bookstore (whether physical or virtual) can unite the reader with in-print books, why not add out-of-print books to the service as well? Why could a reader not enter a bookstore, request an out-of-print item, and leave the store with it 15 minutes later, printed and bound, paying a retail book price? Or why not find that book on one's own computer? The concept of books on demand (or OD, as some industry analysts call it) has been in gestation for some time. For example, in the early 1990s, Xerox partnered with a few large publishing houses in an OD experiment. The products were acceptable, but computer servers and network pipelines were less capacious than today and so the results were slow. The need to resolve rights and permissions issues also posed a significant challenge. The concept needed time to ripen, and ripen it has.

The late 1990s saw breakthroughs that led to such notable developments as Barnes & Noble, one of the world's largest book retailers, buying a 49 percent share in an on-demand publisher called iUniverse.com. iUniverse plans to publish about 1,000 out-of-print titles per month at the outset, and customers ought to be able to browse through iUniverse titles in nearly all of B&N's superstores, eventually to pick up the desired title while shopping in the store. Reliable and affordable on-demand printing is said to be coming within 3 to 5 years.[27] Around the same time, Baker & Taylor, a large book wholesaler, struck a deal with Replica Books, now its on-demand print division, to achieve a similar goal.[28] Of course, acquiring an older title is not just a matter of going to a library or printing books on demand. The Web also offers services such as Bibliofind, at <http://www.bibliofind.com>, through which one can search a database of more than 10 million used books, simplifying remarkably the process of locating and purchasing an original copy of an older or otherwise hard-to-find book.

Both Barnes & Noble and Baker & Taylor are, in their various partnerships, developing capabilities for publishing the works of new authors. In this type of service, the vendors will make available toolkits and services so that an author may self-publish, at a cost of somewhere between $99 and $500, making his or her own materials available online. Given the

---

[27]See "Barnes & Noble Buys Stake in On-Demand Press," *Publishers Weekly*, November 8, 1999, p. 10.

[28]See "B&T in On-Demand Pact with Xlibris," by Calvin Reid, in *Publishers Weekly*, November 15, 1999, available online at <http://www.publishersweekly.com/articles/19991115_82641.asp>.

relative ease, at least prospectively, of publishing books online, some speculate that the U.S. output of books will jump from the current 50,000 per year to hundreds of thousands per year in the coming decade.

At about the same time as the Barnes & Noble and Baker & Taylor announcements were made, R.R. Donnelley and Sons, the nation's largest book printer, under contract with numerous publishers, announced an alliance with Microsoft Corporation to cooperate on e-books: "Together, Donnelley and Microsoft will offer publishers turnkey, hassle-free, end-to-end solutions . . . to create a massive repository on our [Donnelley's] servers to store tens of thousands of titles [and] convert them to e-book formats . . . . We will be working . . . to deliver e-books in whatever format readers ask for."[29]

On January 6, 2000, Barnes & Noble and Microsoft, each a giant in its industry, made a joint announcement about their alliance[30] in connection with software called Microsoft Reader.[31] The announcement was greeted with enthusiasm in some corners and consternation in others. As of July 2000, Barnes & Noble was offering a limited assortment of e-books for download from its Web site free of charge.[32] These e-books can be read with devices using the Microsoft Reader software and accompanying ClearType technology. It was also reported that Amazon will eventually enter the e-book market, but for now it is proceeding cautiously. Apart from the developments above, the publishing-related media have in the past year or two reported announcements of e-book breakthroughs from developers of handheld book reading devices, purveyors of books on the Web, and allied industries.

Thus, in the same January 1, 2000, issue of *Newsweek* that announced a farewell to Charles Schultz ("Good Grief: After 50 Years, the Creator of 'Peanuts' says Farewell to Charlie Brown"), journalist Steven Levy wrote, "It's as inevitable as page two following page one. Books are goners."[33]

---

[29]See "Donnelley, Microsoft Team to Expand eBook Business," by Paul Hilts, in *Publishers Weekly*, November 8, 1999, p. 11.

[30]See "Microsoft Collaborates with barnesandnoble.com to Accelerate Availability of eBooks," press release available online at <http://www.microsoft.com/PressPass/features/2000/01-06barnesnoble.htm>.

[31]The software would be widely available as a free download, enabling large numbers of e-books to flow into the consumer marketplace. Apparently publishers are betting on the success of this venture: Microsoft says it has signed up content from a number of European publishers, with American announcements imminent, and B&N is making its own deals with publishers, who are perceived to be key to the success of the e-book concept.

[32]See <http://ebooks.barnesandnoble.com/pocketpc/index.asp>.

[33]"It's Time to Turn the Last Page," by Steven Levy, in *Newsweek*, January 1, 2000, pp. 96-98. For a longer, more conservative view, see *The Future of the Book*, Geoffrey Nunberg, ed. (Berkeley, Calif.: University of California Press, 1996), especially the concluding essay by Umberto Eco.

BOX 1.3
The Coming of the E-Book

Hardware and software developments in the e-book area burgeon on all sides and will continue to do so. But from a library's point of view, models of publication are more important. A growing number of companies offer online access to electronic collections of books, journals, and other resources. The Library will need to consider when and how to collect such artifacts, how to provide access, and how to integrate them into its broader collections. Here is a snapshot, from early 2000, of some of the players in this territory. These vendors are providing technology and making multiple nonexclusive deals with traditional publishers. One academic press or another may already be found distributing titles through two or more of these vendors:

- *NetLibrary*, at <www.netLibrary.com>, offers a subscription model to libraries, giving restricted access to its titles (over 18,000 so far). The number of copies that can be checked out is limited to the number of copies held by the library, and users can copy only small portions of an e-book.
- *Questia*, at <www.questia.com>, intends to be the first online service to provide unlimited access to the full text of hundreds of thousands of books, journals, and periodicals. The service means to supply the core undergraduate library for students at institutions large and small.
- *Ebrary*, at <www.ebrary.com>, is forming partnerships with scholarly publishers, libraries, and retailers. Users will be able to browse texts free of charge but will pay a fee, set by the publisher, for any passages downloaded, copied, or printed. For those who wish to use substantial amounts of text, Ebrary will offer links to e-retail sites where whole books can be purchased.
- *ITKnowledge*, at <www.itknowledge.com>, concentrates on one field—infor-

---

Most individuals, organizations, and publishers agree that at the very least, the traditional book format (i.e., a hard-copy version of book content) is facing competition from formats that do some things better (see Box 1.3). In 1999, the American Historical Association announced an electronic book prize to be awarded annually for several years to half a dozen brilliant dissertations in various fields of history, dissertations that take full advantage of the converging multimedia capabilities that computers and networks can offer and books cannot. The results will enliven the books, attract readers, promote the new medium as a viable one for serious scholarship, and give young scholars a leg up. The first awards were announced at the AHA annual conference in January 2000. The American Council of Learned Societies, an umbrella association for more than 50 humanistic scholarly organizations in the United States, similarly announced its e-books project, which will digitize some 500 key historical

mation technology. Its comprehensive database will cover topics ranging from programming languages to networking and electronic commerce. The service offers one-step searches that can provide quick answers to complex technical questions as well as cut, paste, and download capabilities.

- *Books24x7*, at <www.books24x7.com>, is creating a library focused on marketing, finance, management, and human resources and geared to corporate professionals. The service also offers summaries and synopses, prepared by its editorial board, of the books it selects. Books24x7 has established relationships with technical publishers and has aligned with a major online retailer to fulfill orders for hard-copy books.

SOURCES: "An Ambitious Plan to Sell Electronic Books," by Vincent Kiernan, in *Chronicle of Higher Education*, April 16, 1999; "NetLibrary Targets an Early Market for e-Books," by Lisa Bransten, in *Wall Street Journal*, November 4, 1999, p. B12; "netLibrary.com," by Christine K. Oka, in *Library Journal*, May 1, 2000, available online at <http://www.libraryjournal.com/articles/multimedia/databasedico/databaseanddiscindex.asp>; "Houston Startup Targets Undergrads," by Steven M. Zeitchik, in *Publishers Weekly*, April 17, 2000, available online at <http://www.publishersweekly.com/articles/20000417_85721.asp>; "Ebrary.com Offers Web as Serious Research Tool," by Paul Hilts, in *Publishers Weekly*, March 27, 2000, available online at <http://www.publishersweekly.com/articles/20000327_85475.asp>; "Ebrary Solves a Very Big Problem," *I/O Magazine*, 2000, available online at <http://www.iowebsite.com/products/3_1.html>; Seybold Seminars Boston Publishing 2000, "The Editors' Hot Picks: Ebrary.com," available online at <http://38.241.81.30/SRPS/froo/hotpicks/ebooks.html>; EarthWeb Inc., "EarthWeb Launches ITKnowledge: Online Services Provider Goes Live with Subscription-Based Online Technical Reference Library for IT Professionals," October 7, 1998, available online at <http://www.internetwire.com/technews/tn/archive/tn981060.htx>; and "New Technologies Transform Publishing Industry: Production Time and Costs Are Being Cut While Publishers Gain More Flexibility," by Barbara DePompa Reimers, in *Information Week*, March 27, 2000, available online at <http://www.informationweek.com/779/ebooks.htm>.

works and commission close to 100 new ones in the coming few years. Both projects are funded by the Andrew W. Mellon Foundation. How will libraries integrate such new book formats?

Digital Music, Digital Video, and the Convergence of Formats

Traditional libraries are most often conceived of as repositories of textual artifacts. High culture constructs itself around artifacts that can be managed and cataloged in particular ways. But the technological changes of the next decade will no doubt challenge that conservatism in new ways. The technical convergence of data, voice, and video technologies, coming to the desktop (or palmtop) through a single network connection, will encourage consumers to think first of data and only secondarily of media. Libraries will then be particularly challenged to decide whether and to what extent their traditional focus on textual or mostly textual artifacts fulfills their responsibility. At the very least, libraries in the year 2000 should be actively assessing the possibility that they will be called upon in the future to be the repositories of whole classes of artifact quite unlike what they owned before, placing very different demands on their various skills. These artifacts will be emphatically commercial in purpose and appeal but no less important than traditional artifacts for document-ing American culture in decades to come and therefore inescapably part of the collecting mission of the Library of Congress as now articulated. In the past, the Library of Congress successfully accommodated the intro-duction of media such as sound recordings and film.

High Initial Cost of the Electronic Environment

Formally published online information resources are expensive to license, often costing more than one would expect to pay for print. Start-up costs for both sellers and purchasers of information are higher than the costs of maintaining traditional print information: (1) information pro-viders are investing in new technologies and skills, and a database or subscription price attempts to recover many, if not all, of the start-up costs over time; (2) institutions are developing their own technological and human capabilities, also with significant new costs; and (3) libraries and publishers are maintaining parallel information systems and re-sources in traditional and electronic media (i.e., the introduction of elec-tronic media has not yet displaced traditional media in most libraries but instead adds cost as it adds functionality). These additional costs will not disappear for some time. But the primary barrier to the use of online information resources is the cost of licensing the electronic resources mar-keted by publishers and vendors. Most libraries are funded on a model for the acquisition of fixed-format materials. License agreements, or even specialized CD-ROM products and services, are being offered at prices that encourage many libraries to consider cooperative purchasing.

Furthermore, the new model for library acquisitions must consider not only the cost of access to the information, but also the cost of main-taining the technical capability (hardware, software, personnel) required to make these resources available to readers.

Various contemporary students of the economics of information have asserted that the only financial survival option of libraries is to scale up into efficient, cooperating entities. Brian Hawkins, now president of EDUCAUSE, wrote as follows: "It is clear that the current unit of analysis . . . cannot survive in the existing environment. The leveraging of our library resources is clearly called for, with the best solution being the largest system-level possible."[34]   How to achieve that scale is an open question. The large consortia that build national catalogs—the large utilities such as Research Libraries Group (RLG) and OCLC—clearly have a part to play in organizing any such meta-system, but the comprehensive libraries, particularly the Library of Congress, will also necessarily be challenged to join such discussions. The question here is whether such scaled-up participation amounts to a continuation of an old role in pursuit of an established mission, a new role in pursuit of an established mission, or a genuinely new function in which libraries may choose to participate or not, depending on their mission, inclination, and resources.

User Demand for Electronic Resources

Although librarians and publishers have, as yet, little quantitative data or user analysis to show how much or even how electronic information resources are used, there is no question that usage, to the extent it can be measured, is shooting up with every passing month.[35]   Readers regularly demand more and more such resources and protest loudly if online

---

[34]The "largest system-level" is the highest level of aggregation or cooperation possible among libraries (from "The Unsustainability of Traditional Libraries," by Brian Hawkins, in *Executive Strategies*, a publication of NACUBO and the Stanford Forum for Higher Education Futures, Vol. 2, No. 3, pp. 1-16).

[35]Members of the committee asked information providers and librarians for usage data and received numerous replies from individual libraries, consortia, publishers, and information intermediaries. These data repeatedly tell the same story: usage is skyrocketing. Kevin Guthrie, president of the JSTOR core periodicals collection, at <http://www.jstor.org>, wrote in a private e-mail letter dated February 4, 2000:

> Usage at JSTOR participating sites more than doubled between November 1998 and November 1999. Overall, usage of the JSTOR database is increasing at a rate of roughly three times per year. Part of this growth comes from the addition of new sites; of course one must control for that. In any case, total 1998 usage was 5,920,398 accesses with 432,714 articles printed, 1999 usage was 17,311,453 accesses and 1,224,400 articles printed. In November 1998, there were 1,063,675 accesses at a little less than 400 sites; in November 1999, there were a total of 2,223,013 accesses from those same sites.

From Min-min Chang, librarian at the Hong Kong University of Science and Technology, the committee learned that the university's Web server usage page recorded 233,848 hits in November 1997; 370,947 in November 1998; and 859,473 in November 1999 (see <http://library.ust.htk.usage/pwebstats/g-index.html>). The Florida Center for Library Automation reports that its Elsevier server's articles were accessed 58,842 times in 1998 and 207,006 times in 1999 (Michele Newberry, assistant director for Library Services, in private e-mail dated January 25, 2000). Indiana's statewide virtual library project INSPIRE delivers journal and periodical databases to everyone in the state and reported serving up 10 million pages of full-text data in 1998 and 20 million pages in 1999; the staff projects that 40 million

access to any index, dictionary, encyclopedia, text, or collection is removed, even if the reasons are seemingly good ones—for example, if a library or institution believes the price is too high or the usage too small to justify continuance. This reaction is no surprise and from the reader's point of view makes perfect sense. Because we live in an age of intense national, institutional, and personal competition, information is essential, and meeting the need for knowledge is an indisputable requirement.

Digital Materials, Ownership Rights, and Libraries

Traditionally, libraries have purchased physical objects for their collections and permitted these to be used as allowed by copyright law and best practices. Many electronic resources, on the other hand, are maintained by publishers, vendors, or others designated by them, and libraries or individuals can obtain rights of access through custom or mass-market licenses. A library's readers then access the works through high-speed information networks. A library's electronic resources licenses generally permit readers a broad range of educational, research, and personal uses, and, increasingly, the book and journal suppliers promise, in the licenses, to deliver ongoing ("perpetual") access or to give the institution a residual "product" should the publisher or vendor discontinue the work, sell it to another supplier, or leave the business altogether.

Nonetheless, this new business and (non)ownership model raises many questions for libraries and for society—issues that are hotly debated wherever information policy and practices are discussed. What future, if any, is there for the largest research libraries in an era when, increasingly, materials that readers want are available without going to the library? More importantly, when libraries or other entities do not have contractual rights to archive and preserve electronic content, can they develop adequate archival and preservation mechanisms for electronic materials? And, finally, will we develop the types of institutions and agreements that can carry electronically communicated knowledge into the far distant future, just as today's libraries have effectively stew-

---

pages will be delivered in 2000 (private e-mail correspondence from Juck Lowe, project manager, dated January 26, 2000). The American Society for Cell Biology reports that the number of hits for its e-version of *Molecular Biology of the Cell* in the 2 years since its release increased about 500 percent; by contrast, the number of subscribers to the print journal increased about 6 percent in the same time (private e-mail from Heather Joseph, dated January 28, 2000). Reference publisher InfoUSA reports a 1,391 percent growth in searching on its Web site from August 1998 to August 1999 (Doug Roesemann, in private e-mail correspondence dated January 25, 2000).

arded knowledge throughout the past centuries? What institutions should have this mission in the future, and how will they carry it out?

These questions speak to large and vital questions of societal well-being. The traditional regime of copyright, enshrined in the copyright law (Title 17 of the United States Code) and its provisions for fair use (section 107) and libraries (section 108), creates for libraries (institutions that for at least the last century have been designated as holders of materials for the public good, materials that they then make freely available to the reading public) a role that now appears to be challenged if not attacked outright. As libraries generally shift toward a service rather than a collection orientation (see above), and as the economics and technologies of publishing (particularly for digital materials) make it harder for libraries to own their materials, the concept of freely accessible information, at least to the academic and public library user at the point of use, may well be at risk.

The Library of Congress has a unique and privileged position in the acquisition of cultural materials. While all other libraries in the United States must find willing sellers and must have the financial wherewithal to become willing buyers in a freely made commercial transaction, the requirement of legal deposit with the Copyright Office gives LC a presumptive right to full ownership of a copy of each and every artifact published in the United States.[36] The publisher in this particular relationship with LC is not a willing seller but a law-abiding citizen paying a kind of "public good" tax on his output. The two questions that arise here are the following: Can LC gain parallel rights for digital information formats? How will it exercise these: to whom and on what terms will LC offer access to the digital works that fall into its purview? This point is central to all discussions of mission and cannot be emphasized strongly enough. The Library is different from all other libraries when confronting the explosion of digital content and the shift from purchase to licensing.

THE GREAT LIBRARIES IN THE ELECTRONIC AGE

The multitude of electronic databases, the rapid growth of Web sites, the increase in the number of electronically available print journals, and the availability of numerous full-text resources such as reports, dissertations, and electronic books all represent a dramatic change in the dissemination of scholarly and cultural content. The history of this revolution is

---

[36]The unique role that the Library of Congress plays in the U.S. copyright system is exceedingly important for the operation of the Library and is discussed elsewhere in this report, beginning in Chapter 2.

short and there is still much to learn, on all levels and in all areas. Not a great deal has been published about how the great libraries are transforming themselves to greet the electronic age, although Maurice B. Line notes that three factors have caused an almost ceaseless questioning of the roles and futures of national libraries: (1) automation, information, and communications technology; (2) the intrusion of the private sector into areas formerly sacred to libraries; and (3) the globalization of libraries. He writes:

> It is always useful to ask, 'If we did not have such-and-such, would we invent it?' From a strictly utilitarian point of view, it is doubtful if we would now invent monumental national libraries; we would find other and cheaper, if less effective, ways of performing national functions. But we do not start from scratch: big national libraries exist, and it is almost unthinkable, on the grounds of cost and logistics alone, to dismember them and distribute their resources among other libraries . . . . Secondly, national pride is a major factor . . . . Another factor is what may be called linguistic pride.[37]

A great deal of information exists about the emerging practices of the largest research libraries in the United States and Canada, particularly in the publications and data gathered by the Association of Research Libraries (ARL).[38] In particular, about 25 of these libraries are also members of an initiative named the Digital Library Federation, under the auspices of the Council on Library and Information Resources (CLIR), which leads its members in exploring various key infrastructure issues and helps them to formulate useful projects and experiments.[39] While the continent's large research libraries in no way begin to compare in collecting scope, mandate, or size with the Library of Congress, they have, nonetheless, begun to move aggressively in the direction of becoming hybrid libraries (i.e., libraries that embrace information in numerous formats, now including electronic formats).[40] How far have they come?

---

[37]"Do National Libraries Have a Future?" by Maurice B. Line, in *LOGOS*, Vol. 10, No. 3, 1999, pp. 154-159.

[38]For additional information, including newsletters, reports, and statistics, see the ARL Web site at <http://www.arl.org>.

[39]For additional information about the Digital Library Federation and its sponsoring organization, CLIR, as well as numerous full-text reports online, go to the Web site <http://www.clir.org/diglib/dlfhomepage.htm>.

[40]For an articulate view from the United Kingdom and its electronic libraries program, funded by the government's Joint Information Systems Committee (JISC), see "Towards the Hybrid Library," by Chris Rusbridge, in *D-Lib Magazine*, July/August 1998, available online at <http://www.dlib.org>.

The transformation of library culture and practice by the adoption of information technology continues apace. An increasing emphasis on service and a decreasing emphasis on collection have already been noted. As the committee surveyed the national scene, it found that libraries are engaging in a broad range of novel activities. It attempts to list them here to give as rich a picture as possible of the nature and momentum of change. Libraries are incorporating electronic technologies and services into the everyday work of all staff by doing a number of things:

• *Working for the broadest possible access for readers in the electronic environment.* Not only are libraries seeking technological standards and presentation of resources in forms accessible to the broadest range of readers, but they are also lobbying to advance the public policy debate in ways that support broad access for the good of society as a whole.

• *Reallocating an increasing and visible portion of collections budgets to the electronic resources needed by their readers.* For example, ARL Supplementary Statistics indicate that in FY98/99, 29 ARL member libraries spent more than $1 million of their collections budgets for licensing electronic databases,[41] representing anywhere from 6 to 22 percent of their library materials budgets.

• *Building collections of digital resources that, while not yet rivaling traditional collections in scope and bulk, are substantial, of high value, and integrated in the traditional patterns of collection and use.*

• *Working to shape and support initiatives such as community education, online course support, Web page design, teaching-specialist electronic resources, and digitizing of materials for these programs—all with a view to making educational opportunities as broad, rich, and accessible as possible.* Lifelong learning is the opportunity and the goal, and "distance learning" is the current buzzword for the tactics librarians seek to support.

• *Finding new ways to measure the usage patterns and behaviors of readers, so as to anticipate and support their needs, bringing the right resources into play for readers.* The digital environment facilitates such measurement and, accordingly, such feedback, giving a better allocation of resources than has ever been possible with print media.

• *Devoting increasing effort to more sophisticated reader services associated with single and multiple electronic resources.* Librarians are more often than ever teachers of how to use electronic resources, and readers spend less time pursuing simple factual information at traditional reference desks.

---

[41]See "ARL Supplementary Statistics 1998-99" (Washington, D.C.: Association of Research Libraries, forthcoming).

- *Cooperating with other libraries in setting up networks that make libraries effectively a single virtual (through the locator tool of interoperable online catalogs) institution that can deliver physical materials, via advanced interlibrary loans and document delivery, to more and more readers more effectively—and more cost-effectively—than ever.*

- *Delivering physical materials by electronic means.* As physical materials become increasingly deliverable at a distance, libraries are putting more and more electronic delivery services into operation.

- *Partnering with other participants in the creation and dissemination of knowledge.* Libraries can, for example, work with individual authors, organizations, publishers (commercial and noncommercial), booksellers, and software companies to create and make available functional and well-used online resources.

- *Digitizing and making available to readers material already in library collections and special collections.* Such materials would include, in particular, out-of-copyright material, image collections, sheet music, maps, and other traditional library treasures.

- *Subscribing to online services that provide statistical data.* Libraries would help readers learn to manipulate services containing anything from historical census data to financial market data.

- *Creating multimedia servers for music, film, and other media.* At the same time, thorny questions of access and permitted use must be addressed, and the technological capability to handle significant quantities of such material must be developed.

- *Using the new generation of library management systems as a springboard not only for integrating forms of access to a wide range of materials and formats but also for reengineering the entire workflow and back-office processes of traditional librarianship.* The technical services of libraries are becoming increasingly business-like, streamlined, and closely managed, with closer links than ever to vendors through electronic data interchange (EDI) and other forms of electronic interaction that work to the advantage of all parties.

- *Working to understand the technical demands, possibilities, and long-term costs and responsibilities of digital media as instruments for the preservation of library information, including material from traditional print media (e.g., the contents of books printed on acid-based paper) and material created in digital form.* When we fully understand the challenges of moving digitally preserved information from format to format, from one hardware and software system to a new hardware and software system, we will have made great progress in solving what many think is the biggest remaining problem in establishing truly functional and satisfactory digital libraries.

- *Working through the issues that must be faced in deciding which kinds of resources are best maintained locally, library by library, and which resources are best maintained elsewhere, whether by publishers, vendors, library consortia, or third parties.* Traditional librarianship achieves security and preservation by having redundant physical copies: the challenge now is to balance redundancy (and thus security) with optimal efficiency and to avoid unnecessary duplication of effort.

• *Understanding evolving legal regimes such as copyright and licensing.* In this arena, librarians seek not only to understand but also to shape and influence developments, thus securing agreements that offer readers high-quality, reliable, and permanent access to resources.

• *Exercising responsible stewardship of library resources, which are usually purchased with public funds or from not-for-profit institutional budgets.* Such stewardship requires keen understanding of the business models and economics of the new information sources in an environment in which libraries find themselves increasingly offered not ownership but access, not a once-for-all price but something closer to annual subscription or by-the-drink pricing.

• *Cultivating an expertise in technology matters.* The technological infrastructure of a library now faces a new degree of volatility and continuing costs as equipment and software need upgrading. The e-marketplace makes it literally impossible to choose not to play the upgrade game: in a very short time, a library's information would simply become unavailable if it persisted in using even slightly outmoded operating systems or software.

• *Continuously upgrading human resources and skills.* The librarians and support staff at this time of transformation must undergo no less arduous a series of "upgrades." As in other sectors of our economy, it is impossible in the library sector for staff to acquire and practice skills and then use them for a lifetime; instead, they must grow and adapt, and there are real and substantial costs for supporting the necessary training and for paying a more highly skilled staff.

• *Seeking new funding sources and opportunities.* Traditional funding sources—annual budgets doled out by the government or not-for-profit organizations with a tiny annual increase—no longer suffice. Librarians are increasingly engaged in entrepreneurial efforts, whether soliciting research and development funding from granting agencies, developing partnerships with other entities in the library sector, or participating in cost-recovery projects with the commercial sector that serves and interacts with the library community.

And libraries do more. There remains an underlying question: Do most consumers of information need the intermediation of libraries? That issue will play itself out in the next few years. But the preservation of the overall collection of human creativity is not something that publishers can achieve unaided. In an odd way, the Library of Congress remains the U.S. library most assured of a future. If that is true, many vital questions remain, including the following:

- What should be the goal of our great libraries, including LC, in this time of technological transformation? (The committee confesses to admiring the view articulated by Anthony Appiah: ". . . the library I never go to is already one of the most important places in my life."[42])
- What sort of institutions should libraries become when every current book, dissertation, journal, and so on is available on electronic servers, potentially never out of print? What is the place of libraries, particularly LC, with its unique copyright role, in such an information-communications system?
- If librarianship is increasingly a matter of public service and LC retains its core mission of collection rather than service, how and where will it differentiate itself from the rest of the library community, and how will it cooperate and collaborate with that community to bring about the greatest societal good?

In short: What will be the future role of the great research, national, and academic libraries? Who will define that role? And what do libraries need to do to play it well? In this period of acceleration, scaling up, and ongoing, hard-to-predict change, developing strategies and continuously adjusting them characterize our new environment. It is complicated and it demands much. It offers immense room for innovation and conceptualization. It is tremendously exciting.

ROADMAP FOR THIS REPORT

This introductory chapter describes some of the remarkable opportunities and formidable challenges created by the digital revolution for the world's great libraries. These opportunities and challenges are most dramatic for the Library of Congress because of the grand scale and scope of its operation. However, while this report focuses on the Library of Congress, much of the discussion in it is applicable to a broad range of libraries, archives, and other cultural institutions that face many of the same challenges. Moreover, because the digital revolution is still unfolding, many of its challenges (e.g., digital preservation) are not likely to be resolved any time soon.

---

[42]"Realizing the Virtual Library," by Anthony Appiah, in *Gateways to Knowledge*, Lawrence Dowler, ed. (Cambridge, Mass.: MIT Press, 1997), p. 39.

As is true for many important libraries, the Library of Congress is a complex organization with multiple purposes and stakeholders. Over time, a distinctive organizational culture has developed, evolved, and become institutionalized at the Library. In Chapter 2, the present-day organization and structure of the Library is surveyed, with some emphasis on the Library Services unit, which most laypersons would regard as "the Library."

For physical artifacts—such as books, periodicals, manuscripts, recordings, films, and numerous other records of the cultural heritage—the core processes for libraries are well established. Materials have to be acquired. They are then organized for two purposes: internal management and use by clients. In the course of organizing, mechanisms such as cataloging exist to make it easy to find materials. Access to the materials is provided by making them available for borrowing and for on-site use in reading rooms. Preservation procedures are implemented to ensure that materials will be available indefinitely. The advent of digital information challenges many of these long-standing practices and raises many questions. Chapters 3, 4, and 5 are dedicated to an exposition of how the core processes of libraries need to evolve, within the special context of the Library of Congress.

In the final chapters the committee's focus returns to the Library of Congress as an organization. Chapter 6 discusses the Library's role within the larger context of the library community and the information industry. Historically, the Library has led or been involved with major initiatives in the library community. How should it continue to do so in the future? Chapter 7 addresses the questions of whether the Library is prepared to play an important role in the larger community today and how it needs to evolve to ensure that it remains a leading institution in the digital future. In addressing these questions, the chapter discusses critical organizational issues such as human resources management and strategic planning. Key operational issues surrounding the information technology infrastructure are addressed in Chapter 8. The revolution in information technology raises a host of questions with regard to networks, databases, computer and communications security, and how LC should manage its development projects—through internal development, the purchase of off-the-shelf software, or contracts with integrated systems vendors.

2
THE LIBRARY OF CONGRESS: FROM JEFFERSON TO THE TWENTY-FIRST CENTURY

Libraries are repositories of the past and so cherish and embody their own histories. They are accretive organizations in principle, constantly expanding from the center as item after item is added to the concatenated shelves and bins in which the collections are stored. Library management tends to be conservative, so library leadership tends similarly to an accretive style. The present management structure of the Library of Congress cannot be understood without a sense of the history that has brought it about.[1] To tell the story in this way, however, is not to suggest that there cannot be critical junctures in history that change sharply the way units are organized or management is done.

A BRIEF HISTORY

The Library of Congress was established in 1800, when the seat of government was moved from New York to the new capital city of Washington. The joint committee that oversees the Library of Congress (LC) was established in 1802 and was the first congressional joint committee. After Washington was burned by the British during the War of 1812, Thomas Jefferson reestablished the Library by selling his own personal

---

[1]A wealth of information about the Library of Congress—past, present, and future—is accessible from the Library's Web site at <http://www.loc.gov>.

collection of 6,487 volumes to Congress in 1815. At the time, Jefferson's library was considered the finest in America.

According to its mission, the Library is "to acquire, organize, preserve, secure, and sustain for the present and future of the Congress and the nation a comprehensive record of American history and creativity and a universal collection of human knowledge." More recently, the mission of LC has been articulated as follows: "To make its resources available and useful to the Congress and the American people and to sustain and preserve a universal collection of knowledge and creativity for future generations."[2]

The initial holdings of the Library were a reference tool rather than any attempt at a comprehensive collection or a collection of American publications. The Library was chiefly a library of legal information that might prove useful to legislators. Twenty percent of the initial holdings were law books in the strict sense. When Jefferson sold his multifaceted, multilingual collection to Congress, he felt the need to defend its diversity by stating that there was "no subject to which a Member of Congress might not have occasion to refer."[3] This combination of missions—LC as a reference for legislators and LC as a comprehensive collection of human creativity—has continued to affect the course of the Library. The legislative and reference function was emphasized in the 1832 legislation creating the Law Library of Congress. This branch of the Library of Congress was housed in the Capitol until 1935 and was administered until that time by the U.S. Supreme Court.

Progress toward the comprehensive collection that Mr. Jefferson had favored was interrupted in the middle of the nineteenth century. In 1851 a fire in the Capitol destroyed 35,000 volumes of the 55,000 in the collection at the time, although Congress responded quickly by appropriating the funds to replace the lost books. The fire was followed in 1859 by a repeal of the law providing for copyright deposits at the Library. U.S. copyright activities became centralized at the Patent Office, which meant that LC and the Smithsonian Institution no longer received copies of the books and pamphlets deposited for copyright under the 1846 law providing for the enrichment of library collections through copyright deposit.

Efforts to build the collection resumed in the 1860s. For example, the Library acquired the 40,000 volumes from the Smithsonian's library in

---

[2]As stated in "The Mission and Strategic Priorities of the Library of Congress: 1997-2004," available online at <http://lcweb.loc.gov/ndl/mission.html>.

[3]Thomas Jefferson to Samuel H. Smith, September 21, 1814, Jefferson Papers, Library of Congress, as described in *Jefferson's Legacy: A Brief History of the Library of Congress*, by John Y. Cole (Washington, D.C.: Library of Congress, 1993). Available online at <http://lcweb.loc.gov/loc/legacy/>.

1866. And by 1870, Congress had passed laws establishing the U.S. Copyright Office as an arm of the Library, thereby centralizing all copyright activities. Even though photography and serial publications were becoming more common and popular in the 1870s and inexpensive prints had been readily available since the beginning of the nineteenth century, the copyright laws were intended primarily to manage and acquire books.

What is now called the Jefferson Building of the Library of Congress was authorized in 1886. The building, with reading and exhibition spaces for the general public, reflects two forces affecting the Library: (1) the obligation, contained in its charter, to "the nation" and (2) the influx of general materials that followed the creation of copyright deposit laws in 1870. In 1897, when the new building was occupied, the staff increased from 42 to 108, and separate divisions were formed for serials, maps, music, manuscripts, and graphic arts.

In 1914, Congress created the Legislative Reference Service, renamed the Congressional Research Service in 1970, to accommodate the research needs of members of Congress. For its first decade, the Legislative Reference Service focused on maintaining indexes relating to laws and legislative acts, a charge arising from work started by the Law Library.[4]

Other congressional creations during the twentieth century emphasized extending the forms of material that fall within the purview of the Library. In 1931, the National Library Service for the Blind and Physically Handicapped was established to create materials for disabled audiences. In 1976, the American Folklife Center and the American Television and Radio Archives were created. In 1977, the Center for the Book followed, with the National Film Preservation Board established in 1988. The American Memory Project, established in 1990 and expanded into the National Digital Library Program (NDLP), with its goal of making 5 million digital items available through the Internet, in some ways extends these activities. The NDLP moves the Library of Congress deeper into content creation and management and addresses K-12 students as well as adult audiences—a new arena for the Library.

The Library played a key role during the twentieth century in the area of cataloging. Dewey's Decimal System was established in 1876,[5] and the Library of Congress began creating index cards around the turn of the century. In 1902, legislation enabled the Library to sell cataloging cards to American libraries to help them to address the expense of doing routine

---

[4]Donald R. DeGlopper, from the section on the Law Library for the "LC Encyclopedia," draft dated July 31, 1998, p. 6.

[5]Melvil Dewey established his classification while at Amherst College and expanded it at the New York State Library.

cataloging. This program led to a uniformity of cataloging across libraries subscribing to the service and some structures to support standard cataloging procedures. Other formal research aids were created and advanced in the Library at around that time. A comprehensive index of legislation from all countries in the world was proposed in 1902 and led to the creation of indexes to federal statutes (1903 to 1910) and various tools for indexing foreign statutes as well through the early years of the twentieth century.

The Library led the development during the 1960s of the machine-readable cataloging (MARC) format for identifying and exchanging information about bibliographic materials, which became a national standard in 1971. As part of a consortium that included the American Library Association and British participants, it developed the Anglo-American Cataloging Rules (AACR), guidelines for cataloging. These efforts were complemented by the creation and management of LC subject headings and the LC cataloging system that replaced the Dewey decimal system in many libraries. Elsewhere, the Online Computer Library Center (OCLC) led in the distribution of catalog materials, while integrated library systems began to be developed. The Library has made substantial efforts to extend the AACR cataloging rules and the MARC format into media besides books and participated in the establishment of an International Standard Book Number (ISBN) for books and an International Standard Serial Number (ISSN) for serials.[6] LC's role in developing tools for managing collections has been as significant as the collections that it has gathered.[7]

UNITS OF THE LIBRARY OF CONGRESS

The Library of Congress comprises four major service units, directed from the Office of the Librarian, which is in turn supported by service units that offer enabling infrastructure to the major service units. The structure is explained by history. In particular, Library Services continues to be the oldest unit of the organization, responsible for the collections and public services that most people think of as the Library of Congress.

---

[6]See Chapter 5 for an in-depth discussion of cataloging—MARC, AACR, OCLC, and related topics.

[7]For additional reading on the history of the Library, see *Jefferson's Legacy: A Brief History of the Library of Congress,* by John Y. Cole (Washington, D.C.: Library of Congress, 1993) and *America's Library: The Story of the Library of Congress 1800-2000,* by James Conway (New Haven, Conn.: Yale University Press, 2000), available online at <http://lcweb.loc.gov/loc/legacy/>.

The Law Library has a slightly different but parallel history, while the Copyright Office and the Congressional Research Service (CRS) arose at different dates in response to quite specific congressional mandates. The major service units have interdependencies and links to each other but still function as loosely coupled organizations, even when the staff for each inhabit different floors of the same building. Figure 2.1 shows the overall organizational structure of the Library of Congress. Figures 2.2 and 2.3 provide detail on the Library's supporting infrastructure and on its Library Services unit, respectively. The remainder of this chapter outlines the organization of LC as the committee found it in 1999. In some cases, the description in this chapter includes recommendations made as part of the committee's overall charge, but for the most part discussion of those recommendations is postponed to the substantive chapters that follow. See Table 2.1 for the budget of the Library of Congress.

Office of the Librarian

The Office of the Librarian is the administrative branch of the Library of Congress and had 728 employees as of September 30, 1999, including 201 employees in the Information Technology Services (ITS) Directorate.[8] This office has overall management responsibility for the Library and includes staff functions such as public affairs and congressional relations. Most of the employees within the Office of the Librarian, however, work in centralized services such as Human Resources Services, Security, Financial Services, or ITS, which fall under the rubric "enabling infrastructure" (see Figure 2.2). The systems and strategies of these services have important effects on the entire institution.[9]

Library Services

Library Services is the largest service unit of the Library of Congress, with 2,304 employees in September 1999. Its specific charge is to develop and manage "the Library's universal collections, which document the history and further the creativity of the American people, and which record and contribute to the advancement of civilization and knowledge throughout the world." The audiences served are the following: "Congress, libraries and librarians, scholars, educators, the general public, the

---

[8]The source for the number of employees—in Library Services and in the other units of LC—is the *Annual Report of the Librarian of Congress*, 1999.

[9]ITS and some other units of the Office of the Librarian are discussed in greater detail in Chapters 7 and 8. The Office of the Librarian is mentioned here for purposes of comparison with the other major offices of the Library.

55

LIBRARY OF CONGRESS

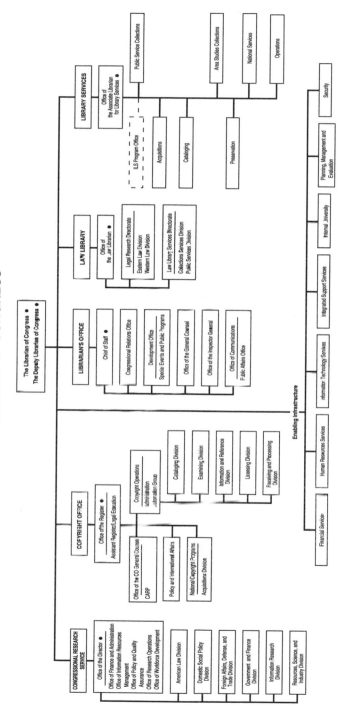

FIGURE 2.1 Organizational structure of the Library of Congress.

● Members of the Executive Committee of the Library of Congress

LIBRARY OF CONGRESS

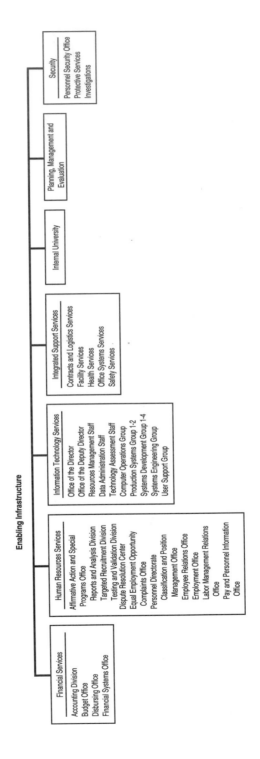

FIGURE 2.2 Enabling infrastructure of the Library of Congress.

LIBRARY OF CONGRESS

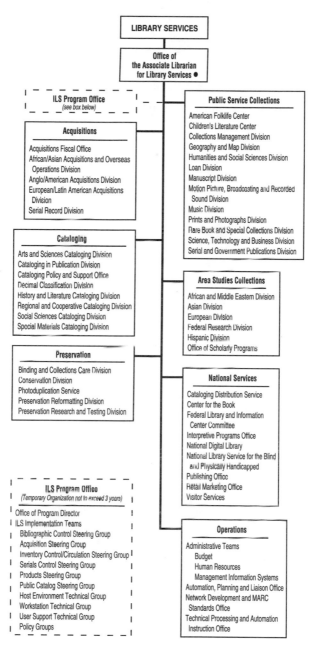

FIGURE 2.3 Library Services and its directorates.

TABLE 2.1 Net Costs by Program Area at the Library of Congress (dollars)

Program Area	Cost	Revenue	Net Cost
Library Services	239,046,427	4,868,749	234,177,678
Law Library	14,562,531	0	14,562,531
Copyright Office	48,039,321	18,218,923	29,820,398
Congressional Research Service	96,017,808	0	96,017,808
National Library Service for the Blind and Physically Handicapped[a]	46,397,702	0	46,397,702
Reimbursable funds[b]	53,661,537	47,897,166	5,764,371
Revolving funds[c]	15,646,988	6,281,721	9,365,267
Miscellaneous			35
Net cost of operations			436,105,790

SOURCE: Adapted from the *Financial Statements for Fiscal 1999*, Library of Congress, March 2000, p. 2-2.

[a]Although the National Library Service for the Blind and Physically Handicapped (NLSBPH) is a unit of Library Services, it receives a separate appropriation from Congress.

[b]The Library manages the Federal Library and Information Network (FEDLINK) and the Federal Research Division, which account for the major portion of the reimbursable revenues. In addition, LC provides accounting services for four legislative agencies under cross-servicing agreements. The net program costs for the Library's reimbursable funds are nearly zero when intra-Library net revenues of $4.3 million are included and adjustments of $1.5 million are excluded.

[c]Under the authority of 2 U.S.C. 160, the Library operates 11 gift revolving fund activities to provide a variety of services.

blind and physically handicapped, and internal clients."[10] The Library fulfills this mandate by providing access to its collection of 26 million volumes, nearly 1 million serials, and many items in other formats. It does this in more than 20 reading rooms in Washington, D.C., alone, as well as through interlibrary loans and Internet access. Not only does Library Services provide access to books, but it also supports the creation and distribution of information about books in direct ways—through the

---

[10]"Information Technology Beyond the Year 2000," presented by LC staff at the committee's first plenary meeting on February 18, 1999.

distribution of catalog materials—and in indirect ways, through initiatives like the Center for the Book and its state affiliates.[11]

One of the most significant features of Library Services from the point of view of information technology is the organization of the Public Service Collections—those divisions organized around the physical form of collections (e.g., the Geography and Map, Prints and Photographs, and Manuscript Divisions), around content centers (e.g., the Humanities and Social Sciences Division and the Music Division), or around functions (e.g., the Loan and the Collections Management Divisions). Figure 2.3 shows the organization of Library Services.

As early as 1902, Library Services began serving its second audience—libraries and librarians—by distributing catalog materials to alleviate the burden of every library having to catalog the same item in more or less the same way. For nearly two-thirds of the twentieth century, this was done through a system of cards and printed volumes providing actual catalog records or references such as LC subject headings. Today, it is largely done electronically, either through the medium of shared resources distributed directly or through services such as OCLC and the Research Libraries Information Network, the services offered to publishers that facilitate cataloging, and the internal Integrated Library System (ILS) of the Library of Congress. The history of these three functions is intertwined.

In 1958, the Committee on Mechanized Information Retrieval began to lay the foundation for the ILS, which was eventually installed in October 1999.[12] An outgrowth of that committee's work was the development

---

[11]The Center for the Book in the Library of Congress, created by Public Law 95-129 in 1977, was established to stimulate public interest in books, reading, and libraries and to encourage the study of books and print culture. Within the Library of Congress, the center is a focal point for celebrating the legacy of books and the printed word.

Outside the Library, the center works closely with other organizations to foster understanding of the vital role of books, reading, libraries, and literacy in society. A partnership between the government and the private sector, the center depends primarily on tax-deductible contributions from corporations and individuals to support its overall program of projects, publications, and events of interest to both the general public and scholars. See <http://lcweb.loc.gov/loc/cfbook/ctr-bro.html>.

[12]The ILS represents a significant step toward resolving the differences among the various systems developed in the Library over the years. The ILS, an off-the-shelf system developed by Endeavor Information Systems, Inc., of Des Plaines, Illinois, finally integrates many of the major component systems of the Library into one application. It supports standard operations such as acquisitions, cataloging, inventory and serials control, circulation, and the online public access catalog. In general, integrated library systems simplify staff tasks, thereby enhancing efficiency, and centralize records, thereby improving collection control and customer service. See Chapter 8 for a detailed discussion of the ILS.

in the 1960s of the MARC format. Together with the AACR cataloging rules that specify which of the elements defined in MARC are to be used for cataloging particular formats, the basic structure of the electronic catalog record was set. MARC records have been readily and consistently distributed to libraries since the late 1960s through the Cataloging Distribution Service (CDS), either directly from the Library of Congress or indirectly through OCLC, the Research Libraries Group, and other large library database managers.

In 1971, the Cataloging in Publication (CIP) program was established to allow publishers to create prepublication catalog records for books that might be expected to be widely distributed. CIP records form a part of the core catalog data distributed through CDS, and they accelerate the dissemination of cataloging data for new U.S. publications, offering a savings in the cost of cataloging and expediting the creation of catalog records. In 1996, the process was expanded to allow electronic transmission of the CIP information from the publisher through the Electronic Cataloging in Publication (ECIP) program.

MARC records have become the norm in library cataloging. Their adoption for use in library systems has been somewhat slower. The Library's first efforts to use electronic records for access during the 1970s led to the Subject-Content-Oriented Retriever for Processing Information Online (SCORPIO) system and the Multiple Use MARC System (MUMS), which provided search, retrieval, and display components. In 1975, the first computer terminal was installed in the main reading room for the use of patrons. In the 1980s and 1990s, the Library moved to more powerful computers and added communications, but SCORPIO and MUMS continued to be the core of its catalog until the installation of the ILS in October 1999. The ACCESS system was implemented in 1991, allowing users to get into SCORPIO and MUMS more easily via a graphical user interface (MS-Windows). The Library of Congress Information System (LOCIS) provided another way of accessing SCORPIO and MUMS in 1993 over the Internet.[13]

Circulation transactions were maintained manually through the 1960s. An attempt to develop an in-house circulation system in the 1970s was abandoned for an interim system borrowed from the National Library of Medicine. In 1988, a circulation control facility (CCF) and an acquisitions module, ACQUIRE, were implemented. Card-based systems for managing the shelf lists and serials check-in have been maintained until the present, along with bound ledgers for the shelf list covering the period before 1940.

---

[13]*Preparing for the 21st Century: Information Technology at the Library of Congress in the 1990s and Beyond,* by Audrey Fischer, undated.

In 1997 plans were made to move to an integrated library system. The product selected was Voyager, developed by Endeavor Information Systems, and it was installed in 1999. All of the primary legacy electronic systems—SCORPIO, MUMS, CCF, and ACQUIRE—have been resolved into the ILS, and in January 2000, they were taken off-line. The shelf list and serials check-in will be converted from their current manual systems into the ILS structure over the next 5 to 10 years.[14]

Geography and Map Division

The Geography and Map Division collects maps, atlases, globes, and CD-ROMs associated with maps and mapping. The division has not yet begun to collect significant numbers of geographical databases or mapping software, although it has been active in deploying tools and cataloging standards for maps. Currently, no robust structure for collecting such nontraditional formats exists in the Library, and this division is no exception.[15] The division has taken the lead in developing the standards to be used within the National Digital Library Program for delivering maps. It is also working with CRS to develop the division's geographical information systems (GISs) resources. The Library has created digital surrogates (with unique cataloged records)[16] for 3,659[17] of the 4.5 million items in the collection, including maps related to the Civil War, railroads in the United States, and panoramic maps of American cities. This division felt keenly the need for more powerful workstations, faster networks, and better access to tools for imaging and for managing the very large images required for making surrogates. This need poses another technical challenge.

The division seems to believe that cataloging with MARC formats makes it sufficiently active in the area of geographic collections management. The committee notes, however, that the area has grown and changed remarkably with the introduction of the computer and with the development of sophisticated GISs. This means that although the division has performed its traditional tasks well, it has fallen behind the cut-

---

[14]The sheer size of the pre-1981 official catalog—a bank of hundreds of cabinets filled with index cards extending what seems to be the whole width of the building—illustrates the challenge of managing legacy systems, to say nothing of the huge amounts of material.

[15]Here, as elsewhere, it can be the case that LC's uniqueness makes it dangerous for LC to wait for others to innovate. However, if LC is the only place, or one of the few places, where innovation might occur, conservatism in innovation is out of place.

[16]By "digital surrogate" the committee means, here and elsewhere, a digital representation of the analog artifact, intended to be not only a representation, but also an item with value and utility in itself. Thus a digital surrogate of a map may (because it can be enlarged, cropped, and compared) offer usefulness not present in the original.

[17]Based on information provided by LC to the committee in July 2000.

ting-edge institutions. There certainly has been no pressure from other LC units for the division to provide anything but MARC-format records for this collection, and the relatively simple demands for metadata placed on it by the NDLP have not pushed the Geography and Map Division further into evolving areas such as those addressed by the Open GIS Consortium.[18]

Manuscript Division

The Manuscript Division collects archival and manuscript material of national significance. It has the papers of 23 presidents, several U.S. Supreme Court justices, and prominent writers, inventors, and intellectuals, as well as the archives of nationally significant organizations such as the National Association for the Advancement of Colored People and the National Urban League.[19] The division has about 12,000 collections, which range in size from a few documents to thousands of boxes of documents. Finding aids (descriptions of collections with listings of the contents of boxes and folders) exist for about 2,000 of the collections, and there are item-level indexes for presidential papers; some 140 of the division's finding aids are online. About 10 percent of the collections have been microfilmed. Very few individual items have been given digital surrogates. NDLP has sampled items from the division (e.g., selected pages from Alexander Graham Bell's papers and portions of Longfellow's manuscripts) and digitized exemplary items. The division has been reluctant to digitize collections, partly because its client researchers generally want more than just a limited selection of materials. The Manuscript Division also has a large backlog of unprocessed collections. The staff considers preparing these collections for use by researchers to have a higher priority than digitization.[20]

---

[18]See <http://www.opengis.org> for information about the Open GIS Consortium.

[19]The Library of Congress collects the papers of private citizens and organizations. The National Archives and Records Administration (NARA) is responsible for collecting historically significant records of the federal government. Presidential papers in the Library of Congress begin with those of George Washington and include most of the presidents through the nineteenth century and into the twentieth century. Then, beginning with President Hoover, twentieth-century presidents established private presidential libraries to house their papers. The presidential libraries are administered by NARA, and since 1981 presidents have been required to deposit the official records of their presidency in a presidential library.

[20]In general, the demands of managing physical materials and of providing access— digital or otherwise—to them are more acutely at odds in manuscript collections than other parts of libraries. The Library of Congress is no different in this regard. Microfilm has made it possible for whole collections to be quickly and easily captured (and for researchers, whole collections are usually the most important) rather than just a few highlights, which is the extent to which digitization can realistically go at this date.

While initiatives such as that for encoded archival description (EAD)[21] provide a standard mechanism for sharing archival finding aids online, the division is only beginning to experiment. Like so many LC units, this division is set up to continue to receive traditional materials. There are no structures for, and little thought has been given to, cataloging, storing, managing, or offering access to a collection that arrives as a set of computer files, e-mails, and other digital materials. Even a mixed collection containing some traditional material and some electronic material cannot be easily accommodated with the existing tools.[22]

Motion Picture, Broadcasting, and Recorded Sound Division

The collections of the Motion Picture, Broadcasting, and Recorded Sound Division include roughly 1,000,000 audio recordings and 200,000 cans of film. The limited applicability of MARC for cataloging the materials of this division led to the development of specialized cataloging and collections management tools, so these collections as cataloged were not part of the initial ILS installation.

Most of the materials in these collections are still under copyright, which restricts LC's ability to create digital surrogates, but such digital surrogates are important for preservation purposes. Some material—especially early motion picture footage—has accordingly been digitized and showcased in the National Digital Library (NDL). The creation of the National Audio-Visual Conservation Center at Culpeper, Virginia, along with thoughts of distributing assets to multiple non-LC locations (e.g., a jazz museum in Harlem), has helped to generate ideas about distribution of digital collections as a way to preserve originals in remote storage facilities while still serving the needs of the public.

There is no systematic plan for collecting content developed exclusively for distribution on the Internet (e.g., MP3 format music or streaming video), and, like the Manuscript Division, the Motion Picture, Broadcasting, and Recorded Sound Division has no plan for housing such digital content.

---

[21]See Chapter 5 for a discussion of EAD.

[22]The Library of Congress could join forces with other interested parties (e.g., NARA) to find ways of dealing with issues of this sort. This theme—LC reaching out to others facing comparable challenges with respect to digital information—is discussed at length in Chapter 6 and throughout the report.

Prints and Photographs Division

The Prints and Photographs Division has had a long-standing program for creating digital surrogates for preservation and access. Currently, approximately 575,000 images (out of a collection of 13.5 million) are available digitally, and 445,000 of these are within the scope of NDLP. They are accessible through the Prints and Photographs Online Catalog (PPOC), a custom cataloging system that was developed by the division to collect and distribute such information.

The division does not yet collect images that are created as digital works.[23] There are no structures in place for capturing, storing, or managing such materials. To the committee's knowledge, there has not yet been any consideration of the implications for the future of the MARC format of its inadequacy for dealing with this important class of library materials.

Serial and Government Publications Division

The collections of the Serial and Government Publications Division include 70,000 periodicals and 1,400 newspapers along with publications of the federal government (including those received as a federal depository library). Access to electronic versions of newspapers and to various electronic journals has been provided via links to archives of such material (e.g., *The Christian Science Monitor*). The division provides access to online journals and newspapers in its reading room, but only for so long as the publisher keeps the material online. It has not begun to collect or allow access to digital-only serials or digital forms of serials in any significant sense. Microfilm and microfiche versions continue to be collected because they are considered the "best edition" for long-term preservation and access. The division has had little involvement with NDLP, partly because of copyright issues with private-sector publishers and partly because of technical problems. NDLP and the other divisions of LC have

---

[23]In this division as in others, the fact that more and more born-digital objects are being created that are analogous to physical artifacts suggests either expanding the scope of the divisions or creating another division. One could argue for either approach. Just because a digital image might be published like a print or photograph (in fact, it might be nearly indistinguishable in its published form from either a print or a photograph) may not mean that it is within the purview of the Prints and Photographs Division. We tend to classify digital materials by the analog forms they are realized in rather than by their native digital forms. This may not be the best way to do it. Certainly, having a division for collecting digital materials—no matter what analog forms of presentation they take or imitate—would address some of the knottier technical issues that must now be solved by the various divisions where this content would otherwise be kept.

developed appropriate ways of presenting digital content (zoomable maps, pagination for multipage items, etc.), but no satisfactory way of presenting materials such as newspapers has been developed. Implementation of the ILS will continue to preoccupy this division, for the serials check-in list is still managed as a manual file. Automating this important function would be an important first step to making the holdings more widely accessible.

National Library Service for the Blind and Physically Handicapped

The National Library Service for the Blind and Physically Handicapped (NLSBPH—NLS, for short) was established in 1931 by an act of Congress to serve the particular needs of blind and physically handicapped people who cannot use ordinary printed texts. The NLS, which has 131 employees,[24] offers free Braille and recorded materials to 780,000 individuals each year, most of whom (90 percent) are blind. The emphasis is on the production and distribution of general or popular publications rather than scholarly works. Each year approximately 2,000 titles in various formats are produced by NLS, and through a network of 85 regional offices, NLS circulated 23 million items in a recent year. Special provisions in the copyright law allow the NLS to select, produce, and distribute these materials. NLS produces recorded materials in 86 languages for distribution to handicapped patrons in their native languages. In addition, NLS designs and oversees the manufacture and servicing of the specialized equipment that is used to play back the audio recordings.

NLS has been largely self-contained with respect to developing and using information technologies (such as the circulation system and specialized databases for producing print or audio resources and for tracking loaner equipment and borrower preferences). It anticipates integrating its catalog and online retrieval system into ILS. NLS has throughout its history been involved in the specification and deployment of technology related to audio recording, audio playback equipment, production of recorded materials, and shipping of recordings. The changing population of blind users influences the technical solutions. For example, in 1945 a disproportionately large segment of the target population were veterans of the Second World War; today the largest segment is elderly individuals who are losing their sight and acquiring other infirmities.

Digital technology offers powerful new opportunities for extending the service, but there are special challenges associated with the dissemination media. The existing audio system depends on the use of a non-

---

[24] As of September 30, 1999, from the *Annual Report of the Librarian of Congress*, 1999.

standard tape format played on special hardware, a mechanism that encourages publishers to allow recording and disseminating their works without fear that the tapes will be reproduced without authorization and used beyond the intended audience. The creation of a similar digital delivery channel for the blind will raise formidable technical and—more important—social issues. NLS has considered various strategies for using digital technology and has been actively participating in the creation of a National Information Standards Organization (NISO) standard to ensure compatibility among the several systems under development. The timetable, file specification, and interface characteristics of a playback device for compressed digital audio are still being developed.[25]

A Web-based delivery of audio files from a digital library supported by improved voice synthesizers capable of turning digital text into functional audio without the expense of recording and distributing a "performance" of a given book can be envisioned, although there are some obstacles to achieving such a vision:[26]

- Publishers' reluctance to allow the uncontrolled dissemination of text in such forms,
- Physical difficulties involved in the use of current and next-generation Web-based systems for the visually handicapped, and
- Economic difficulties associated with ensuring access to suitable technology by a population whose members would tend to be on the disadvantaged side of the "digital divide."

Other Divisions

Library Services is a large and complex organization that the committee could not fully explore. For example, the committee was able to visit only briefly the African and Middle Eastern Division, Asian Division, European Division, Hispanic Division, and the Office of Scholarly Programs. Other units, such as the Science, Technology, and Business Division, the Humanities and Social Sciences Division, and the Music Divi-

---

[25]The Web site at <http://www.niso.org/commitaq.html> indicates that NLS staff are leading the Task Force on a Digital Talking Book, which includes manufacturers of hardware devices and software tools as well as many individuals from organizations serving blind people. The standard will be applicable to all types of users. The challenges for NLS include meeting the needs of the severely disabled and the elderly population, as well as making the transition in hardware and distribution of audio files.

[26]Despite the challenges, the NLS is making some progress on digital initiatives. See, for example, "Library of Congress Launches Web-Braille on the Internet for Blind and Visually Impaired Library Users," at <www.loc.gov/nls/nls-wb.html>.

sion, were studied through documentation provided by the Library or obtained through published sources.

Law Library

The primary function of the Law Library is to "serve as the foreign, comparative, and international law research arm of the U.S. Congress, the Judiciary, and Executive agencies."[27] The Law Library ensures that a staff member is physically present in the Law Library whenever Congress is in session in case there is a need to look something up.[28] The Law Library is divided into two directorates with a total of 97 employees (as of September 30, 1999). The Services Directorate provides on-site access to a range of materials relating to foreign law and to a comprehensive collection of U.S. bills and associated materials, including the *Congressional Record* and the publications that preceded it. The reference collection in the reading room numbers 65,000 volumes, and the entire collection contains roughly 2.3 million items. More than half the items are in languages other than English, in accordance with the mandate to collect primary legal material from around the world. The Legal Research Directorate provides research into foreign, comparative, and international law for members of Congress and (as resources permit) to other governmental bodies and the general public as well.

Starting in 1902, the Law Library developed strategies for managing and indexing its complex materials. The index of federal statutes, which started as a Law Library project but eventually became a responsibility of CRS, and comparable indexes of international collections (most notably the Latin American indexes that have been maintained since the 1950s) have served as the basis for the Law Library's current initiatives in technology, including development of the Global Legal Information Network (GLIN).

Public access to U.S. legislation has been achieved through the THOMAS system. The materials entered into THOMAS, however, are within the purview of the Law Library, which maintains the most complete set of federal and state legislative materials in any one place. The congressional materials run from 1774; the complete set of U.S. Supreme Court records runs from 1832.

---

[27]"Services of the Law Library of Congress," brochure dated December 1996.

[28]From outside the Law Library, this requirement, which grew from an incident in the nineteenth century when the Law Library was housed in the Capitol and someone wanted a publication after it had closed, has the charm of tradition. From within, given the reality that meeting twenty-first-century information needs seldom requires physical access to the Madison Building by members after hours, it is a burden on a staff already overtaxed.

The challenge of providing access to foreign legislative materials led the Law Library to establish GLIN, for which it gathers materials in their native languages. To search this corpus effectively requires either (1) a structure for abstracting into English the contents of each document or (2) multilingual search engines. Since the latter solution, the technological one, is not viable in even the limited areas where it has been tested, the choice has been to abstract. To do this requires adding staff to do the abstracting or creating structures to capture abstracts from the participating countries. This abstracting requires training and a considerable amount of oversight by Law Library staff. The comparative ease of getting THOMAS up and running has not been possible with GLIN.

Because GLIN has turned out to be so complex and because much of the software that was being imagined for it either did not exist in off-the-shelf form or could not be easily adapted to the needs of GLIN, the Law Library had to partner and raise funds to realize what has been developed so far. The World Bank has emerged as a major sponsor, so the main participating countries are developing nations such as Albania and Brazil. (GLIN's managers have also decided, sensibly, to defer work on the laws of more developed countries, on the assumption that those countries will have the means and the will to create similar resources for themselves, with GLIN helping to establish standards and interoperability.) Given the difficulties and constraints, the Law Library has made good progress in transferring the concepts underlying the THOMAS system to international law.

GLIN would be far more valuable if it had a higher priority and if it were autonomously funded—in which case it could select for itself the countries with which it deals and could work with the rest of the Library to build the standards and technology needed to do a complex job in the most appropriate way. For example, GLIN would benefit from LC investments in foreign language text representation, editing, search, and retrieval. GLIN's dependence on external funding marginalizes its potential.[29]

In other areas, the Law Library has been an active partner in advancing technology. For example, the installation of the ILS by Library Services was received with enthusiasm by the Law Library staff, who expect it will make their collection easy to manage.

The Law Library took advantage of the NDL to digitize a considerable amount of its early holdings. One of the largest projects in the NDL is from the Law Library, namely, the Century of Lawmaking project, which includes many of the popular documents relating to the founding

---

[29]Depending too heavily on donors or sponsors to select program focus or determine technology selections is a theme that will be revisited in subsequent chapters.

of America, as well as complete photo reproductions of large portions of the publications that were predecessors of the *Congressional Record*.

Copyright Office

The Copyright Office had 505 employees as of September 30, 1999. Like the Law Library, it operates under mandates that were based on an earlier set of circumstances. While the letter of the law that moves the Copyright Office forward may be out of date, its spirit is not. The basic outlines of copyright were created for a bibliocentric world that had a manageable, if diffuse, number of works and number of creators. Scalability was not a primary concern when the fundamental tenets were outlined, and the problems of identifying rightful copyright holders had to do with the complexities of communicating over large areas with a limited set of tools rather than with handling great numbers of things about which a great deal can be known using sophisticated tools. When the copyright system under which our country continues to operate was enacted, a physical certificate (like a diploma or a stock certificate or a banknote) was typically the tangible way to present a verifiable status (without having to resort to validation in each instance). A small number of books and other materials were being copyrighted, and one of the biggest challenges the Copyright Office had to face was the size of the country and the difficulty of administering something as regional or even local as publishing was in the 1870s. In the year 2000, we have many ways of verifying authenticity (and while certificates of various kinds have the power of law, they are seldom used for verification). The number of books and other items copyrighted has risen considerably, and contemporary shipping and communication make the most out-of-the-way corners of the country part of a national (and even global) system. The requirement that each work be examined physically and that a certificate proving the copyright be created and distributed and the idea that making a copy of the copyright application is critical in the process may be troubling to the outsider, but those steps are part of the process that has governed copyright for the last 125 years.

For all works published in the United States, two copies must be deposited according to the law.[30] Registration is an optional procedure

---

[30]While there can be a question of whether something is "published" or not in the analog world, the question of whether a digital work is published or not can be even more difficult to answer; for a discussion of considerations in what constitutes publication, see *The Digital Dilemma: Intellectual Property in the Information Age*, by the Computer Science and Telecommunications Board, National Research Council (Washington, D.C.: National Academy Press, 2000).

that copyright holders can pursue to strengthen legal assertion for both published and unpublished works. To register a published work, one must submit two copies (which also satisfies the mandatory deposit requirement). To register unpublished works, one copy is sufficient. Each submission must be examined in the Copyright Office to determine whether it is eligible for copyright protection. Selection officers from the Law Library and Library Services review published materials and select those that meet the criteria for inclusion in the Library's permanent collection. The Copyright Office is obliged by regulation to retain unselected published works for 5 years. It retains unpublished work for 70 years after the author's death.

The Copyright Office operates largely separately from the rest of the Library. There is, however, a critical link between the Copyright Office and Library Services (and the Law Library to a lesser extent): the majority of materials obtained for LC's collections are received from the Copyright Office. In the world of physical artifacts, it is not a problem that the respective organizations are loosely coupled. Selectors can physically sort through the materials. In the digital world, especially with born-digital content, a more coordinated, specified interface will be needed to ensure that digital materials can be read and tracked in a reasonable way.

Because of the large numbers of works it must deal with (the office processes more than 600,000 claims each year), because of the examination and retention requirements, and because it must be able to verify that on a particular date a particular object was deposited or registered or both, the information systems maintained by the Copyright Office are necessarily management and cataloging tools. Until 1978, a copyright card catalog was used to record every item registered. Since 1978, the Copyright Office Publication and Interactive Cataloging System (COPICS) has been used to record all registered works, as well as transfers and assignments of rights submitted for recordation by copyright owners. It uses a set of MARC-like elements to catalog each entry, and copyright catalogers do not follow generally accepted cataloging rules. For internal management, the Copyright Office In-Process System (COINS) tracks applications for registration and other work requests within the Copyright Office and includes all fiscal processing of fees and maintenance of deposit accounts for high-volume remitters. Both systems have been upgraded over the years, and COINS is to be substantially revised in the near future. The Copyright Office uses an imaging system to facilitate preservation of the applications for copyright registration as well as the assignment and transfer documents. The system also produces the certificates of copyright registration and makes the applications and documents available for viewing by the public. ITS developed the imaging system in 1994 using the same proprietary software used for the CRS imaging system. This system is slated for replacement in 2001. Since 1993, the Copyright Office has been developing (in a project with the Corporation for National Research Initiatives, discussed in Chapter 3) the Copyright Electronic Recordation and Deposit System (CORDS) to accept deposits and registration of digital materials.

None of the procedures that constitute the registration process is well integrated with the others. Tools were built to deal only with parts of problems, the relentless flow of material continues to grow, the steps in the copyright process are idiosyncratic, and the works that arrive in the Copyright Office offer the examiners multiple complexities and ambiguities. None of these parameters is likely to change very rapidly. Digital works will add layers of complexity; a single tangible, created entity in the age of digital content that changes with additions to databases or that is intentionally fugitive or that allows regular or continuous updating is not consistent with the current procedure for delineating a copyrightable object.

Congressional Research Service

The Congressional Research Service is responsible for providing Congress with "comprehensive and reliable research, analysis and information services that are timely, objective, non-partisan, and confidential" through its 720 employees (as of September 30, 1999). It is the arm of LC that most nearly and exclusively performs the original function of LC, the support of Congress and its legislative needs. It has had a history of more or less close association with the rest of the Library, but there are numerous points of disjunction. For example, the staff of CRS make much less use of LC collections than the committee had expected, and CRS employees have their own union, quite separate in identity and organization from the unions to which other Library staff belong.[31]

The Congressional Research Service is organized into six research areas: American law, domestic social policy; foreign affairs, defense, and trade; government and finance; information research; and resources, science, and industry. In addition, of the five staff offices in CRS, Information Resources Management handles legislative information, including the Legislative Information System (LIS) (see Box 2.1), and Research Operations manages technology application development, imaging, and infrastructure for CRS.[32]

---

[31]CRS staff even have business cards with a design distinctly different from that of other LC staff business cards.

[32]Special Announcement 99-4, available online at <http://lcweb.loc.gov/staff/ogc/sa/sa99-4.html>.

BOX 2.1
The Legislative Information System

As Speaker of the House of Representatives, Newt Gingrich directed the Library of Congress (LC) to develop a system for making legislative information available to the public through the Internet by January 1995. The Library did this using existing data and systems and creating a Web interface with a new search engine. Congress (through appropriations language) also requested that LC conduct a study in 1995 of the duplication of legislative systems across all legislative branch agencies. The study found considerable duplication, whereupon Congress asked LC to prepare a plan for a new system to serve as Congress's primary legislative information system (LIS). The LIS was to be developed and maintained collaboratively by all the offices and legislative support agencies that serve the Congress. The Library and the Congressional Research Service were given responsibility for coordinating the retrieval component of this effort among all congressional offices (House, Senate, LC, Government Printing Office, Congressional Budget Office, General Accounting Office) and for making the information accessible. The result has been an ongoing reengineering of the collection, storage, and retrieval of legislative information across Capitol Hill, beginning with the clerks on the chamber floors and in the legislative counsels who draft the bills and extending through retrieval of the information through either the LIS (for members and staff of the Congress) or THOMAS (for the public). As a result of these efforts, there is now one coordinated, distributed system that provides legislative information to Congress and the public. Both the House and Senate retired their legacy retrieval systems and provide data directly to the LIS. This was one of the most remarkable successes LC has had in digital information management systems. Some of that success reflected the nature of the materials (legal texts are "flat" and structured at the same time) and some reflected the ability of the organization to react to significant outside pressure with a nimbleness and agility that are not seen in day-to-day life at LC.

CRS produces primarily two kinds of products:

- Material distributed broadly throughout the Congress, including issue briefs that require regular updates and reports that were formerly static documents but increasingly are updated periodically. All issue briefs and a growing number of the reports are available to Congress via the CRS Web site.
- Confidential work, which is guided by the principle that clients own the answers as well as the questions. Such work necessitates tracking multiple "original" works on similar or identical topics.[33]

---

[33]Since members of Congress are apt to use the results of this type of research in public statements, one can imagine that it is important that the results seem original. Simply distributing the same report with the same language and examples might create some embarrassing situations.

In FY99, CRS responded to almost 546,000 congressional requests, produced roughly 1,000 new CRS reports and issue briefs, and created over 1,700 custom confidential memoranda.

CRS benefits from a clear sense of mission and of customer identity. Although members of Congress and congressional staff can and do ask about an amazing variety of subjects, the CRS staff know from whom the questions will come, and the protocol for providing answers is comparatively clear. In some ways, CRS resembles a remarkably large staff of reference librarians, answering sophisticated inquiries in immense detail and with great professionalism; in others, it resembles a university faculty, performing original research on issues of public policy. Members of Congress and their staffs are generally pleased with the service received.

Because CRS requires quick access to information, it manages its own digesting services, it considers electronic forms as the best edition for its business, and it has an interest in such things as geographical information systems. In some ways, its agenda pushes other parts of the Library. The Geography and Map Division will benefit from its partnership with CRS, which wants the kind of GIS that Geography and Map has been wanting. In other ways, however, its special needs set it apart. Both CRS and the Law Library have research arms that prepare reports for their clients, but CRS requires a degree of confidentiality that makes it inappropriate even to share tracking systems for research. CRS might well be a client for newly acquired digital materials in the Copyright Office, except that the pace of the Copyright Office and the rate at which its materials find their way into the Library's collection are generally too slow for CRS. Accordingly, CRS has been an early adopter of technology but has often done so independently of the rest of LC.

CRS has its own cataloging and information retrieval system—Star ILS—that it intends to integrate into the new Voyager ILS. It has the Public Policy Literature File, an online abstracting system available to Congress and CRS staff. The Inquiry Status Information System (ISIS), introduced in 1978 and upgraded in 1996, manages requests received from Congress and tracks their status as the work is performed. The congressional mandate to provide access to large bodies of text material—bills, the *Congressional Record*, and related materials—along with the requirement to reduce duplication of effort among congressional units led to the implementation of the LIS and THOMAS systems, which use a natural language query engine that gives online access to these legislative materials in a convenient and timely way. LIS and THOMAS have proven to be two of the most effective of LC's forays into the distribution of online materials. They were implemented very shortly after the mandate and have continued to function—with occasional enhancements and regular expansion—very effectively. CRS maintains an active Web site and has an interest in multimedia distribution, maintaining secure networks, increasing bandwidth, and serving its audience better.

National Digital Library Program

Between 1990 and 1994, the Library experimented with a pilot project called the American Memory Project to make digital surrogates of key documents held by the Library. Out of that project, the National Digital Library Program was born. The NDLP had more than 100 employees as of April 1999 and an annual budget of $12 million. Its goal is to digitize 5 million items within 5 years.[34] The NDLP has made astute use of the tremendous popular appeal of the documents in its collection to garner private support. It aims to provide materials for educational purposes for children from kindergarten through high school—audiences that have hitherto been largely outside the focus of the Library (see Box 2.2). To meet this challenge, the NDLP has depended on a mix of LC staff and contractors. As a project-based program, the NDLP is not required to provide the long-term service functions that LC must normally provide.

Apart from working to achieve its immediate goals, the NDLP has worked to bring in outside sources of support and content. Ameritech has supported creating collections that are physically located at other institutions but intellectually integrated with NDLP resources at LC. The Mellon Foundation is seeking to make available digital content that does not reside at LC. Digital materials created by projects such as the Making of America (Cornell University and the University of Michigan) are under consideration for inclusion. The NDLP has a general vision but no formal, central plan for selecting materials or creating links between various materials. For some collecting areas, having digital surrogates available is a benefit—in the Prints and Photographs or Geography and Map Divisions, for instance. In others, the capability would be apt to provide access to materials otherwise difficult to see on account of access restrictions or concerns for preservation—the materials from the Law Library, for instance. For still other areas, such as the Manuscript Division, having digital surrogates provides exposure but in and of itself does not yet benefit users.

Thompson Technology is providing repository software for the NDLP with an Oracle database system, a search engine, and tools for managing metadata. The Library's Information Technology Services Directorate has been involved in an advisory capacity in this development but has not

---

[34]An "item" in the NDLP collection is not equivalent to an item in LC's collections. Instead, it is a digital image, and one Web page may contain one or more digital images.

BOX 2.2
Opportunities to Expand the Library's Audiences

The advent of digital information and networks offers substantial opportunities for making the Library of Congress (LC) more visible and valuable to a wider audience. There is great virtue in using technology to extend the accessibility of the Library's rich resources beyond Capitol Hill. Clearly, new audiences such as the K-12 community also offer new opportunities for partnerships and funding. At the time this report was being prepared, a $25 million advertising campaign contributed by the Ad Council of America was under way to expand the audience.

At the same time, however, reaching out to new audiences poses challenges. For example, reaching a significant portion of the K-12 community directly (i.e., developing resources that are to be used by students and teachers directly) is difficult, especially for an organization that does not traditionally possess such expertise. Partnerships with intermediaries who have experience working with this community may be a more effective approach; in the case of the National Digital Library Program, such intermediaries include public and school libraries and publishers that serve this community. Such a strategy would allow LC to leverage its investments in digitization by having an impact on a much broader segment of society than if it had reached out to students and teachers directly. An additional benefit is that the packaging and interpretation of digital resources to be used for teaching would be developed primarily by intermediaries experienced in making such judgments, thereby avoiding criticism for having the federal government interpret history for schoolchildren or use public resources to compete with the private sector (i.e., educational publishers). In the spring of 2000, the America's Library Web site (<http://www.americaslibrary.gov>) began addressing a school-age audience even more explicitly.

played a leadership role here and has certainly not played the role of application developer. Guidelines for developing particular media have been created as each media type is tackled. The procedure has been to get the program working and to be successful, but as the program develops, more planning will have to be done. The NDLP has been especially valuable to the Library in the areas of creating (converting from analog to digital) and managing digital materials. Because none of the collecting arms of the LC have much in the way of structures for gathering digital materials, the NDLP has set itself the daunting task of managing the 5 million items once they are digitized. This is being done in an open fashion so that the collecting arms can make use of links to that imagery. So far, however, the Geography and Map Division seems to be the primary division taking advantage of this opportunity; the committee hopes that the ILS and other systems (e.g., the Prints and Photographs cataloging system) will link to this imagery at some point. While the bulk of the materials being accumulated under the umbrella of the NDLP are still images, the NDLP has tackled issues having to do with formats for delivering materials, longevity of approaches, and the like. Though not widely published and certainly not widely emulated within LC, the basic methods for creating each type of surrogate—still images, sound recordings, audio recordings, and maps—have been carried out in a thoughtful and developmental way. These methods should be examined for their applicability to other LC activities and publicized more assertively in the larger community.

The NDLP and the Library need to do much more work in developing metadata beyond MARC formats. This would allow the metadata to be readily communicated as formats and managed over time. Much of the captioning for imagery seems to be original captioning, written for particular audiences. These captions live within the structure of the NDL but have no direct bearing on the production data stored as a part of the catalog records. Similarly, attendant data such as information on ways of managing subjects, chronology, place names, and so on need to be pursued in a clearly replicable way. The point may seem to be a fine one, but in some respects the management and delivery of narrative content constitute the logical next step after the development of the MARC format for management and delivery of formatted content. The Library has an opportunity to play a leadership role in examining the complex relationship between narrative materials that are acceptable for public access and the formal content of the catalog. The committee believes very strongly that LC should participate in the dialogs that are springing up in this area of information management.

LOOKING TO THE FUTURE: THE LIBRARY OF CONGRESS IN 2010

The Library of Congress resembles many other established institutions in confronting the possibilities and challenges presented by information technology. The institution has thought carefully about its mission over the years and has a reasonable sense of where it wants to go, even though it is a somewhat loosely coupled organization. But implementing that mission at a time of rapid change in the fundamental technologies on which the institution relies requires that the LC's sense of mission be even clearer and that the choices be understood well. This section summarizes what the committee sees as the particular challenges it believes need to be addressed.

It should go without saying that LC exists to support the information needs of the Congress. For the fulfillment of this fundamental mission, both the organization and technology are largely at hand, although change is constant. The Congressional Research Service is like a large and highly specialized research department in a library that knows its customers very well indeed. Such a tight link between library and customer is unusual (tighter even than in universities and colleges), enviable, and a good source of guidance and direction for the CRS. The committee does not mean to minimize the challenges for CRS, but compared with those facing other departments of the Library, they are relatively straightforward.

It is Library Services—the unit of LC that most people think of as "the library"—that faces the most pointed questions. If it seeks to continue to accumulate a "comprehensive record of American history and creativity and a universal collection of human knowledge"[35]—in other words, a comprehensive collection of the nation's creative output and at the same time a broadly inclusive collection of research materials brought from around the world—it must manage to deal with the old and the new together. The first implicit question—never clearly resolved—is how far LC really is a "national library" like those in other countries; the second consequent question, already being faced here and abroad, is what becomes of a national library in the digital age. The following parameters are the most relevant:

- Old technologies continue to flourish. No decline in paper publication has yet been discerned. Existing systems for acquiring and managing that body of material must be maintained at current volumes or higher for the foreseeable future. LC is typical of great libraries in that it continues to need substantial space for physical collections even as funding agencies labor under the vague but mistaken assumption that digital publication will obviate such need.

- Materials collected using old technologies now need to be made more accessible through the resourceful use of IT. The new ILS is an important step in this direction, but nowhere near the whole of LC's collection is accessible that way. Electronic indexing and abstracting services, for example, are key tools for using print journals in a wide variety of fields. Business process redesign around the new ILS is an important step, but fresh consideration of other tools and how they may be made accessible (and to whom) is also needed.

- Older materials cry out to be reviewed for digitization by projects similar to the National Digital Library. First, digitization can make materials of great interest accessible to far wider audiences than ever before. Second, for some older materials, digitization is the preservation strategy of choice (and for some older preservation media—for example, micro-

---

[35]From the LC mission statement.

film—digitization is a next step in achieving real usefulness of materials).[36] The NDLP is completing one milestone phase this year and looking to move ahead: the decisions made now will have important long-range impacts.

• New materials published and made commercially available in digital media (with or without paper counterparts) need to be collected, made accessible, and preserved. This endeavor requires new forms of purchase and lease arrangements with publishers and new forms of access for readers and poses new questions about best edition and preservation. LC has just begun to address these questions.

• A much larger body of material than ever before and even much larger than has been collected by LC is available on the World Wide Web and sometimes in digital libraries without having been "published" in the traditional sense. To what extent does this material fall under the collecting aegis of LC? There are, as well, the further questions of copyright registration, deposit, and selection for a continuing collection. It is here that issues of ownership, access, and responsibility for preservation arise. Here, LC has made less progress than have some other large institutions and—more to the point—it has failed to play the leadership role that it has the power to play in the library community as a whole. Through digital initiatives, major research libraries have demonstrated their awareness of these concerns and moved to act on them. LC has held back, and for the host of libraries without the resources or skills to address these complex issues, that lack of leadership is and will continue to be a problem.

To absorb the impact of the new while continuing to distinguish itself by discharging its traditional responsibilities, the Library will require keen management and new resources. But management will still be pressed to deliver the services demanded of LC without inordinate budgetary requests for new money. The committee sees several areas in which the impact of the new and the survival of old responsibilities will challenge LC most.

First, LC will need to think and rethink the audiences it chooses to address. Beyond Congress, there has traditionally been an overlapping set of publics defined first by access to the buildings of LC on Capitol Hill in Washington. Research scholars have had the strongest incentive to make their way to LC, but a wider public has been welcomed on remark-

---

[36]The committee believes that the subject of digital preservation is sufficiently important to warrant its own chapter (Chapter 4).

ably generous terms.[37] But when access to the buildings is no longer a condition for the use of at least some of the collections, whom then should LC address? The issues of audience are most clearly drawn at present for the National Digital Library Program, but these issues will eventually be raised by all areas of library service mediated beyond the buildings of LC by information technology.

Second, the Library of Congress has a special function that most national libraries elsewhere do not have: responsibility for managing copyright registration as well as deposit.[38] At present, copyright registration is a function that overlaps the deposit of printed materials, but within LC the systems used to support the Copyright Office and Library Services are very different. The physical materials are registered for copyright in one department of the Library and then are moved to a room where selectors extract the volumes likely to be added to the Library's collections. At that point, a separate process of documentation and cataloging begins. Can the copyright registration and deposit processes be more closely integrated with acquisition, selection, cataloging, and preservation of materials for the Library's collection?

Third, within LC, the Law Library risks being neglected because of its size and specialized function. Its distinctive feature is its support of research into the laws and judicial systems of other countries, although it does provide a wider range of traditional law library services. The Global Legal Information Network program is making progress in providing electronic access to international legal materials, but its impact has been limited by funding and personnel constraints. Are there ways to enhance that project's impact and link it more closely to other LC functions? At the same time, before a GLIN service is developed that would compete with the private sector, careful consideration should be given to whether it is appropriate for the federal government to provide the proposed service.

So far, the committee has outlined problems that press on the Library from the point of view of service to its traditional users—readers and researchers from a variety of walks of life. But LC has another vitally important set of customers, ones it has served with distinction for many

---

[37]The mission statement lists the audience as Congress, the government, and the wider public, without further differentiation except to observe that digital media allow LC to reach a wider audience than before. Historically, the Library did not consider children to be a part of its clientele, and as of this writing, most on-site LC services may be accessed only by those 18 years of age and older (guided tours are an exception).

[38]In a number of other countries, this responsibility is carried out by organizations that are distinct from the national library.

years: libraries. While LC's function as a source of interlibrary loan materials has actually been relatively modest, it has led in setting standards and leading collaborative enterprises. LC's history of consolidating and standardizing the cataloging of library materials has been distinguished, and it has played an important part in making librarianship here and abroad more economical and more effective. Now the challenge is to find appropriate ways to participate in the planning and execution of new standards and the creation of new infrastructure. The committee heard repeatedly from librarians around the world that LC must take the lead role in this area, but defining that role takes some thought and decision making in the new environment libraries face.

Organizing the services and infrastructure of LC to respond flexibly and efficiently to the new challenges is the last area this report addresses. The committee naturally offers some observations about specific technical directions, but at the same time it has studied closely the organizations and interactions that bring technology to the librarians and users. Technical questions are not solved well unless there are planning and implementation structures in place to optimize outcomes. At present there are both a central ITS Directorate and IT-specialist personnel in units throughout the Library. Do those units interact as well as they could and should? Are technology decisions made according to a broad strategic view of the future? Are technology decisions made in a way that is open and transparent to the library's management as a whole? Do those decisions successfully anticipate need or only respond to it? The committee was particularly asked by LC's senior managers to revisit a question raised by an earlier study: Does LC need to appoint explicitly a chief information officer to oversee management of its technology resources?[39]

It is important to emphasize at this point what should be obvious from the way in which the problem has been stated: namely, the committee judges the limitations and challenges LC faces to be structural and strategic, and they need to be thought of in that way. The committee did not approach this study by looking for things that are broken and trying to find ways to fix them, much less by seeking to assign blame for shortcomings. It is most concerned about those limitations that appear to be most intractable: human resources policies and practices that limit inno-

---

[39]In December 1995, the Government Accounting Office, at the request of the Senate Appropriations Committee, contracted with the consulting firm Booz-Allen & Hamilton to perform a management review of LC's operations and to deliver a report within 6 months. This report was delivered in May 1996. Along with relevant congressional testimony and an accompanying Price Waterhouse financial statement, it is available online at <http://www.gao.gov/special.pubs/loc.htm>.

vation and flexibility, government pay scales that restrict access to the best talent, and statutory requirements (particularly in the area of copyright) that may compel the Library to engage in activities that would be better off restructured. But even those areas can be addressed if there is support at the highest levels in the Library and in the Congress.

Mainly, however, the committee has chosen to concentrate on the problems and opportunities that are presented by the times we live in. This is an exciting moment for those who care about the preservation and transmission and dissemination of cultural heritage and cultural innovation. The excitement translates into real challenges for traditional institutions like LC and should be preserved and harnessed so as to launch a new century of innovation and service.

3

BUILDING DIGITAL COLLECTIONS

TRADITIONAL COLLECTIONS: SCOPE AND RESPONSIBILITY

Collectors of books are cautious about virtualization. The artifact and the content of the artifact are so closely allied in users' minds that the necessary theorization of virtuality—made long since by most citizens of Western nations when it comes to their own money, from banknotes and coins to credit cards and account balances—has been slow in arriving. For a library of the twenty-first century, building collections will consist necessarily of a range of activities, from the acquisition of traditional materials to something much more like what we do when we own stocks in companies whose printed share certificates we never see. Thinking through what it takes to be a great library in this new world is the central challenge librarians face in this new century.

The Library of Congress's collection is the largest in the world. The collection is renowned not only for its scale and scope but also for its diversity and its depth in many areas. Books and serials constitute only a minority of the 119-million-item[1] collection. The Library holds the world's largest collections of motion picture films and newspapers and enormous quantities of manuscripts, prints, photographs, sound recordings, and maps. The committee heard and observed repeatedly on its visits to the Library that the Library's collections are its primary asset.

---

[1]This was the size of the collections in FY99, as indicated in the *Annual Report of the Librarian of Congress* for 1999 (Washington, D.C.: Library of Congress, 2000).

As the largest research library in the world, the Library of Congress has had a very expansive collection policy, which it describes as follows:

> The Library's acquisitions policies are based on three fundamental principles that the Library should possess:
>
> 1. All books and other library materials necessary to the Congress and the various officers of the Federal Government to perform their duties.
> 2. All books and other materials which record the life and achievements of the American people.
> 3. Records of other societies, past and present, especially of those societies and peoples whose experience is of the most immediate concern to the people of the United States.[2]

In another place, LC describes its policy as follows:

> The extent of the Library's collection building activities is extremely broad, covering virtually every discipline and field of study, and including the entire range of different forms of publication and media for recording and storing knowledge. The Library has always recognized that its preeminent role is to collect at the national level. It has striven to develop richly representative collections in all fields, except technical agriculture and clinical medicine (where it yields precedence to the National Agricultural Library and the National Library of Medicine, respectively).[3]

The Library's policies and practices in respect to traditional materials are sophisticated and highly evolved, reflecting decades of experience and infrastructure development. The Library uses a variety of mechanisms to build its collections (see Box 3.1), including the following:

• Selecting published works for the permanent collection from materials that authors and publishers submit on their own initiative to satisfy the mandatory deposit requirement of the copyright law. Receipts from the Copyright Office constitute the core of the collection, particularly those in four divisions: Geography and Map; Music; Motion Picture, Broadcasting and Recorded Sound; and Prints and Photographs.[4] Selectors examine the cartloads of materials in the Copyright Office to identify those items that will be retained for the permanent collections; approximately one-half of the published materials (and virtually none of the

---

[2]See <gopher://marvel.loc.gov:70/00/research/collections.catalogs/collections/about/general>.

[3]See <http://lcweb.loc.gov/rr/collects.html>.

[4]Data derived from the Acquisitions Frequently Asked Questions list, available online at <http://lcweb.loc.gov/faq/acqfaq.html>. Some of the materials received through the Copyright Office are transferred to other institutions (e.g., National Library of Medicine).

BOX 3.1
The Acquisitions Directorate at the Library of Congress

The Library of Congress (LC) acquires materials in all formats, languages, and subjects (except technical agriculture and clinical medicine) from all over the world, under the guidance of LC's collection policy statements.[1] On average, 22,000 items are received by the Library every working day; of these, approximately 7,000 items are selected for the permanent collections.[2]

The Acquisitions Directorate is organized into a fiscal office and four divisions— the African/Asian Acquisitions and Overseas Operations Division,[3] the Anglo/ American Acquisitions Division, the European/Latin American Acquisitions Division, and the Serial Record Division. There are about 300 employees in the Acquisitions Directorate in the Washington, D.C., area and 300 staff members based abroad.

---

[1]See <http://www.lcweb.loc.gov/acq/> for information about the Library's collection policy statements and other aspects of the Acquisitions Directorate.

[2]These data are based on a presentation made at a site visit to the Library in July 1999.

[3]The Library operates offices in New Delhi, Cairo, Rio de Janeiro, Jakarta, Nairobi, and Islamabad to acquire, catalog, preserve, and distribute materials in regions where conventional acquisitions methods are not effective. In addition to serving LC, these offices conduct cooperative acquisitions programs on behalf of 105 participating institutions, primarily academic research libraries.

---

unpublished materials) are selected for the permanent collections.[5] The remaining items are earmarked for exchange or disposal;

• Demanding copies of selected works published in the United States from publishers who failed to submit the copies, as per the mandatory deposit requirement;

• Selecting from works submitted for the Cataloging in Publication (CIP) program. The CIP program serves the nation's libraries by cataloging books in advance of publication, using page proofs. It requires that publishers submit a copy of the published book to LC;[6]

• Purchasing materials that add to the depth and breadth of LC collections. The Library has an acquisitions budget of approximately $10 million per year, much of which goes for purchases abroad;[7]

---

[5]The Copyright Office retains unpublished work that it receives off-site for 70 years after the death of the author, but such materials are not cataloged or integrated into the Library's collections.

[6]For additional information about the CIP program, see <http://lcweb3.loc.gov/cip/>.

[7]As reported to the committee during a site visit to the Library in July 1999. In 1999, the median acquisitions budget for members of the Association for Research Libraries was $6.3 million (see <http://www.arl.org/stats/arlstat/1999t4.html>). The Library estimates the annual value of copyright deposits selected for the collections at $23 million, and its direct purchases amount to $10 million, for a total of $33 million in acquisitions for the Library.

• Exchanging surplus copies with selected partners around the world. Surplus duplicates that the Library obtains are traded with U.S. educational institutions and with other selected exchange partners; LC has exchange arrangements with more than 12,000 institutions throughout the world;

• Receiving donations (some of which are solicited) of rare books, photographs, films, sound recordings, and manuscript collections; and

• Selecting surplus publications that are transferred to the Library from libraries in government agencies. Under long-standing policy, federal libraries are encouraged to transfer their surplus library material to LC, which has stipulated that it will accept from surplus only soft- or hard-bound books in certain categories.[8]

Two principles underlie the development of the collections: careful selection and stewardship. Selection has always been important in building LC's collections, even though its mission is to acquire, organize, preserve, secure, and sustain—for the present and future use of the Congress and the nation—a comprehensive record of American history and creativity. The Library organizes its collections either by topical area or into special collections that are further subdivided by media or form of material (see Box 3.2). Selectors on the Library staff use their expertise in subjects, area studies, and special formats and their knowledge of LC's collections to guide decisions about which materials should be added to the Library's physical holdings. Once materials are selected for inclusion in the collections, the Library assumes a number of associated stewardship responsibilities that include preserving collections to ensure long-term viability and providing for intellectual access to materials. These responsibilities are discussed at length in Chapters 4 and 5.

THE CHALLENGES OF DIGITAL COLLECTIONS

The rapid growth of digital materials will challenge the Library in what it tries to collect, how it carries out its collecting role, and when and how it permits users to access its collections. Although there are many direct analogies between digital and physical collections, there are also significant differences. The digital era has brought with it a wide range of new types of intellectual creations and new means for authors to distribute their works. Some of the most important digital resources today

---

[8]In particular, LC does not have responsibility for selecting or preserving records of the federal government; that task is within the purview of the National Archives and Records Administration (NARA).

BOX 3.2
Collections at the Library of Congress

1. General
2. American studies
   African-American studies
   American history
   American literature
   American political science
   American popular culture
   Asian- and Pacific
     Islander-Americans
   Hispanic American studies
   Indians of North America
3. Area studies
   Australia/New Zealand
   Anglophone/
     Commonwealth literature
   Canada
   China
   Europe
   Great Britain/Ireland
   Hebraica and Judaica
   Japan
   Korea
   Luso-Hispanic studies
   Near East
   Southern Asia
   Sub-Saharan Africa
   Tibet
4. Science
   Environmental and earth
     sciences
   Life sciences
   Mathematics and
     computer sciences
   Physical sciences
   Science and technology
   Technology
5. Social sciences
   Anthropology
   Business
   Education

Family studies
International relations
Sociology
Sports
Women's studies
6. Humanities
   Children's literature
   Classics, Byzantine, and
     medieval studies
   Dance
   Decorative arts
   Fine arts
   Genealogy and heraldry
   Library science and
     bibliography
   Linguistics and languages
   Music
   Philosophy and religion
   Theater
7. Law and government
     publications
   Law
   International organizations
8. Special materials/formats
   Architecture, design, and
     engineering
   Computer files
   Geographic and
     cartographic materials
   Graphic arts
   Manuscripts
   Microformat collections
   Motion pictures
   Newspapers
   Photography
   Radio
   Rare books
   Sound recordings
   Television

SOURCE: Derived from <gopher://marvel.loc.gov:70/00/research/collections.catalogs/collections/about/outline.of.collection.overviews>.

represent new types of materials without easy analogy to the world in which the Library's collections policies were written, such as social science datasets, geographic information systems, scientific data with visualization tools, digital images, and the ubiquitous Web page.[9] Many of these new materials do not fit easily into traditional collecting categories because they cross the boundaries of established topical areas, nor do they coincide with the conventional categories in "special formats."

Not only are many new types of materials being created, but the way in which they are distributed also differs significantly from the methods of the past. The Library's collecting methods are now tuned to books, serials, and other tangible artifacts that flow into the Library through a variety of well-established channels. Some new digital materials are following different paths; others never arrive. These materials frequently are being distributed by different types of organizations, using new business and economic models. E-journals and e-books, which today bear a fair resemblance to their paper predecessors, are being distributed primarily through Internet-based subscriptions in which the publisher or distributor permits access to a remote site rather than providing a copy of a journal or book. A collecting model that relies on vendors providing copies of resources for processing and storage at the Library will not suffice for digital materials, especially when the item in question is dynamic and changes frequently.

Probably the most active area of digital publishing today is taking place on the World Wide Web. Much of this publishing does not follow the dominant commercial model of the past century. Individual authors and organizations make a wide variety of information available through the World Wide Web in order to disseminate their ideas, to gain recognition, and possibly to provide a venue for advertising. Often there are no publishers, at least in the traditional sense, to act as intermediaries between the creator of the works and the Library. Yet some of these digital works are as important as records of current research and creativity as were the journals and books of the eighteenth, nineteenth, and twentieth centuries.

Traditionally, libraries have served geographically or institutionally local audiences. Local residents visit a library building to access books and artifacts in its collection. If a particular artifact is not available locally, it can be obtained through elaborate procedures developed to locate the desired item and transport it to the customer—but even then, the basic

---

[9]Compounding the challenges are those materials that are closely linked to computer applications, such as a Mathematica notebook, which can be viewed properly only in tandem with the Mathematica application.

library model is essentially unchanged from a century ago. With the advent of a wide range of new computing and communications technologies, however, this traditional model will probably not survive the present decade. In the future, most objects will no longer exist in a specific physical space, and access to digital objects will no longer be limited to those who present themselves at a particular location. Over time, the new technologies will eliminate the association between geography and a library's customers. Of course, the physical artifacts of the past will persist, and many will not be committed to digital form for a long time, if ever.

This shift from artifact to virtual information has only just begun to influence the Library. For example, most of the people seeking access to LC collections are required to visit the Library in Washington, D.C. Whether they wish to read a foreign newspaper, search out an unusual journal, inspect a rare book, or do in-depth research in a particular subject area, they have to transport themselves to the desired resources. There have been some limited exceptions, such as access for members of Congress and the visually handicapped and borrowing through interlibrary loan. But in an increasingly wired world, the balance between on-site and remote access has the potential to shift radically. Digital materials, regardless of where they are physically housed, could, in principle, be accessible from any location where the appropriate constellations of technology are available. In addition, these materials could be accessed by many people at the same time, or an individual could easily access multiple sites concurrently.[10]

Providers of information protect their intellectual property rights in ways that complicate the task of providing access to digital materials. Where a traditional book has a natural limit of one user at a time, digital information can, in principle, be used by unlimited numbers of people more or less simultaneously, to such an extent that publishers fear a substantial loss of sales. Academic and other research libraries have addressed this issue primarily by negotiating licensing agreements with publishers and distributors of digital works. Licensing agreements can define the community of users who at any given time have access to a resource; for example, they may allow access only to members of a well-defined community, such as the students, faculty, and staff of a particular

---

[10]Collections of national importance, such as presidential papers, could then transcend current distinctions of "ownership," which now force users to visit multiple institutions (e.g., the Library, the National Archives and Records Administration (which manages the National Archives and the presidential libraries), and the Smithsonian Institution).

university.[11]   But apart from members of Congress and federal government employees who need access to the Library's collections to carry out
their work, the Library lacks an easily definable user community. Today's
fundamental changes require a reexamination of what a library needs
physically to collect, what it can rely on others to hold while providing
users with remote access, and under what conditions it can provide access
to which users. There are experiments abroad with "national site license"
models that seek to ensure the broadest possible access, but neither libraries nor publishers have pursued such models with any success in the
United States.[12]

Because of the dynamic, rapidly changing nature of many digital
resources, the Library also needs to be more energetic in its approach to
collecting digital information. Much of the information that was available
at one time on the Web is already lost because no institutions had the
foresight to copy and preserve it before it was changed or deleted. Estimates of the average life of a Web page vary, but the basic conclusion is
the same: it is short.[13] Within a matter of a few weeks or a few months,
much of the information available on the Web is updated, augmented, or
simply deleted. In the digital environment, all libraries have to decide
quickly what information should be included in their collections and then
negotiate with rights holders over the terms and conditions for managing
and providing access to these materials. The committee believes that
these differences require the Library to reexamine its policies and to de-
vise new infrastructures reflecting the very different nature of digital
materials.

The committee believes that LC needs to be not only more ambitious
but also more selective in the methods it uses to build digital collections.
Increased attention to selection is necessary because of the explosion in
digital information of widely varying quality and interest. The Library
cannot be expected to collect everything, especially if collecting carries

---

[11]Because digital materials can be easily copied and viewed by a large number of people,
publishers have a legitimate concern about their accessibility. Any number of economic
models are being investigated, including pay-per-view and licensing arrangements that put
restrictions on which and how many users may view the licensed materials. Publishers fear
that, in the worst case (from their point of view), an institution like LC could obtain a single
digital copy of a journal and make it available over the Internet, at which point the market
for additional copies could effectively disappear.

[12]See <http://www.library.yale.edu/~llicense/national-license-init.shtml> for current
information about such initiatives.

[13]Brewster Kahle pointed out that research at the Internet Archive finds half of the Web
disappearing every month—even as it doubles every year. "The mean life of a Web page is
about 70 days," he said. See "No Way to Run a Culture," by Steve Meloan, in *Wired News*,
February 13, 1998. It should be noted that estimates of the mean life of a Web page vary.

with it an obligation to preserve what it collects. The number of authors and publishers in the existing print publication environment is large, heterogeneous, and distributed. Nonetheless, after several centuries of bibliographical development, a great deal of control has been achieved to provide libraries and users with thorough and systematic information about what has been published. By comparison, the world of Internet publishing is new, raw, and wild. New models for defining Library collections require a redefinition of what constitutes a library's "collection." With digital materials, no longer is it necessary for a library to hold an item physically to provide its users with access. Remote access challenges one of the fundamental assumptions of current collection policies: that a library needs physical control of an item to assure its users access. Nowadays, a library may provide intellectual access to distributed digital works without ever owning them or hosting them on its systems. A library might provide access to current materials for a limited period of time and then relinquish long-term preservation responsibilities to another organization. It might enter into cooperative arrangements and partnerships with other libraries, publishers, consortia, and commercial service providers for some or all of the activities associated with stewardship of physical items.

DEFINING AND BUILDING COLLECTIONS
IN THE DIGITAL ERA

Defining the Scope of "Collecting" Responsibility

Traditionally, the boundaries of collections have been determined by the ownership of tangible objects. Most of the decisions made about collections—about acquisition and deaccession, cataloging, preservation, and access—have been made by the local institution that houses and/or owns them. This makes sense for collections comprising discrete physical objects—books, serials, maps, and the like. For collections of digital objects—either born digital or digitized from other media—the notions of collection and collection maintenance need to change because ownership and physical proximity to collections are no longer prerequisites for access to materials. Technically at least, copies of items in a digital collection can be accessed from anywhere, provided the right combination of hardware and software is available. With digital resources, the issue of access can be separated from that of stewardship. Therefore, an important question facing LC and all other libraries is how to define their digital collections. This question has significant implications for LC in terms of what to collect, which mechanisms to use to build its collections, and how to sustain over time those digital materials that constitute part of the comprehensive record of American history and creativity.

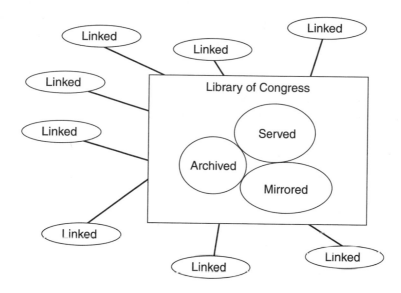

FIGURE 3.1   Digital collections and the universe of information—a possible model.

The Digital Library program of the University of California at Berkeley offers one possible model for defining a library's responsibilities for collecting and maintaining digital works (see Figure 3.1).[14]   That digital library identifies four levels of collecting defined by where the information resides and what level of commitment the library makes to management and long-term preservation:

• *Archived*—The material is hosted at the Library and the Library intends to keep the intellectual content of the material available on a permanent basis.
• *Served*—The material resides at the Library but the Library has not (yet) made a commitment to keep it permanently.
• *Mirrored*—The Library hosts a copy of material that also resides elsewhere and the Library makes no commitment to maintaining the contents. At this level, another institution has responsibility for the content and its maintenance.
• *Linked*—The material resides elsewhere and the Library points to that location but has no control over the information (the portal model).

---

[14]"Digital Library SunSITE Collection and Preservation Policy," University of California at Berkeley, available online at <http://sunsite.berkeley.edu/Admin/collection.html>.

One underlying principle is that material in any category other than the archived collection may be shifted from one category to another to meet changing user needs, to improve remote server responsiveness, to address intellectual property issues, or to reflect changing assessments of the value of the material. Some such model must emerge if the Library is not to become an island cut off from increasingly large portions of the creative output of American and world cultures.

The burden of preserving digital collections is enormous. The committee believes that this burden must necessarily be shared among a variety of archiving institutions (see Chapter 4). To ensure that all important research materials are preserved for future generations, it is important that archiving institutions understand the scope of each other's stewardship roles, as is the case with hard-copy publications.

> **Recommendation: The Library should explicitly define the sets of digital resources for which it will assume long-term curatorial responsibility.**

Fulfilling the archiving and preservation responsibility is a long-term effort that will serve researchers for generations to come. The Library also has a responsibility, however, to provide access to a much wider and more comprehensive body of resources for current use. Its current acquisitions policy identifies Congress and various government officials as one specific audience. The extent to which the Library can or should emphasize audiences beyond this core set of users is of considerable significance for the overall collecting strategy.

> **Recommendation: For digital resources for which the Library does not assume long-term curatorial responsibility, the Library should work with other institutions to define appropriate levels of responsibility for preservation and access. Some materials that the Library acquires and makes available to its users may have only temporary value; other materials may be hosted on a Library site for more efficient access, with long-term archiving responsibilities accepted by another party.**

> **Recommendation: The Library should selectively adopt the portal model[15] for targeted program areas. By creating links from the Library's Web site, this approach would make available the ever-increasing body of research materials distributed across the Internet. The Library would be responsible for care-**

---

[15]Portals serve as gateways to information. On the Web, Yahoo! is an example of a portal.

fully selecting and arranging for access to licensed commercial resources for its users, but it would not house local copies of materials or assume responsibility for long-term preservation.

Mechanisms for Building Digital Collections

Libraries have built complex infrastructures to handle physical collections. People and systems are in place to order, receive, process, and catalog materials. There are stacks in which to store materials, binding services, and systems for identifying and locating materials and for circulating them to users. The people who keep libraries running have a deep knowledge of their physical collections, where to find new materials to add to the collections, and how to assess their value. All of these functions have analogues in the digital world, but the specifics of the required infrastructure differ, reflecting the differences in the nature of the objects, the suppliers and users, and the business and service models involved. How digital materials are identified and selected, how they are received and inspected for quality, where they are stored, how they are described in metadata (see Chapter 5), and how they are made available to users— all require the redesign of existing systems, new systems and new relationships with providers, and new skills on the part of library staff. Many of the mechanisms that the Library of Congress will use to build its digital collections resemble those used by other large libraries. But LC also has some unique responsibilities (e.g., acquiring a comprehensive record of American life, achievement, and creativity) and unique mechanisms to help it meet these responsibilities, especially copyright deposit.

Copyright Deposit

The Library's role in registering copyright and enforcing the mandatory deposit law (discussed at length in Chapter 2)[16] creates a unique opportunity for it to collect digital information that might otherwise vanish from the historical record. In conjunction with the Corporation for National Research Initiatives (CNRI) and the Defense Advanced Research Projects Agency (DARPA), the Library has been working on the Copy-

---

[16]This report focuses on copyright deposit because it is the aspect of the copyright law that is most important for LC. However, the copyright issue, especially in the digital domain, includes many diverse and complex issues that are often at odds with one another. It is beyond the scope of this report to discuss these issues here; readers are referred to *The Digital Dilemma* by the Computer Science and Telecommunications Board, National Research Council (Washington, D.C.: National Academy Press, 2000) for additional information.

right Office Electronic Registration, Recordation and Deposit System (CORDS) project since 1993. The current intent of CORDS is to permit certain applicants to prepare copyright registration applications, deposit digital materials, and handle transactions with the Copyright Office via the Internet. Approximately $900,000 is spent on CORDS per year: about $600,000 is provided to CNRI (through a DARPA contracting mechanism, to which DARPA itself has contributed a total of more than $1 million for development costs), with the balance allocated within LC for two full-time equivalents (FTEs) in ITS, staff in the Copyright Office, and hardware and software.

As a research and development activity, the CORDS project has helped the Copyright Office staff develop and evolve their thinking on information systems, and for that reason, CORDS has been helpful. However, the committee is concerned about the current and planned scale of deployment. A very small percentage of the Copyright Office's workload in the year 2000 is handled by CORDS, and the expansion plan for the year 2004 projects only 100,000 digital deposits (less than 15 percent of the projected total of 725,000 deposits) will be handled through CORDS.[17] CORDS is currently available to a handful of publishers with copyright accounts and the appropriate technological infrastructure. Individuals and most publishers wishing to deposit digital materials electronically cannot use the system. An operational system is urgently needed (whether it is CORDS or something else) and must be deployed in an expeditious manner. The Copyright Office plans to draft a statement of work in FY01 and to obtain the services of a vendor to develop a production system beginning in FY02. It is imperative for the Library's digital future that this vendor solicitation process take place as scheduled or, preferably, sooner. The drafting of the statement of work should be informed by the lessons learned from the Integrated Library System project and completed carefully, considering the needs of the Copyright Office and Library for ongoing technical support, maintenance, and flexibility (in the context of the evolving digital environment and reengineering within the office[18]).

The production system for digital registration and deposit, whether it

---

[17] A rough estimate of 100,000 submissions through CORDS and 725,000 total submissions in the year 2004 was provided during a site visit to LC in May 2000. It is likely that the majority of the currently projected 100,000 submissions will be processed as "mixed" CORDS (electronic registration coupled with the submission of a physical artifact) rather than as fully electronic submissions.

[18] As of this writing, a contractor to conduct business process reengineering is about to be selected, and in April 2000 the senior managers at the Copyright Office completed seminars in reengineering.

is an evolved CORDS or a new system, must fit into an infrastructure that would help the Library augment its comprehensive physical collections with digital works. The Copyright Office is one of the primary points of entry for physical materials into the Library's collections, and one would expect CORDS to be carefully integrated with a repository system where the Library's electronic collections will be maintained.[19] Selectors from Library Services must be able to select digital works for the Library's collections, to transfer them to the permanent collection, or to preserve them. Electronic copyright deposit is a strategic tool the Library will require in the digital world. It cannot risk being technically unprepared to deal with electronic copyright deposits and the smooth addition of such materials into its permanent collections.

The design for the Library's production system should not be unduly constrained by current work processes for the registration and deposit of physical artifacts, because the new system needs to support the Copyright Office of the future (and also because those processes are likely to evolve under the planned reengineering effort in the Copyright Office). However, the rapid proliferation of digital objects (described in Chapter 1) demands that the design for the production system move forward in parallel with reengineering efforts at the office.

The committee addressed the specific technical question of whether the production system should be developed anew or based on an evolution of CORDS. It interviewed the principals at LC and CNRI and former staff of CNRI. Given that these discussions resulted in varying points of view and that the committee did not assess the CORDS architecture or program code directly (such an assessment was thought to be beyond its charge), the committee did not arrive at a consensus on the question of technological revolution or evolution, although the members did agree that a new system deserves serious consideration.

Finding: The Library urgently requires a production-quality system for receiving and managing digital objects deposited with it and registered for copyright. Such a system will enable the Library to enforce the deposit requirement for born-digital materials.

Finding: The new production system needs to integrate well with other Library systems; the new system should at the same

---

[19]Determining who may access work digital works is not an easy matter, given the challenges posed by copyright and licensing issues.

time make it easier for providers of information to register and deposit their works.

Recommendation: The Copyright Office should complete the statement of work for a production system in FY01, as planned, and as soon as possible (e.g., by the end of calendar year 2000). To achieve this goal, the resources and attention of Library-wide senior management should be directed to the Copyright Office, perhaps on a scale and with visibility comparable to those of the Integrated Library System implementation. The committee urges the Congress to support and fund the acquisition of a production system for receiving and managing digital objects.

Another copyright issue has to do with the preferred format for the deposit of materials available in electronic form. Current deposit requirements discourage the digital deposit of complete digital works, except for those represented in a tangible form, such as on a CD-ROM. According to its best-edition statement,[20] the Library generally favors tangible items over digital versions, illustrated by its preference for CD-ROMs and printouts of digital information. Authors wishing to register copyright for digital work may deposit either a complete version of the work on CD-ROM or a printout of selected portions of the work. The deposit requirement for registering software is a printout of the first and last 25 pages of the source code. This policy, developed before the Internet made it easy to transfer digital information through networks, is no longer justifiable or effective.

Finding: The Library's mechanisms and policies for the deposit of digital works currently favor printouts or tangible forms (such as CD-ROMs) over digital editions of digital works. This strategy is shortsighted because an increasing amount of born-digital information cannot be represented in tangible form and is much less useful if reduced to print or analog form. Tangible physical objects also require extensive physical handling for registration, cataloging, shelving, retrieval, and use.

Recommendation: The Library should set new standards for

---

[20]When materials are published in more than one format, the Library specifies the format to be registered and/or deposited. This is referred to as the "best edition." The applicable circulars are available online at <http://www.loc.gov/copyright/circs/>.

the appropriate formats for digital materials acquired through copyright deposit, purchase, exchange, and donation and should review those standards annually. The concept of "best edition" must be revisited to remove the present bias in favor of paper versions. Each class of materials should be considered separately, depending on its specific physical and digital properties for current access and preservation purposes.[21] The complexity of these issues will increase as the digital environment evolves. Accordingly, the Library must have an ongoing capacity to monitor these issues closely and systematically and have sophisticated staff involved in the deliberations.

Licensed Resources

The Library's mandate for copyright registration and deposit provides a unique opportunity to capture and preserve digital information. But voluntary deposit is only one of several methods that the Library must use more aggressively to build its digital collections. One of the most important applications of CORDS thus far has been the copyright registration of dissertations. Through a cooperative agreement with ProQuest (formerly Bell & Howell Information and Learning or University Microfilms, Inc.), dissertations and theses can now be registered and deposited electronically. The agreement designates ProQuest's Digital Dissertations database as the official off-site repository for the more than 100,000 dissertations and theses converted to digital form since 1997 and registered electronically. The agreement also provides for the Library to obtain a digital copy of the dissertations and theses should ProQuest cease to maintain the database. This is an example of an LC collection that resides off-site but that would move to the Library's archived collection if ProQuest stopped maintaining it. The agreement illustrates one way of controlling access to a linked collection: users who come into the Library's reading rooms can gain access to the ProQuest Digital Dissertations database, but they may not access the database remotely through LC.

The committee is concerned, however, that sufficient attention has not been given to the mechanisms by which LC would respond if a provider failed to maintain the material. It is also unclear whether the ProQuest arrangement, even if it proves successful, is scalable as a gen-

---

[21]See the discussion in Chapter 1 on the recent and dramatic rise of e-books. Consideration will have to be given in the very near future to the question of when the best edition of a popular new novel is the digital file from which both paper and electronic copies are derived.

eral-purpose model for the Library. Nevertheless, the committee commends the Library for taking this initiative and urges it to view the ProQuest arrangement as an experiment—that is, it should also consider alternative models (e.g., the inclusion of a third-party agent that would hold digital information in escrow and release it to the Library if the vendor ceased operations).

> **Recommendation: The ProQuest agreement serves as an interesting experiment in how the Library might handle digital collections. In such arrangements, the Library must pay particular attention to its legal rights and responsibilities in the event of default. It must establish and regularly test its capacity to accept and make available such collections if it should be called on to do so.[22]**

Today, many publishers and distributors enter into licensing agreements that permit registered users to access digital materials online. Most licensing agreements prohibit wholesale copying and redistribution and place limits on printing or downloading digital information. The Library already licenses many electronic information services, both for CRS and for on-site Library users. Depending on the terms of the license, when such a subscription is canceled the information may no longer be accessible to the Library of Congress's users. Where licensed digital distribution is the only means of access, business decisions by the publishers and distributors may determine what information is preserved and remains available in the long run—which poses the risk that important scientific or cultural information could be lost because its retention was not profitable. If it concludes that a work makes an important contribution to the national collection, the Library may need to enforce aggressively the copyright law that requires publishers to deposit copies of works published in the United States. Capturing important digital content that is controlled by licensing agreements will require LC to take aggressive measures, including negotiating special licenses with publishers.

---

[22]The committee has one worry about using the ProQuest agreement as a model, however. The Library chose in this case to deal with a commercial service provider to find ways to handle its "content." But there is no sign that LC recognized in undertaking the project that the academic community has a substantial interest in the way dissertations are managed. The committee urges that future arrangements take into account content as well as form and that LC seek to include stakeholders broadly in designing future arrangements for specific classes of information.

Recommendation: The committee believes that the Library is in a unique position to demand the deposit of some digital materials and to require agreements for shared custody or fail-safe preservation should the materials become unavailable; it should do so.

Collecting Web-based Resources

The Web has become a powerful new paradigm for the dissemination of information of many kinds. While it is used to distribute commercial and licensed products, much of what is available is being freely distributed by its creators. Web publishing is one of the most original features of contemporary American life. It is hard to imagine how the scholars of the future will analyze and document American culture at the end of the twentieth century and beyond without having access to a great deal of this material. No effort to maintain a comprehensive collection of American creativity will be credible without it.

Some national libraries are using their countries' mandatory deposit laws actively to collect digital documents. One of the most aggressive programs to collect and preserve digital documents is the Web archiving program operated by the Swedish Royal Library. Using Web crawler technology similar to that developed by the Internet Archive (see Box 3.3), the Swedish Web archiving project is creating a digital collection of all publicly accessible Swedish Web sites. The Swedish Royal Library considers publicly accessible Web sites "publications" that are subject to mandatory deposit.[23] A similar effort is under way in Finland, and the Canadian National Library and the Australian National Library have programs for selectively collecting and preserving national content distributed via the Web.[24] The challenge of capturing significant American content on the Web is much more daunting than any of the efforts mentioned here,[25]

---

[23]The Swedish Web archiving project is described at <http.//kulturarw3.kb.se/html/projectdescription.html>.

[24]Information about Project Eva in Finland may be found at <http://renki.lib.helsinki.fi/eva/english.html>; information about digital projects at the National Library of Canada may be found at <http://www.nlc-bnc.ca/digiproj/edigiact.htm>; information about the Pandora project in Australia may be found at <http://www.nla.gov.au/pandora/>.

[25]While the size of the U.S. portion of the Web is unknown, it is certainly enormous. Perhaps half of the Web sites in existence today are based in the United States. In October 1999, researchers at OCLC estimated that the World Wide Web had about 3.6 million sites, of which 2.2 million offer publicly accessible content. These sites contain nearly 300 million Web pages. The largest 25,000 sites represented about 50 percent of the Web's content, and the number of sites and their size are climbing (see "OCLC Research Project Measures Scope of the Web," an OCLC press release, Dublin, Ohio, September 8, 1999. Available online at <http://www.oclc.org/oclc/press/19990908a.htm>).

BOX 3.3
The Internet Archive

The Internet Archive is a nonprofit foundation located in San Francisco and founded by Brewster Kahle. Since 1996, it has been collecting HTML (and some FTP and gopher) pages monthly. It currently contains 14 terabytes (i.e., a billion pages). A recent Web crawl collected about 450 million pages. The staff believes that it collects about 90 percent of the public static HTML pages. The Internet Archive hopes to record audio, video, and other Web content soon. It is starting to collect all the images on the Web pointed at by the pages it collects and also to explore the possibility of recording television broadcasts.

The collection is open to anyone over the Internet, but some programming skills are required to use it. Notable Internet Archive users include the Smithsonian Institution, which built a collection of the 1996 presidential election Web sites. The archive has also worked with IBM Corporation researchers and intellectual property lawyers, and it is collaborating actively with researchers from Compaq and Nippon Electric Co. (NEC). The Internet Archive is still evolving: the staff want it to be a center for research, a destination, and a catalyst for innovation. It hopes to be both a service organization and an active community of scholars exploring the archive's contents.

When asked what lessons they had learned, the staff replied that building the archive is technically much harder than one might imagine. Managing data volumes measured in terabytes puts them well beyond the scale of off-the-shelf tools. Everything must be done with great attention to scalability. Most tools break immediately when used on this scale.

The archive has worked closely with Alexa[1] (now a subsidiary of Amazon.com), which has provided it with various Web crawls over the last 4 years. The archive has its own building, computers, and storage and maintains close ties to Alexa but is now operating independently of it. It is slated to have a staff of between 20 and 50 (as of May 2000, it had a staff of 5).

SOURCE: Testimony at the committee's September 1999 plenary meeting, information at the Internet Archive's Web site at <http://www.archive.org>, and a site visit to the Internet Archive by committee members Jim Gray and David Levy on December 14, 1999.

[1]Information about Alexa may be found at <http://www.alexa.com>.

---

yet the initiatives in other nations offer solid technical and policy models for active collecting programs led by U.S. national institutions.

The Library of Congress recently launched a project with researchers at Cornell University to capture Web sites from the year 2000 election campaigns. The committee applauds this effort. Not only will it bring important documentation of American life and culture into the Library's collections but it will also allow Library staff to become familiar with techniques for pulling materials from the Web and will expose the Library to a variety of policy and technical issues associated with proactively collecting materials from the Web. This effort will also help to articulate a definition of digital publication, thereby helping to clarify which digital materials are subject to mandatory deposit. The committee recognizes that such an undertaking is fraught with legal, technical, intellectual, and practical difficulties (see Box 3.4).

Recommendation: The Library should aggressively pursue clarification of its right to collect copies of U.S.-based Web sites under the copyright deposit law. If questions about this right remain, then LC should seek legislation that changes the copyright law to ensure that it has this right. This right would not necessarily include the right for LC to provide unlimited access to the Web sites collected.

Recommendation: The Library should conduct additional pilot projects to gain experience in harvesting and archiving U.S.-based Web sites. Such projects should be carried out in partnership with experts or organizations that have the requisite expertise.

Recommendation: The Library should quickly translate the experience gained from pilot projects into appropriate collecting policies related to U.S. Web sites.

Building Infrastructure for Digital Collections

To acquire, organize, service, and preserve digital collections of the same breadth, depth, and value as its physical collections, the Library of Congress needs to develop an infrastructure of systems, policies, procedures, and skilled staff equivalent to the infrastructure in place for its physical collections. The Library has begun to address some of its infrastructure needs as part of the NDLP. However, the committee believes this effort needs to be increased significantly and reoriented from meeting the specific needs of its own digitized special collections (which has dominated the focus of the NDLP) to the purchase, deposit, and aggressive collecting of born-digital materials. The elements of this infrastructure include reorienting existing methods of acquisition, such as copyright deposit, to the acquisition of digital materials.

The Library requires a generalized infrastructure to support a much wider set of heterogeneous digital resources from a wide variety of sources. The NDLP gave the Library a great deal of experience in receiving and integrating into its systems materials that had been converted under contract by vendors. It also has gained very limited experience

BOX 3.4
Archiving Web Space

Archiving Web space is an enormously challenging task, one that is only beginning to be taken on and in only a small number of institutions. The key issues that an archiving effort must address include the following:

• *Scope*—Although estimates of the number of Web sites now extant vary, there is no question that the total is huge and growing rapidly. Even the well-funded and very sophisticated "harvesting" facilities of the Internet search engine vendors can cover only a small percentage of all sites. To be successful, any archiving effort will need to limit its scope.

• *Scale*—A corollary to the observations above about the scale and growth of Web space is that any archive hoping to cover more than narrow slices of the Web will quickly grow to enormous size. How to maintain such a huge corpus and how to make it useful pose a significant research challenge.

• *Change*—Web sites are created, change, and disappear at an astonishing rate. An archiving effort must be able to expand to cover relevant new sites and cope with sites that appear to be gone; for example, is a nonresponding site gone, temporarily off-line, or moved elsewhere? Archived sites need to be rechecked regularly and decisions need to be made about when to maintain different generations of a site.

• *Links*—The interconnectedness of the Web is one of its key features. In some cases a key part of the content of a site is carried largely in its links to other pages. When must an archive preserve not only a site but also pages to which that site links? How will an archive maintain such links when a collection contains numerous generations of linked-to pages?

• *Databases*—An increasingly large portion of Internet resources is not stored directly in HTML pages available for harvesting with the technologies currently used by Internet search engines. Rather, content is stored in databases and HTML pages are generated on the fly in response to user requests. What part of such sites should be archived? Will such sites cooperate in ways that make it possible to harvest the appropriate content from their databases automatically and reliably?

• *Technical evolution*—Today's Web is far from mature, with less than a decade of widespread use. It will evolve rapidly, adding functions and features. Maintaining the utility of older Web pages will probably mean migrating them to newer formats, which may not always provide easy ways to preserve the content of the older pages. Migration is a particularly difficult issue for pages that contain active elements composed of computer programs providing functions such as animation and custom user interactions. Preserving the functionality of such programs while support for the underlying software disappears will present a significant technical challenge. Another challenge is whether to support a large and increasing number of formats or to select a few favored formats and map all content to the selected formats. The convergence of media and equipment for audio, video, and textual materials over the next few years will only make these questions more pressing.

• *Intellectual property rights*—Web pages are protected by copyright. Creating an archive of such materials without explicit permission of the owner raises obvious issues of copyright violation. In some countries changes to copyright law to permit such archiving are planned. The situation in the United States with respect to such activity by the Library of Congress (as the site of the national copyright deposit) seems to be unclear.

with taking in digital copyright deposits (see discussion of CORDS above). The problems of taking in and making available heterogeneous materials from a wide variety of sources of varying technical sophistication will be challenging. The Library will need to develop significant expertise in an ever-expanding list of varied digital formats and the ability to transform received items into supported formats. The experience of libraries that have loaded commercial electronic journals into local systems has demonstrated the need for good tracking and quality control systems to ensure the receipt, completeness, and functionality of electronic information. Furthermore, if the Library is to pursue the collection and preservation of Web-based publishing, then it will need to build specific skills and facilities to harvest and validate such data. Finally, bringing more digital materials into the Library's collections will inevitably raise questions about the terms and conditions under which users will be able to access materials remotely. The Library will need expert staff to manage negotiations with publishers and other rights holders and to administer complex licensing agreements.

Neither this committee nor any group of consultants can recommend details of the technical infrastructure that the Library needs until the Library refines its collecting aims and stewardship responsibilities for digital collections. For example, the number, size, and technical specifications for one or more digital repositories will depend on the characteristics and relative size of the collections that the Library decides to host on its own systems as opposed to creating links to remote sites or entering into partnerships with third parties that will serve as off-site repositories, as in the ProQuest agreement. The committee agrees on the general outline of features that would be highly desirable for such an infrastructure. Mechanisms for depositing digital materials, whether through copyright deposit, licensing, or purchase, should be highly automated and easy to use. Repositories for storing digital materials will need to support long-term preservation requirements (discussed in Chapter 4) and the various metadata schemata for organizing, describing, and managing heterogeneous digital collections (discussed in Chapter 5). Robust security to prevent loss, alteration, and unauthorized access, in conjunction with complex rights management requirements, will also be needed.

Recommendation: The Library should put in place mechanisms that systematically address the policies, procedures, and infrastructure required for it to collect diverse types of digital resources and to integrate them into its systems for description and cataloging, access, and preservation.

Recommendation: Throughout the Library and particularly in Library Services, the acquisition and management of digital collections will require that the professional librarians have high levels of technological awareness and ability. The Library needs to undertake job redesign, training, and reorganization to achieve this goal.

4

PRESERVING A
DIGITAL HERITAGE

A library is not a last resting place for the books contained there but a place where information and ideas live and breathe in new minds. To continue to do so, the materials collected—whether books or Web pages—must themselves be alive and fresh, in forms and formats that preserve their character and make them accessible to new readers. The digital age brings, here as elsewhere, opportunities and challenges.

Chapter 3 describes mechanisms that the Library of Congress (LC) could use to collect digital materials aggressively and coordinate the development of distributed virtual collections. This chapter discusses the nature of LC's preservation mission in the changing digital context. The Library can now provide access to some objects without assuming any responsibility for preserving them. It can distinguish "research collections," for which LC serves as a portal for access, from more focused "curatorial collections," for which LC would assume primary long-term preservation responsibility. The committee's focus here is on the curatorial collections, but see Chapter 6 for its remarks on the Library's obligation and opportunity to play a part in assuring the quality and preservation of collections it does not directly control.

PRESERVATION:
TRADITIONAL SCOPE AND RESPONSIBILITIES

The acquisition of materials and their integration into a library's collections traditionally have implied a responsibility to preserve those items for use by future generations. The Library of Congress has carried out its preservation responsibilities using a variety of professionally accepted practices:

- Providing adequate storage conditions (e.g., proper environmental controls and appropriate binding and shelving);
- Reformatting materials from their original fragile formats and media to more stable media (e.g., microfilming newspapers and brittle books, transferring audio recordings to more stable media, and copying content on nitrate and acetate film to more stable polyester film bases); and
- For a small percentage of rare and unique materials with intrinsic value in their original formats, restoring originals through conservation treatments.

The Library also has a long history of providing leadership in the broader field of preservation. Over the last two centuries, it has conducted research and led efforts in areas such as binding and shelving books, proper environmental conditions for storage, use of microfilm for preservation, and mass deacidification of paper. The Library has also contributed to national preservation efforts, such as the development and adoption by many publishers of a standard for permanent paper and the coordination of preservation efforts under the Brittle Books Program, funded by the National Endowment for the Humanities, and the National Newspaper Project.[1]

PRESERVATION CHALLENGES FOR DIGITAL COLLECTIONS

The Library faces challenges in digital preservation that are widely recognized and shared by many other libraries and archives. They include the following:

- *Fragile storage media*—Digital materials are especially vulnerable to loss and destruction because they are stored on fragile magnetic and optical media that deteriorate rapidly and that can fail suddenly from exposure to heat, humidity, airborne contaminants, faulty reading and writing devices, human error, and even sabotage.
- *Technology obsolescence*—Digital materials become unreadable and inaccessible if the playback devices necessary to retrieve information from

---

[1]For additional information on LC's preservation efforts for analog materials, see <http://lcweb.loc.gov/preserv/>.

the media become obsolete[2] or if the software that translates digital information from machine- to human-readable form is no longer available.

• *Legal questions surrounding copying and access*—Libraries, archives, and other cultural institutions have limited and uncertain rights to copy digital information for preservation or backup purposes, to reformat information so that it remains accessible by current technology, and to provide public access.[3]

All organizations with responsibilities for preserving digital information are seeking better technical solutions, model policies, best practices, and clearer guidelines regarding legal and intellectual property issues. The committee found few examples of LC providing leadership or contributing actively to solving critical problems of digital archiving and long-term preservation. Until now, LC seems to have assumed a wait-and-see attitude toward its role in preserving digital information created outside the walls of the Library itself; this was probably exacerbated by the absence of a director for the Preservation Directorate. The committee observed a circular logic operating at LC with regard to born-digital materials: "We don't have much born-digital content because we don't know what to do with it; we don't know what to do with born-digital content because we don't have very much of it." Yet because of the Library's national stature and visibility and its past record of leadership, its participation in digital preservation efforts would be of great value and indeed is sorely missed.

The Library's collecting policies and mechanisms with regard to born-digital materials are closely tied to its preservation capabilities. As long as traditional collecting mechanisms guarantee a steady stream of print, other analog materials, and tangible digital objects such as CD-ROMs into the Library's collections, there is an illusion that little significant content is being lost. The absence of significant digital content in the Library's collections removes a sense of urgency about digital preservation, and the lack of organizational capacity to preserve many types of born-digital information discourages the Library from taking on responsibilities that it

---

[2] It is worth noting that analog materials also suffer from this problem.

[3] For additional discussion on copyright and digital preservation, see Chapter 3 of *The Digital Dilemma*, by the Computer Science and Telecommunications Board, National Research Council (Washington, D.C.: National Academy Press, 2000); "Digital Preservation Needs and Requirements in RLG Member Institutions," by Margaret Hedstrom and Sheon Montgomery, Research Libraries Group, available online at <http://www.rlg.org/preserv/digpres.html>; and the film "Into the Future," by the Council on Library and Information Resources, description available online at <http://www.clir.org/pubs/film/film.html#future>.

is not prepared to fulfill. In order for LC to break out of this dilemma, it needs to be aggressive in building collections of born-digital materials, as argued in Chapter 3. The methods for doing this include traditional collecting and custodianship and developing relationships with publishers, other research libraries, other national libraries, bibliographic networks and utilities, government agencies, and archives.[4]

ORGANIZATIONAL ISSUES: DEFINING THE SCOPE OF THE LIBRARY'S PRESERVATION RESPONSIBILITIES

Traditionally, the acquisition of materials through purchase, exchange, or deposit and their cataloging into the Library's permanent collection entailed a commitment to preserve those materials. In the digital environment, LC will assume a wider variety of roles and responsibilities with regard to preservation. One of the first steps that LC needs to take in adapting its collecting practices to accommodate born-digital information is to delineate clearly its responsibilities for preserving digital information. These preservation responsibilities may be loosely classified into three categories:

- LC as creator, active collector, and primary custodian;
- LC as key player in a fail-safe mechanism; and
- LC as a partner in preserving distributed digital collections.

As LC identifies the areas in which it will assume the lead responsibility for digital preservation, other organizations can adjust the scope of their digital collections accordingly. Just as the Library cannot ignore the problem of digital preservation, so also it cannot be expected to do it all. If LC does not set clear boundaries around its digital preservation responsibilities, then many people may assume unrealistically that the Library will be the repository of last resort for everything worth keeping.

The Library of Congress As Owner and Primary Custodian

The Library of Congress must act as the owner and primary custodian for the digital collections it creates.[5] This is a logical extension of

---

[4]The relationships that LC needs to foster are discussed in Chapter 6.

[5]The notion of "creation" in the context of digital collections is admittedly ambiguous. A model of sole creation may be too simplistic, and in fact it may be more common that LC creates digital material in concert with other partners or that is interlinked with content from other partners. In these cases, the Library needs to ensure that the custodial responsibilities of all parties are clearly delineated.

the Library's current efforts to preserve the digital resources that it creates through the retrospective conversion of materials for the National Digital Library Program (NDLP), compilation of public-domain materials, and cataloging. The THOMAS system maintains a comprehensive full-text database of legislation introduced into the U.S. Congress since 1989 and bill summaries and status data from 1973 to 1989. The Law Library's Global Legal Information Network (GLIN) maintains an online database composed primarily of searchable legal abstracts in English of foreign laws and regulations enacted in selected countries since 1976 and over 20,000 full texts of legal instruments since 1995. In addition, LC has preserved its bibliographic database of some 12 million machine-readable catalog records representing the books, serials, maps, sound recordings, manuscripts, and visual materials in its collections by migrating these data successfully from older legacy systems to the new Integrated Library System.

The Library can also logically be expected to serve as owner and primary custodian of materials for which it has a unique mandate and of digital resources that it has unique responsibilities for acquiring. The Library's role in registering copyright and enforcing mandatory deposit law creates a unique opportunity for the Library to collect digital information that might otherwise vanish from the historical record. To fulfill its role and meet its responsibilities, LC urgently needs to develop the organizational and technical capacity to preserve digital deposits of long-term value, as discussed in Chapter 3.

One particular concern with regard to preservation is how deposited items will be identified for integration into LC's permanent collection and which parts of LC will look after long-term preservation requirements. It is not clear when (or if) CORDS will begin retaining and preserving complete digital objects in a systematic way rather than maintaining only registration information and a digital signature of the object being registered. In some cases, only the digital signature will be kept in CORDS, to verify potential alterations to a digital document or copyright infringements. It is also unclear whether the Copyright Office will assume responsibility for the long-term preservation of the digital content deposited in CORDS or whether some or all of this task will pass to Library Services. The Library needs to determine whether CORDS is intended to serve solely as a registration and deposit mechanism or whether it should also include a repository for digital materials with long-term value. If CORDS is not the most appropriate place to preserve deposited digital works—and the committee doubts that it is—then what other provisions will LC make for digital deposits?

The Library of Congress As a Fail-safe Mechanism

The Library of Congress will continue to provide a fail-safe mechanism for preserving materials that no other library has the mandate, resources, or will to maintain; however, it will do so in a new way for digital information. In the paper world, each library that decided to provide its users with a given resource both obtained and conserved its own copy of the object. This replication in the paper world served as a powerful fail-safe mechanism, helping to ensure long-term accessibility through the uncoordinated but distributed maintenance of independent copies. (The only coordination between libraries took place when materials deteriorated to the point where reformatting was required. At that point, a library would check in national databases to see whether another library had already reformatted the item.) In the digital environment, in which much content is distributed through the centralized services of a publisher, it is not clear where the preservation responsibility lies. If libraries can provide timely services to their users without the complexity and expense of locally storing and preserving the content, then who is to assume preservation responsibilities?[6] If the creator, publisher, or distributor is willing to preserve digital resources as long as it is financially viable, when should libraries step in to ensure long-term preservation? The Library has begun experimenting with arrangements that may help clarify its role in these instances. It is now necessary to move from these early experiments to the development of a coherent, overarching strategy for digital preservation. The committee found two noteworthy examples where LC is experimenting with its role as a fail-safe mechanism. The first is in the context of the National Digital Library Program, which—as mentioned above—is investigating a repository system to preserve the content and associated indexing and retrieval capabilities of this rich collection. The NDLP begins to diverge from the strict ownership and custodial model because nearly 30 other institutions besides LC have contributed digital content. NDLP staff reported to the committee that the

---

[6]Many publishers who provide direct online access to their materials today explicitly disclaim long-term preservation responsibility. Others say they will keep resources available, but there is a growing consensus that the dynamics of the commercial world do not favor long-term archiving. As content ages and use declines, it is far from clear that a commercial publisher will be willing to invest in keeping old content alive, migrating it as technology changes and retrofitting old content to take advantage of the ever-increasing functionality from advances in technology (as users will expect). Further, content will be threatened whenever it is in the hands of a single institution. Companies evolve, combine with others, change their orientation as markets evolve, and (a particular threat in this time of upheaval and dramatic technological change) go out of business.

Library would take responsibility for preserving digital content from partner institutions should any of them become unable to maintain their portions of the collection. This is a good example of the Library agreeing to serve as a fail-safe mechanism.

The committee nevertheless has several concerns about this arrangement. There are no formal arrangements that define LC's role in long-term maintenance and preservation of the portions of the NDLP that are currently in the custody of other participating institutions. Although the committee does not question the participating institutions' commitment, in principle, to preserving the digital content they have contributed, a variety of unforeseen circumstances could prevent them from doing so. This is a particular concern because of the funding model for the NDLP and the emphasis to date on digitization and the development of access mechanisms. While the committee encourages LC to function as a fail-safe mechanism, it believes that LC does not understand that it is placing itself in a risky position when it expresses a willingness to do this without adequately calculating the scale of the commitment and developing the capacity to fulfill it. Also, as the NDLP grows and as more institutions contribute content, the Library will have a larger number of relationships to manage. An important next step for the NDLP is to develop standards and agreements for long-term stewardship that define when and under what circumstances LC will serve as the fail-safe mechanism or repository of last resort.[7]

The committee also notes that the requirements and technical standards for the repository have not yet been defined. Repositories are systems for storing digital objects in a robust and managed fashion. They protect data from inappropriate access, facilitate the recording of appropriate metadata to allow the management of objects, and provide delivery facilities for both curatorial and user access. The Library has recently acquired, through a gift, the TEAMS system developed by Thompson Publishing. TEAMS supports both object and metadata storage and maintenance and has been implemented in a variety of corporate settings (for example, it is used by the *Washington Post* to manage its digital content). Its use by LC represents the first implementation of TEAMS in a traditional library application. The committee supports the development of a repository system as an important next step for the NDLP and agrees that this work needs to be stepped up, but it has reservations about the direc-

---

[7]As an implementation issue, the role of LC as a fail-safe mechanism or repository of last resort does not necessarily have to be fulfilled by having the digital content resident on LC servers only. Redundancy across locations (whether at LC servers at other sites or at the servers of cooperating organizations) is desirable.

tions that LC is taking. Is it in the best long-term interest of LC or the participants in the NDLP to use a commercial product developed for a commercial application? Although accepting donated hardware and software helps to mobilize private support for LC and may reduce expenditures in the short run, contributions like these can also commit LC to proprietary systems and methods that in the long run will limit the Library's ability to federate its collections with those of other repositories and interoperate easily with potential partners. Where long-term strategic purposes are involved, selection should be based on a full review of the technical architecture, costs, and long-term value.

One approach is for LC to coordinate its efforts to develop a repository system with those of other organizations that are using the reference model for the Open Archival Information System (OAIS) (Box 4.1). This high-level model does not specify any particular implementation of an archival information system, nor does it define standards accession, description, data management, or distribution. The OAIS model is important for digital preservation standards and strategies because it defines the functions and requirements for a digital archive through an international standard that vendors and producers of digital information can reference. If the OAIS reference model is widely adopted (and there are indications that it will be), then it may provide the framework for a network of cooperating and federated repositories. The National Archives and Records Administration is adopting this model for some of its digital archiving requirements and is working with the San Diego Supercomputer Center on one specific implementation.

In general, for LC to develop the capacity to serve as a fail-safe mechanism, it will need to acquire a much more extensive technical infrastructure and greater expertise in a wide variety of file types and formats. While they are important experiments, neither the NDLP repository nor CORDS yet offers solutions to LC's responsibility to preserve born-digital content created outside the Library. In the case of NDLP, LC has been working with materials *converted* to digital form, and for these materials it has taken the lead in setting standards for formats, metadata, naming conventions, and other technical attributes. But for born-digital materials, especially those created outside the Library, LC is unlikely to have the leverage to define or limit the formats and structures that are used. In the experimental period of the dissertation project, ProQuest is presenting dissertations in the portable document format (PDF) directly to the Copyright Office.[8] These are being accepted as the best edition, cataloged using the cataloging specifications offered by

---

[8]See Chapter 3 for a discussion of the ProQuest arrangement.

BOX 4.1
Open Archival Information System

The Open Archival Information System (OAIS) is a high-level reference model developed by the Consultative Committee for Space Data Systems with representatives of the leading space science agencies in North America, Europe, and Japan.[1] The OAIS reference model provides a unifying set of concepts for an OAIS archive. It consists of an organization of people and systems that has accepted responsibility for preserving information and making it available to a designated community. The OAIS model provides terminology and concepts for describing and comparing the architectures and operations of archives, defines the responsibilities of an open archival information system, and offers detailed models for the functions, components, and processes necessary to support long-term preservation and access to digital information. Although the model was developed originally to assist organizations with the preservation of large databases of space science information, it has been used in several other contexts, including in Project NEDLIB and in archival program development at the National Archives and Records Administration. Building on the OAIS model, the Council on Library and Information Resources (CLIR) began an initiative in the year 2000 involving the preservation of digital scholarly journals.[2]

---

[1]Information about the OAIS reference model is available online at <http://ssdoo.gsfc.nasa.gov/nost/isoas/>.
[2]For additional information, see <http://www.clir.org/diglib/preserve/presjour.htm>.

ProQuest, verified by examiners in the Copyright Office, and stored at ProQuest. That is, registration is handled by the Copyright Office but the deposit is virtual. This arrangement presents LC with no immediate need to preserve the materials.

Finding: Because of intellectual property law and the uncertainty of some publishers regarding the deposit of copies of digital works, institutions with long-term preservation responsibilities must seek and develop new means of ensuring continuing access to the valuable documentation of history, culture, and creativity. One possible approach is contractual agreements with rights holders who maintain digital information in off-site repositories, with provisions for deposit in a library or other institution should the publisher cease to maintain the information. Some publishers have agreed to provide perpetual access to their materials as one of the conditions of a license. The Library has initiated an experiment in reaching such an agreement with ProQuest. The committee believes that

such arrangements need to be tested carefully and that other models need to be explored as well.

Recommendation: The Library should establish contractual arrangements (i.e., projects) in 2000 and 2001 with a pilot set of publishers and distributors of significant digital content, in order to conduct additional experimental programs for storing and maintaining digital information in off-site and on-site respositories.

Recommendation: For all fail-safe arrangements, the Library must regularly test the integrity of the materials and systems and its capacity to accept responsibility in a timely way. Such tests will demonstrate whether LC has the appropriate technical capability and whether the arrangements with publishers are realistic ones.

The way in which librarians work must be totally reconceptualized for these fail-safe mechanisms to work. The Library should coordinate such efforts with institutions doing related work, including other research libraries, the National Libraries of Agriculture and Medicine, the National Archives and Records Administration, other national libraries working to preserve their nations' digital heritage, and other organizations that have a legal mandate for long-term preservation or a commercial interest in it.

The Library of Congress As a Participant in Shared Responsibilities for Long-term Preservation

The committee's analysis suggests that the Library needs to articulate carefully a policy identifying the subset of digital materials for which it will assume long-term curatorial responsibility, taking into account the following:

• The burden of preserving digital collections is daunting and must be shared with other archiving institutions.
• The archiving and preservation of digital resources normally accessed over the Internet will not take place as a by-product of normal access but must be explicitly pursued. Simply assuming that preservation will be carried out somewhere across numerous replicated research collections will not be a solution for networked resources.

Both considerations argue for libraries to define the scope of their archiving roles, in order that responsibilities be distributed across the archiving libraries of the world.

The archiving and preservation responsibility is a long-term one that will serve researchers in generations to come. One advantage of digital materials is the potential to distribute preservation responsibilities among a wide variety of partners so that each institution preserves only a designated portion of the global digital record. With careful planning, coordination, cooperative agreements, and clearly articulated boundaries around its curatorial collection, the Library could assume long-term preservation responsibility for a much smaller portion of the digital corpus than it did for the paper one. Some redundancy is necessary for backup and security purposes, but less redundancy is needed for digital collections than was required in the past because access no longer requires physical proximity to materials. Distributed curatorial responsibility will be achieved only with leadership from LC and cooperation with many partners. A variety of roles can be envisioned for the Library in a collaborative effort among libraries, publishers, government agencies, and other stakeholders to define the parameters of distributed digital collections and delineate the roles and responsibilities of various parties for access and long-term maintenance of important digital works (see Box 4.2).

One of LC's roles could involve coordination with other national libraries. As mentioned above, several European national libraries and the national libraries of Canada and Australia have launched programs to collect and preserve the digital portions of their national bibliographies. If the mechanisms to acquire and preserve the digital national bibliographies of some countries succeed, LC could be relieved of responsibility for preserving most digital materials from those countries. At that point, it could concentrate its curatorial efforts on works created or published by Americans or that reflect important aspects of U.S. history, policy development, and culture. Some other countries would need help. For the foreseeable future, many developing countries will not have the resources to preserve their digital heritage. Curatorial responsibility for these collections could be shared by LC and other libraries that have well-developed repository systems rather than assuming that LC will serve as the repository for all significant materials globally.

There are many other opportunities to divide up long-term preservation responsibilities by subject area or domain. This is not unprecedented: LC already cedes responsibility for materials in medicine, agriculture, and education to the national libraries set up for those subject domains. In addition, the National Archives and Records Administration preserves records of the federal government that have long-term value for documenting U.S. government, policy development, and history. A clear delineation of LC's long-term curatorial responsibilities would be critical as

BOX 4.2
Research and Experiments in Digital Preservation

• *The CEDARS project* aims to provide guidance in best practices for digital preservation by both developing practical demonstrator projects and sponsoring strategic working groups. Funded by the British Joint Information Systems Committee (JISC), with work carried out at Leeds, Oxford, and Cambridge universities, its main objectives are to promote awareness; to identify, document, and disseminate strategic frameworks for the development of appropriate digital collection management policies; and to investigate, document, and promote methods appropriate for long-term preservation. (For more information, see <http://www.leeds.ac.uk/cedars/>.)

• For *Project NEDLIB*, several European national libraries have joined forces to develop strategies, programs, and infrastructure for digital deposit and archiving. Project NEDLIB—Networked European Deposit Library—started in January 1998 with funding from the European Commission's Telematics for Libraries Programme. Project partners include deposit libraries, archives, developers of information technology, and three large publishers (Kluwer, Elsevier, and Springer-Verlag) that contribute to the project and will supply electronic publications for demonstration purposes. The project aims to construct the basic infrastructure upon which a networked European deposit library can be built. Key issues to be investigated are standards and interfaces for the generic architecture; electronic document technical data; and access controls and archival maintenance procedures. Information technology developers and publishers will assist in defining standards, methods, and techniques. The commercial and copyright interests of publishers will be handled through access controls implemented when the publications are stored and activated when they are accessed. (Information on NEDLIB projects, working papers, and reports is available online at <http://www.konbib.nl/coop/nedlib/>.)

• *The PANDORA project* (Preserving and Accessing Networked Documentary Resources of Australia) is an initiative of the National Library of Australia that aims to develop policies and procedures for the selection, capture, and archiving of Australian electronic publications and the provision of long-term access to them. One of its priorities is the fostering of working partnerships with other national libraries and overseas agencies that are also undertaking research and development in this area. To date, it has developed a working proof-of-concept archive (<http://www.nla.gov.au/pandora/archive.html>) and a collection of policy documents outlining the conceptual framework for a permanent electronic archive. It is now developing a working model for a national collection of Australian electronic publications. (See <http://pandora.nla.gov.au/pandora/>.)

• *Project PRISM*, at Cornell University, is a 4-year effort to investigate and develop the policies and mechanisms needed for information integrity in distributed digital libraries. A collaboration of librarians, computer scientists, and social scientists, it is funded by the Digital Library Initiative, phase 2 (see <http://www.dli2.nsf.gov/>). One of its five foci is digital preservation; it aims to investigate the long-term survivability of information in digital form. Another focus is to investigate policies and mechanisms for preserving digital content, especially when that content is not under direct curatorial control. (For more information, see <http://www.prism.cornell.edu/main.htm>.)

• *The CAMiLEON Project* is a joint undertaking between the University of Michigan and the University of Leeds (United Kingdom) and is funded by the Joint Information Systems Committee (JISC, which also funds the CEDARS project) and the National Science Foundation. It aims to evaluate emulation as a digital preservation strategy for retaining the original functionality and look and feel of digital objects and to locate emulation within a larger suite of digital preservation strategies. Its deliverables include cost comparisons of different levels of emulation; a set of emulation tools that will be available for use and further testing in libraries; and preliminary guidelines for the use of different strategies (conversion, migration, and emulation) for managing and preserving digital collections. (See <http://www.si.umich.edu/CAMILEON/>.)

• *The Data Provenance Project* at the University of Pennsylvania is exploring methods for keeping track of the source (the provenance) of digital information as it is extracted from databases, translated, transformed, and combined with other information. Funded by the Digital Library Initiative (DLI), it aims to identify the central issues of digital provenance and to contribute to the development of new data models, new query languages, and new storage techniques that will lead to the creation of a substrate for recording and tracking provenance. (See <http://db.cis.upenn.edu/Research/provenance.html>.)

• *The NARA Project: Persistent Archives and Electronic Records Management,* a project of the San Diego Supercomputer Center and the National Archives and Records Administration, is working on an approach to maintaining digital data for hundreds of years by developing an environment that supports the migration of collections onto new software systems. It is developing both the technologies and the preservation and management policies needed to define an infrastructure for a collection-based persistent archive. The project's current focus is the creation of a 1-million-message persistent e-mail collection. (See <http://www.sdsc.edu/NARA/>, <http://www.dlib.org/dlib/march00/moore/03moore-pt1.html>, and <http://www.dlib.org/dlib/april00/moore/04moore-pt2.html>.)

• *LOCKSS* (Lots of Copies Keeps Stuff Safe), a project of Stanford University's HighWire Press, has funding from Sun Microsystems and the National Science Foundation. LOCKSS is testing the feasibility of preserving digital documents by storing multiple copies on different computers. Each computer in the LOCKSS network looks for and corrects errors in its copy by comparing it with other copies in the LOCKSS system. The system is currently being tested at the libraries of Columbia, Harvard, and Stanford universities, the University of California at Berkeley, the University of Tennessee, and the Los Alamos National Laboratory. If these tests are successful, the Stanford researchers hope to expand the project to libraries overseas. (For more on LOCKSS, see <http://lockss.stanford.edu/>.)

• Like LOCKSS, the *Intermemory* project, based at the NEC Research Institute, aims to preserve digital information by replicating it at multiple sites. It is performing basic research in the area of Internet-distributed algorithms and protocols. (See <http://www.intermemory.org>.)

a means to avoid unachievable commitments to long-term preservation and enable the Library to preserve materials that it is best suited or uniquely able to collect and maintain.

Finding: Many national libraries, university research libraries, national archives, bibliographic utilities, and organizations with large holdings of digital information are actively pursuing solutions to the problems of digital preservation. Although the Library of Congress might have been expected to provide leadership in this area as it once did in others, LC has at best played only a minimal role in these initiatives. As a consequence, it has little awareness of potential solutions that are emerging from joint research and development projects and has not contributed much to this important national and international problem for the library community.

Recommendation: Ensuring its leadership in digital preservation will require the Library to hire or develop relevant expertise. The Library should join and, where possible, lead or facilitate national and international research and development efforts in digital preservation. There are opportunities for the Library to learn from and contribute to such efforts in preserving born-digital information and converting certain types of information to digital form as a preservation strategy.

Recommendation: To make it a safe haven for preservation purposes,[9] the Library should take an active role—including working with the Congress if necessary—in efforts to rework intellectual property restraints on copying and migration.

---

[9]In *The Digital Dilemma*, p. 210, it was similarly recommended that "Congress should enact legislation to permit copying of digital information for archival purposes, whether the copy is in the same format or migrated to a new format." LC is currently investigating intellectual property rights in the digital domain under a mandate from the Digital Millennium Copyright Act of 1998, which asks the Librarian of Congress to determine whether technical protection measures are having an adverse effect on the ability to make noninfringing uses of copyrighted works.

WHAT DOES THE LIBRARY OF CONGRESS NEED TO DO TO FULFILL ITS LONG-TERM PRESERVATION RESPONSIBILITIES?

Even if LC carefully defines its roles and responsibilities along the continuum from serving as a portal to acting as the primary custodian for digital materials, there is an urgent need for it to enhance its technical capacity and expertise in digital preservation. Such preservation will involve a wide range of activities, including the following:

- *"Protecting the bits"*—The making of backup copies, periodic re-copying to new media, and regular checking of object coherence and validity are required to make certain that rarely accessed materials remain technically sound. Access will be enhanced to the extent that archived materials remain online rather than, say, being stored on media such as tapes, which must be mounted manually.
- *Archiving appropriate copies*—For many digital materials, the format most useful for current services (say, a PDF file or a GIF image) is not the most robust for long-term archiving (SGML, XML, or TIFF may serve better). A preservation program must encompass the selection and archiving of the appropriate formats for long-term use and then the derivation of current-use copies appropriate to the technological base of today's users. It must also work with users to help them undertake these tasks.
- *Maintaining appropriate metadata*—All preservation activities will depend on the completeness and quality of the metadata for the objects to be preserved. It will be critical for the Library to monitor developments in metadata standards and follow best practices for metadata as they develop.
- *Migrating formats*—Even the most careful selection of archiving formats cannot ensure that objects will be useful in the decades to come. It will be necessary to migrate objects periodically from one archival format to another. Such processes must be carefully designed and executed to ensure minimal loss of content (it is impossible to ensure that all such migrations will be loss-free). Some works, such as those that include active software (e.g., Java applets), may raise particularly difficult issues.
- *Conducting research and development*—Only a handful of institutions are likely to face digital preservation challenges on the scale or scope of those that LC faces in the coming years. This makes it unlikely that LC will be able to import models and solutions for all of its preservation needs. An active program of research and development in digital preservation is needed to solve immediate preservation problems—technical, legal, and economic—at LC and to provide guidance to other libraries and archives.

- *Educating the relevant communities*—Especially in this transitional period, when digital materials are new and preservation practices are still in flux, institutions and particular communities will need to be educated about digital preservation: What is the state of the art? What factors must be taken into account in planning for preservation? LC is well situated to participate in such efforts and possibly to take the lead.

A robust preservation program will employ curators and preservation staff with knowledge of the formats of materials in their collections and of appropriate metadata standards and practices and an understanding of the issues involved in migrating objects from one format to another. It will require well-developed production services for creating the specified metadata, sound and robust repository services, and periodic quality checking and copying of objects in the collection. Technical staff will be required to build or implement many pieces of the necessary infrastructure and to create the custom migration facilities that a digital collection will need to endure over time. It is not imperative that the Library itself carry out all of this activity. The curatorial responsibility can be met by ensuring that appropriate activities are carried out by contractors or other libraries and archives.

In the future, LC will also need to make much more extensive use of digitization for preservation. Some professionals consider digital objects—whether born digital or turned digital—unacceptable as preservation masters because their longevity is uncertain.[10] In some cases, however, digital conversion may offer the only viable means of salvaging and preserving certain materials, such as audio recordings in obsolete analog formats. The Library has used digitization to preserve severely damaged black-and-white negatives and some audio and video records on magnetic media. Just as LC will need new capabilities to collect and maintain born-digital materials, so also will it need to develop new capabilities to preserve all of the digital information under its control.

The challenges of digital preservation make it easy to overlook the benefits that LC could enjoy by rapidly enhancing its capacity to collect and preserve digital information. Digital storage media are very compact, making it possible to store enormous quantities of information in a very small amount of space. Digital information can be managed and handled more automatically. More significantly, whatever LC collects and preserves in digital form has the potential to be made accessible to

---

[10]*Why Digitize?* by Abby Smith (Washington, D.C.: Council on Library and Information Resources, 1999).

anyone, anywhere, on any day of the week or at any time of the day (as rights permit under the copyright law or terms of licenses). Unless LC develops the capacity to integrate digital materials into the mainstream of its collecting and access programs, it will forgo all of these benefits and will cede its position as one of the world's leading libraries.

Finding: The Library of Congress lacks an overarching strategy and long-range plan for digital preservation. (In recent years, it has also been without a permanent head for its Preservation Directorate.) Although the Library has preserved many of its own digital resources, including the full-text databases of the THOMAS system, its own bibliographic databases, and the content, descriptive information, and retrieval capabilities of the National Digital Library Program, these efforts are not coordinated with each other or with efforts to address the larger problem of capturing and preserving born-digital content, nor is there any strategy, plan, or infrastructure to capture, manage, and preserve born-digital information that originates outside the Library.

Recommendation: The Library should immediately form a high-level planning group to coordinate digital preservation efforts and develop the policies, technical capacity, and expertise to preserve digital information. The hiring of someone who is knowledgeable about digital preservation as a new head of the Preservation Directorate must be given high priority.

Recommendation: The Library should put a digital preservation plan in place and implement it as soon as possible, taking into account life-cycle costs and minimizing the need for manual intervention. The Open Archival Information System (OAIS) reference model provides a useful framework for identifying the requirements for a digital archiving system. The initiative by the Council on Library and Information Resources that builds on the OAIS should also be consulted.

5
ORGANIZING INTELLECTUAL ACCESS TO DIGITAL INFORMATION: FROM CATALOGING TO METADATA

Libraries not only collect and preserve material; they also provide access to it. The intellectual basis of providing such access is the organization and cataloging of materials under their aegis. The Library of Congress, even more than most libraries, invests heavily in cataloging its collections. It probably has the largest cataloging operation in the world[1] and is a source of both cataloging data and standards for much of the library community. In the world of paper-based publication, its role is second to none.

One enduring role of libraries during the transition from physical to digital information will be the intellectual task of cataloging—imposing order[2] on diverse resources with the goal of making those resources easier to discover and manage. As the chair of this committee said, "The librarian [in the digital age] will have to be a more active participant in staving off 'infochaos' by playing a role in selecting information resources and describing them in the 'information waterfall' of the 'virtual library.'"[3]

---

[1]The Cataloging Directorate at LC employs approximately 550 people. Cataloging functions also take place in other units at LC.

[2]"Cataloging in the Digital Order," by David M. Levy, paper presented at Digital Libraries '95: The Second Annual Conference on the Theory and Practice of Digital Libraries, available online at <http://csdl.tamu.edu/DL95/papers/levy/levy.html>.

[3]*Avatars of the Word: From Papyrus to Cyberspace*, by James J. O'Donnell (Cambridge, Mass.: Harvard University Press, 1998), p. 43.

The first section of this chapter reviews the longtime leadership role of the Library of Congress in developing and maintaining cataloging standards for physical resources. The chapter then looks at the implications of the new digital milieu for these traditional cataloging mechanisms. It closes with some observations on how the Library seems to be addressing these changes, arguing that it is not treating them as the strategic issue the committee believes them to be.

A HISTORY OF LEADERSHIP IN CATALOGING STANDARDS

The Library of Congress has a well-earned reputation for its leading role in the development and administration of cataloging and associated standards. Before reviewing these standards efforts, it is worthwhile to answer briefly two questions: Why are standards important? What role have they played over the past century?[4]

Cataloging is arguably among the most expensive tasks in the library. Current estimates range from $50 to $110 for the creation of a single full cataloging record.[5] What is responsible for this high cost? While some of the tasks of cataloging—for example, recording a title—are indeed mundane (in the majority of but not all cases), others are intellectually challenging and time consuming:

• *Subject analysis*—The usability of library catalogs for finding resources "about" a particular subject depends greatly on the nontrivial task of understanding the content of a resource and tagging it with a controlled subject heading.[6]

• *Authority control*—While the subject of assigning authorship may

---

[4]The original goals of cataloging as expressed by Charles Cutter at the end of the nineteenth century were to enable readers to do the following: (1) to find all works by a particular author, (2) to find any work by title, (3) to find all editions of a work, and (4) to find all works on a subject. These goals were originally conceived of as applying to works held by a particular library.

[5]Based on testimony to the committee and the personal knowledge of committee members. However, a "full" cataloging record is not generated for many materials; less thorough cataloging records will naturally cost less.

[6]Any user of a library catalog, either in card or online form, is familiar with this subject tagging. For example, the book *Avatars of the Word*, by James J. O'Donnell, is tagged with the three subject headings *Communication and technology—History; Written communication— History;* and *Cyberspace*, which are elements of the Library of Congress subject headings (see <http://lcweb.loc.gov/catdir/cpso/wlsabt.html>). The advantages of this tagging are twofold. A user of the library catalog can search for resources on the basis of the subject classifications, and once a resource is found, related resources (by subject classification) can be located.

seem superficially simple, it is confounded by the fact that people frequently use different forms of their name, and different people frequently have very similar or identical names. There is the problem of the multiple spellings of historical figures (is it "Shakespeare" or "Shakespere" or "Shakespear" or ?), the problem of aliases ("Mark Twain" and "Samuel Clemens"), and the seemingly random use of initials, shortened names, and the like ("Samuel Langhorne Clemens," "Samuel L. Clemens," "Sam Clemens," etc.). Authority control, in the context of author names, is the task of, first, associating these name variations with a canonical name in the cataloging record to show that the variations are indeed the same person and, second, differentiating between ambiguous and overlapping names.

The development of standard cataloging practices from the end of the nineteenth century through the twentieth century made it possible to share cataloging records, leading to a significant cost savings for libraries. "Copy cataloging" exploits the fact that the overwhelming majority of resources in an average library are not unique. Rather than produce original cataloging records for the duplicated resources, libraries can use cataloging records from other libraries. In fact, in preautomation days, the Library of Congress was in the business of supplying physical catalog cards to many other libraries across the United States.[7]

The following subsections, while not exhaustive, give an overview of the Library's involvement and leadership in cataloging and resource discovery standards.

Machine-Readable Cataloging

The development of the machine-readable cataloging (MARC) record[8] by the Library of Congress, in concert with the library community, in the 1960s was a landmark event in the automation of library operations. As recalled above, preautomation catalog sharing involved the physical shipment of catalog cards to fellow libraries. The introduction of computers into the library environment allowed

---

[7]The LC cards were also an important source of information for the purpose of selecting new titles to be added to a library's collection.

[8]There are in fact many separate dialects of MARC used across the world. For simplicity's sake, this report uses the term "MARC" to denote the USMARC standard. When other dialects are intended, their specific designation is used. For additional information on MARC, see *Understanding MARC Bibliographic: Machine-Readable Cataloging*, by B. Furie (Washington, D.C.: Cataloging Distribution Service, Library of Congress, 1998).

sharing computer catalog records among libraries by exchanging magnetic tapes. MARC consists of both an encoding scheme for labeling cataloging elements (e.g., "author" or "title") and an exchange format for packaging the encoded bibliographic data into a record for transfer purposes. The MARC record remains a critical technical foundation of existing integrated library systems (e.g., the Endeavor ILS recently installed at the Library of Congress) and permits the transfer of records (now via networks) among these systems.

The Library's Network Development and MARC Standards Office[9] leads and coordinates international efforts to further develop MARC as a standard for the efficient and long-term interchange of bibliographic information. In recent years, the office has been analyzing the relationship of MARC to standard generalized markup language (SGML)[10] and the use of MARC for digital media.

One important aside to this discussion of MARC is the potential that the widespread and rapid adoption of MARC presented for the migration of the National Union Catalog to electronic format.[11] A number of the individuals interviewed by the committee said that the Library had missed an opportunity in the late 1960s and early 1970s to provide online access to shared catalog records. Such a catalog could have been a natural product for a national library and, perhaps, could have provided a revenue stream to underwrite the Library's cataloging operation. In fact, the Library, for reasons not entirely obvious to the committee or the individuals, failed to take advantage of this key opportunity and ceded it to the Online Computer Library Center (OCLC) and the Research Libraries

---

[9] Its Web site is at < http://lcweb.loc.gov/marc/>.

[10] A markup language is one that allows tags to be intermixed with standard text to instruct a computer about how that text should appear when rendered (presented) or to indicate the structure of that text (its division into chapters and sections, for example). The markup language most well-known to users of the Web is hypertext markup language (HTML). HTML was preceded by SGML, which is used mainly in the publishing community but has proven too complex for general use. The recent development of extensible markup language (XML) in the Web community represents an attempt to find a standard that mediates between the low functionality but simplicity of HTML and the overwhelming complexity of SGML.

[11] The National Union Catalog (NUC) is a record of publications held in more than 1,100 libraries in the United States and Canada, including the Library of Congress. Major portions of the NUC are published in two principal series: one covers post-1955 publications and the other pre-1956 imprints. Since 1983, the NUC has been issued on microfiche. For additional information, see <http://lcweb.loc.gov/rr/main/inforeas/catalogs.html#union>.

Group (RLG).[12] The Library should learn from this experience to identify and secure for itself appropriate strategic leadership roles (see Chapter 6).

General Cataloging Standards

While MARC provides the markup and transfer syntax for bibliographic records, the Anglo-American Cataloging Rules (AACR2)[13] provide the rules for the actual description of a bibliographic item. The Library of Congress plays a major role in coordinating activities in AACR2, and its *Library of Congress Rule Interpretations*[14] defines common practice for the use of AACR2 in cooperative cataloging. The result, in combination with the MARC standard, is that both the meaning and encoding of cataloging records can be shared among a large number of libraries. These activities are centered in the Library's Cataloging Policy and Support Office (CPSO), which provides "leadership in the creation and implementation of cataloging policy within the Library of Congress and in the national and international library community."[15] Among the cataloging standards coordinated by CPSO are authority files (both names and subjects) to support MARC data elements, the Library of Congress classification rules, and Library of Congress subject headings, all described above.

Encoded Archival Description

In general, archival and manuscript items are handled differently from monographs and serials. Whereas the latter are cataloged at the item level, the former are described at a coarser level of granularity (for example, a manuscript box or folder). Tools for locating such items are

---

[12]OCLC (<http://www.oclc.org>) and RLG (<http://www.rlg.org>) are nonprofit corporations, each having a union catalog product that it markets to libraries. Combined, OCLC's WorldCat (<http://www.oclc.org/oclc/menu/colpro.htm>) and RLG's Union Catalog (<http://www.rlg.org/cit-bib.html>) are the basis of cooperative cataloging among the world's libraries. Many of the original cataloging records in these products came from the Library of Congress. One possible reason why LC did not take advantage of the commercial opportunity is that such an initiative would have taken it far afield of its primary mission of serving Congress.

[13]*The Concise AACR2, 1988 revision,* by Michael Gorman (Chicago: American Library Association, 1989), p. 161.

[14]*Library of Congress Rule Interpretations,* 2nd ed. (Washington, D.C.: Cataloging Distribution Service, Library of Congress, 1989).

[15]Library of Congress Cataloging Policy and Support Office; see <http://lcweb.loc.gov/catdir/cpso/cpso.html#tools>.

referred to as "finding aids." The encoded archival description (EAD)[16] was the product of a project at the University of California at Berkeley in the early 1990s to develop a standard for machine-readable finding aids.[17] The EAD standard utilizes SGML to mark up structured descriptions of units of archival information. The Library's Network Development and MARC Standards Office serves as the maintenance agency for the EAD standard, an excellent example of the Library stepping in to play an important role in the new metadata environment.[18]

THE DIGITAL CONTEXT AND ITS CHALLENGES TO TRADITIONAL CATALOGING PRACTICES

A user of the Web who has sampled any of the numerous search engines (e.g., Google, AltaVista, Excite[19]) might argue that digital content, networks, and full-text indexing have made human-mediated organization through cataloging obsolete. Web search engines demonstrate the great utility of such searching and the benefits of over 30 years of research in information retrieval[20] and, to a lesser degree, natural language processing.[21] However, there are numerous inherent limitations to the technology underlying them:

- *Scalability*—Most Web search engines accumulate indexes by scanning the Web and downloading full content from sites.[22] As the volume of Web content grows, it has become increasingly difficult to keep these

---

[16]"Encoded Archival Description," by D. Pitti, paper presented at Mid-Atlantic Regional Archives Conference, 1997, Wilmington, Del.

[17]This notion of machine-readability for finding aids can be compared to the role that MARC plays with AACR2. That is, finding aids have semantic content (in the same sense that AACR2 defines the "meaning" of bibliographic cataloging) and a syntax for encoding that information in computer files and exchanging it between computers (in the same sense that MARC provides a "markup" for AACR2 records).

[18]Encoded Archival Description official Web site at <http://lcweb.loc.gov/ead/>.

[19]See <http://www.google.com>, <http://www.altavista.com>, and <http://www.excite.com>, respectively.

[20]*Readings in Information Retrieval*, by K. Sparc-Jones and P. Willett (Los Angeles, Calif.: Morgan Kaufmann Publishers, 1997).

[21]*Natural Language Understanding*, 2nd ed., by J. Allen (Redwood City, Calif.: Benjamin/Cummings, 1995), p. 654.

[22]The model followed by existing Web search engines is known as Web crawling. This involves downloading individual pages, analyzing the content of those pages and indexing it in full-text search engines, and then following the hyperlinks on those pages to determine additional pages to download.

indexes current or complete. One study[23] indicates that even the best search engines index only about 12 to 15 percent of Web content.[24] Even more problematic are the limitations of the information retrieval (IR) technology used in most popular Web search engines. The nature of the Web as a corpus presents some difficult scalability challenges for IR and often leads to poor results. The sheer size of the corpus is a notable problem; a typical Web query will retrieve a very large set of potentially relevant documents. In addition, the Web corpus is usually presented as a single, unorganized collection of documents, which makes synonym clashes inevitable.[25] Synonym clashes are well understood and can be addressed with a variety of techniques (e.g., thesauri, user feedback, local context analysis, phrase structure), but these techniques are generally not exploited by Web search engines.

• *Access limitations and databases*—While a great deal of useful content is freely available on the Internet, there is a growing and equally valuable portion of Internet content that is proprietary and held in protected systems. Much "valuable" content (from the point of view of the rights holder) is held in databases on special servers that require a password or other means of authorization for access. These databases also provide enhanced functions beyond what can be done with simple, static Web pages. However, they do not in general support access via crawling, the method used to build most Internet search services. Thus, while Web indexers are able to access and index a large percentage of the total content on the Web, an ever-growing percentage of the most-sought-after material is not available from Internet search facilities.

• *Format*—Existing Web search engines are limited to textual content. They index words in documents and process textual queries—for example, "digital imaging"—returning lists of documents ranked according to the appearance of the query words in their content. Extending this approach to images will require tools to analyze image content and re-

---

[23]"Search Engines Fall Short," by S. Lawrence and C.G. Giles, in *Science*, Vol. 285 (1999), No. 5426, p. 295.

[24]This low proportion of indexed pages is caused by a number of factors. Among them are the simple scale of the number of Web pages and limitations on accessing all of them in a reasonable time, problems of occasional server unavailability, and policies of certain Web sites (voluntarily followed by Web crawlers) that prevent crawling of that site.

[25]Any user of Web search engines quickly becomes aware of the problem of synonym clashes, in which a search term has multiple meanings and results are returned for all these possible meanings, producing false hits that overload the results relevant for the query. For example, a user might want information about the planet Mercury and enter a query with that term. In addition to sites about the planet, the search engines will intermix results about the element Mercury, the car brand Mercury, the Roman god Mercury, and various other meanings or uses of that term.

spond to queries such as "find images with cars in them" or, at an even more advanced level, to queries that ask for images with features similar to those of another digitized image. The tools to retrieve images, video segments, voice, and music are being actively researched[26] but are currently beyond the capabilities of Internet search engines.

- *Context*—At a more abstract level, the usefulness of indexing based solely on the text content of a resource is compromised by lack of context. The best tools to help a person locate a resource are those that are tailored to the context in which the resource occurs and to the knowledge context of the searcher. For example, content-based searches of MEDLINE (the medical index at the National Library of Medicine) might be appropriate for a professional familiar with medical terminology and with the body of medical literature indexed by MEDLINE. However, a high-school student might not be able to select documents that are appropriate to his or her background and might not be familiar with medical terms, so he or she might find content-based searching to be difficult. The lack of context is a problem for both human and automatically generated representations, but different representations can often be combined to good effect.

- *Markup*—HTML, the main markup language of the Web, provides only a very simplified set of tags for labeling the parts of a document. These are primarily oriented to supporting the appropriate display of the document and in general tell little about the meaning of the various sections of the document. Many search engines utilize smart markup to provide more powerful retrieval facilities, allowing users to limit which parts of a document are used to satisfy the search argument. The simplicity of HTML markup severely constrains Internet search engines' use of such facilities, which are very useful for limiting and refining search results.

The creation of structured descriptive records for resources (e.g., traditional cataloging records or, more generally, surrogates) can help to address some of these limitations.[27] Scalability can improve if surrogates are used instead of the full content for indexing. Content providers may be more willing to distribute freely descriptive surrogates for indexing, in

---

[26]*Advances in Information Retrieval: Recent Research from the Center for Intelligent Information Retrieval,* by W.B. Croft, ed. (Boston: Kluwer Academic Publishers, 2000).

[27]Surrogates that augment the full text of documents are common. Abstract and indexing services routinely add terms to make documents more accessible to a given audience. It is not uncommon for a journal article to be indexed by two or three secondary indexing services, each of which characterizes the article in terms that will be meaningful within its subject domain.

lieu of the full content. Surrogates can be created, and standards are being developed for describing all manner of digital objects. Finally, surrogate records may include descriptive information that is not part of the document itself (usually the result of human analysis). For example, surrogates to facilitate searching MEDLINE by high-school students might associate more common medical subject terms with the resources, thus making searching easier for this community.[28] On the other hand, there is broad agreement among the committee members and in the general information community that the nature of resource description needs a thorough examination in the context of digital resources. Traditional cataloging is one kind of resource description, which, in turn, is one kind of "metadata"[29] (information that describes the structure or content of a document but is not part of the document). The nature and use of metadata are evolving to accommodate the great variety of digital objects.[30]

The following sections examine some of the new challenges presented by the Internet and the Web, to help explain the expanding role of metadata and the requirements for expressing and delivering it.

Scale

Traditional library cataloging has scaled up to serve institutions of great size—prominent among them the Library of Congress. However, over the past year the number of resources on the Web has grown to the point that they exceed the number of books in even the largest of libraries and even the number of book pages in the average library.[31] The growth rate of these networked resources substantially exceeds the growth rate of traditional physical resources. Sheer size presents considerable challenges

---

[28] Abstracting and indexing services index material for a specific community, with its terms and its knowledge base. It is not unusual to have a journal indexed by two or three or even more secondary services, with each putting the spin of its own subject expertise and the needs of its audience into the indexing and classification of the journal's articles.

[29] "Summary Review of the Working Group on Metadata," by T. Baker and Clifford A. Lynch, in *A Research Agenda for Digital Libraries: Summary Report of the Series of Joint NSF-EU Working Groups on Future Directions for Digital Libraries Research*, P. Schauble and A.F. Smeaton, eds. (Paris: European Research Consortium for Informatics and Mathematics, 1998).

[30] See, among others, <http://www.nla.gov.au/meta>, <http://www.ifla.org/II/metadata.htm>, <http://domino.wileynpt.com/NPT_Pilot/Metadata/mici.nsf>, <http://www.ukoln.ac.uk/meta-data/>, and <http://www.w3.org/Metadata/>.

[31] Estimates of the size of the Web vary, but a reasonable estimate is about 2 billion publicly available Web pages as of mid-2000. See <http://censorware.org/web_size/> and the articles referenced there.

to the economics of traditional library cataloging, in which metadata records are characterized by great precision, detail, and professional intervention. The high price of traditional library cataloging makes it impractical in the context of such growth, and less expensive alternatives are needed for many, if not all, of these resources. There has always been a trade-off between the cost of creating metadata and its value in facilitating access to document collections. Large print collections generally cannot be accessed without some sort of metadata, so the value of the metadata is high. The appearance of digital objects in commercially interesting collections during the 1970s changed the economic model. Then, access could be provided with relatively little investment in metadata, although higher-quality metadata could still be justified for high-value materials. Now, the steady increase in the volume of electronic materials has increased pressure to reduce the cost of metadata, although manually produced metadata are still common.

Permanence

The lifespan of networked resources differs dramatically from that of physical resources. The well-known problem of "dangling URLs"[32] bedevils any librarian who is trying to incorporate Web pages into a collection. The impermanence of networked resources is rooted in the economics of networked dissemination. The cost of distributing networked content is low compared with the cost of printing and distributing hardcopy content, so there is little benefit to the publisher of maintaining older versions of a document.[33] With no incentive to retain older versions, the management of objects is haphazard and object permanence is problematic. Such an environment has a strong impact on the economics and incentives for producing metadata and also points out the critical need for preservation-oriented metadata and mechanisms to manage the preservation of digital objects.

Credibility

The breakdown of traditional publishing roles has disrupted some of the traditional mechanisms for establishing the credibility of an informa-

---

[32]This is the problem familiar to many a Web user whereby a link to a resource through a URL returns an error indicating that the resource has not been found or, even more insidious, that the returned resource has changed, changing the semantics of the link in ways not obvious to the user.

[33]However, in general it is unclear whether the overall cost of networked electronic publishing is significantly lower than the costs of publishing in traditional media.

tion source. In the traditional print model, the pedigree of a document derived in part from the credibility of the publisher (e.g., publisher X publishes good computer books) and the credibility of the information intermediary—library or bookstore—that made the material available. Because the information intermediaries are being circumvented, it has become increasingly difficult to assess the integrity of information resources. A further problem is that information can be viewed in ways that were never intended by an author or publisher. An excerpt from an otherwise credible source may be misleading when viewed out of context.

Since metadata is itself an information resource, the credibility issue applies to the quality of metadata created by external sources (outside the traditional library cataloging community). The creation of bad metadata can be nonmalicious: for example, an author who lacks training or who doesn't care may assign a bad subject classification to a descriptive metadata record. It can also be malicious: so-called "index spamming," whereby content creators seed metadata fields with misleading or incorrect information to affect the ranking of their pages by search engines, is a real problem on the Web.[34] An important challenge for networked information is developing the mechanisms and policies to verify the origin of any information, including metadata.

Variety

The Library of Congress, like all libraries, deals with a considerable variety of resources, including books, serials, maps, software, movies, images, and, now, digital resources. The Library's efforts to create metadata for this spectrum of resources can be divided into two categories. First, much attention has been paid to enhancing the traditional cataloging mechanisms—AACR2 and MARC, for example—to accommodate these new genres. These efforts are motivated by the central role that the traditional cataloging formats play in the Integrated Library System and in the cooperative cataloging efforts described above. Notable among these efforts in the context of a discussion of digital resources is the creation of a new field to handle links to electronic resources[35] and a set of

---

[34]Index spamming is of considerable concern to search engine providers in that it interferes with the usefulness of their search engines. For a look at what one search engine provider, AltaVista, says about index spamming, see <http://www.altavista.com/av/content/spamindex.htm>.

[35]The 856 field in MARC—see <http://lcweb.loc.gov/marc/bibliographic/ecbdhold.html#mrcb856>—was created in the early 1990s to contain information needed to locate and access an electronic resource. Typical information stored in the 856 field includes a URL, the relationship of the item referred to by the URL, and the resource described by the MARC record itself.

draft interim guidelines for cataloging electronic resources[36] published and disseminated by the Library's Cataloging Policy and Support Office.

Second, the Library has employed a number of other vehicles for resource description—metadata schemata tailored for individual resource characteristics. Some schemata have been coordinated with external communities; others have been developed internally. The use of other metadata vocabularies raises the issue of how these vocabularies interact to provide integrated information spaces for users of digital libraries. After all, one of the major strengths of the standardization on AACR2 and its expression in MARC records has been the uniform search interface provided by library catalogs to large and heterogeneous collections. The subject of multiple metadata vocabularies is the focus of further attention below in this chapter.

METADATA AS A CROSS-COMMUNITY ACTIVITY

As mentioned above, the field of metadata has exploded into a major area of investigation and development over the past several years. As information becomes more of a commodity item—and, as many would argue, is the largest product of the "new economic paradigm"[37]—its management is of interest to a broad spectrum of organizations. This stands in rather strong contrast to the situation in the pre-Internet era, when the standardized management of information was more or less restricted to libraries, with the Library of Congress playing a key leadership role. This broadening of the metadata environment will include many new players and applications and require the Library to think in new ways if it is to reassert its leadership in this area.

Descriptive cataloging, exemplified by the traditional library cataloging record, is but one of many classes of metadata. Real-world applications need to make use of a much broader range of metadata than descriptive cataloging. Some other metadata types are listed below to provide a sense of this range. The list is not in any way comprehensive, nor are all of these types of data appropriately within the scope of the Library of Congress.[38]

---

[36]See <http://lcweb.loc.gov/catdir/cpso/elec_res.html>.

[37]*Information Rules: A Strategic Guide to the Network Economy,* by Carl Shapiro and Hal R. Varian (Boston: Harvard Business School Press, 1999), p. 352.

[38]"Metadata: Foundation for Image Management and Use," by Carl Lagoze and S. Payett, in *Moving Theory into Practice: Digital Imaging for Libraries and Archives,* A.R. Kenney and O.Y. Rieger, eds. (Mountain View, Calif.: Research Libraries Group, 2000), p. 250. Also see *The Warwick Framework: A Container Architecture for Aggregating Sets of Metadata,* by Carl Lagoze, Clifford Lynch, and Ron Daniel, Jr., Technical Report TR96-1593 (Ithaca, N.Y.: Cornell University Computer Science Department, 1996).

• *Terms and conditions*—metadata that describe the rules for use of an object. Terms and conditions might include an access list of who may view the object, a conditions-of-use statement that might be displayed before access to the object is allowed, a schedule (tariff) of prices and fees for use of the object, or a definition of the permitted uses of an object (viewing, printing, copying, etc.).

• *Administrative data*—metadata that relate to the management of an object in a particular server or repository. Some examples of information stored in administrative data are the date of last modification, the date of creation, and the administrator's identity.

• *Content rating*—a description of attributes of an object within a multidimensional, scaled rating scheme assigned by some rating authority; an example might be the suitability of the content for various audiences, similar to the well-known movie rating system used by the Motion Picture Association of America. Note that content ratings have applications far beyond simple filtering on sex and violence levels. Content ratings are likely to play important roles in future collaborative filtering systems, for example.

• *Provenance*—data defining the source or origin of some content object, for example, of some physical artifact from which the content was scanned. The data might also include a summary of all algorithmic transformations that have been applied to the object (filtering, reductions in image density, etc.) since its creation. Arguably, provenance information might also include evidence of authenticity and integrity through the use of digital signature schemes; or, authenticity and integrity information might be considered a separate class of metadata.

• *Linkage or relationship data*—data indicating the often complex relationships between content objects and other objects. Some examples are the relationship of a set of journal articles to the containing journal, the relationship of a translation to the work in its original language, the relationship of a subsequent edition to the original work, or the relationships among the components of a multimedia work (information on synchronization between images and a soundtrack, for example).

• *Structural data*—data defining the logical components of complex or compound objects and how to access those components. A simple example is a table of contents for a textual document. More complex examples include the definition of the different source files, subroutines, data definitions in a software suite, SGML or XML tagged books, or other complex works.

The need for additional metadata types and for traditional metadata for a larger volume of materials challenges traditional means of metadata creation—manual techniques cannot be scaled up to meet demand. But automated techniques are available that can help in the production of metadata (natural language processing, automatic classification, document clustering). These techniques have yet to be integrated with more traditional manual techniques; such integration will be a huge task for the library community.

The following sections summarize a number of the current efforts that address these metadata requirements, the goal being to show the breadth of communities involved in this endeavor. While the Library is involved in a number of these efforts, it by no means plays the same prominent role it plays in traditional cataloging.

Dublin Core Metadata Initiative

The Dublin Core Metadata Initiative (DCMI),[39] begun in 1994, hoped to create a simplified metadata convention that would provide more effective resource discovery on the Web. Over the past 5 years, it has developed and refined a set of 15 elements—the Dublin Core Element Set (DCES)—for resource description to facilitate discovery. The DCMI has broad international participation from librarians, digital library specialists, the museum community, and other information specialists. Its advocates claim that the DCES has distinct advantages over traditional cataloging methods in terms of simplicity, interoperability, and extensibility.

DCMI, which is hosted by OCLC, represents a concerted effort by OCLC to extend the leadership role it has played with physical resources into the world of digital resources. The DCES plays an important role in one of OCLC's latest projects, the Cooperative Online Resource Cataloging (CORC) project,[40] which is examining the use of new Web-based tools and techniques for cataloging electronic resources. One important aspect of CORC is that it examines the mechanics and economics of different levels of representation, whereby resources can be described simply using the DCES and, when appropriate and economically feasible, described more completely using traditional cataloging techniques (MARC).

The Library of Congress does participate in the DCMI: a member of its Cataloging Directorate has long played a role. Not only did the Library host the sixth Dublin Core meeting in November 1998, but its Network Development and MARC Standards Office has also developed "crosswalks" (translations) between the DCES and MARC.[41]

---

[39]See <http://purl.org/DC>.
[40]See <http://www.oclc.org/news/oclc/corc/about/about.htm>.
[41]See <http://lcweb.loc.gov/marc/dccross.html>.

Geospatial Metadata Standards

The geospatial community's interest in metadata stems from the difficulty of managing and locating the burgeoning amount of data being produced by geographic information systems (GISs),[42] remote sensing initiatives (e.g., satellites), and the defense and intelligence community. The U.S. Federal Geographic Data Committee[43] has been working for several years to create a complete and complex metadata format for describing geospatial entities—Content Standards for Digital Geospatial Metadata.[44] The Open GIS Consortium, which comprises technology companies, universities, and government agencies, manages consensus processes with the goal of achieving interoperability among diverse geo-processing systems.[45]

Content Rating

The motivation for content-rating metadata grows out of the proliferation of adult material on the Internet and the desire for filtering mechanisms to keep certain individuals (e.g., children) from accessing certain content (e.g., pornography).[46] Faced with this challenge, the World Wide Web Consortium (W3C)[47] developed a description standard, Platform for Internet Content Selection (PICS).[48] The PICS standard enables content providers to label (voluntarily) the content they create and distribute and "enables multiple, independent labeling services to associate additional labels with content created and distributed by others."[49]

E-commerce and Rights Management

The burgeoning of content available over the Internet has stimulated interest in the business community in mechanisms for managing, controlling, and receiving remuneration for providing access to digital intellec-

---

[42]GIS systems include a broad class of software systems for storing, representing, and analyzing geospatial data. They are widely employed by governmental agencies such as planning departments, public utility companies, surveying and engineering concerns, and a spectrum of other parties.

[43]See <http://www.fgdc.gov>.

[44]See <http://www.ifla.org/documents/libraries/cataloging/metadata/meta6894.txt>.

[45] See <http://www.opengis.org>.

[46]"Filtering Information on the Internet," by Paul Resnick, in Scientific American, 1997, pp. 106-108, available online at <http://www.sciam.com/0397issue/0397resnick.html>.

[47]The W3C <http://www.w3.org> is an international organization that develops and maintains the standards by which the World Wide Web operates. These standards include the protocols for exchange of data over the Web, markup languages for structuring that data (e.g., HTML), and the metadata standards discussed here.

[48]See <http://www.w3.org/PICS/>.

[49]See <http://www.w3.org/PICS/principles.html>.

tual property.   So-called "rights management" is among the most active topics in digital library research and Internet business development. One initiative—<indecs> (Interoperability of Data in E-commerce Systems)[50]—is an international initiative of rights owners formulating metadata standards to govern the exchange of digital intellectual content.

Resource Description Framework

The proliferation of standards for metadata has motivated W3C to examine a general infrastructure for associating multiple metadata records with Web resources and packaging those records for exchange (as MARC does for AACR2 descriptions).   The result is the resource description framework (RDF),[51] a major initiative by W3C to facilitate descriptions of Web resources.   The intellectual underpinnings of RDF lie in a variety of knowledge representation efforts.[52]   The RDF is based on two key assumptions: (1) the diverse metadata needs of networked objects argue for a modular, not a monolithic, metadata solution and (2) the different metadata modules should be created and managed by individual communities of experts (e.g., let the librarians construct the bibliographic descriptions). RDF is an area of intense development within the Web community, and the associated tools and standards promise to enhance significantly the functionality of the Web over the next several years.

INTEROPERABILITY OF METADATA STANDARDS

Cataloging has evolved from primarily a library practice into an activity engaged in across the Internet economy. As described above, the Library itself, faced with a proliferation of resource types and management needs, has undertaken and participated in a variety of metadata initiatives outside traditional cataloging. This proliferation of metadata types and standards raises a pressing need for intensive work, both technical and organizational, on issues of metadata interoperability.

The problem of interoperability is not new. Specialized metadata standards have been developed in many domains (e.g., law, medicine, chemistry) to help normalize the description of knowledge in each. Interoperability problems are exacerbated by the nature of the "Internet Commons,"[53] where multiple communities intermix and interact in nontradi-

---

[50]See <http://www.indecs.org>.

[51]See <http://www.w3.org/RDF>.

[52]*Knowledge Representation: Logical, Philosophical, and Computational Foundations,* by J.F. Sowa (Pacific Grove, Calif.: Brooks/Cole, 2000), p. 594.

[53]The term "Internet Commons" was coined by Stuart Weibel of OCLC, founder and leader of the Dublin Core Metadata Initiative.

tional ways. By eliminating physical barriers, the Internet encourages interactions among formerly separate communities. In such interactions, one community may have good reason to use the work of another. For example, an art museum may put a digitized map, which is the product of the geospatial community, on its Web page to provide directions for visitors. These spontaneous interactions underlie the need for common metadata standards to support finding, evaluating, and managing content across traditional boundaries.

Metadata interoperability has three dimensions:

• *Semantic interoperability*—Every metadata scheme defines its own set of data elements or categories for data. For example, the DCES defines a set of 15 categories for resource discovery. Semantic interoperability is the extent to which different metadata schemes express the same semantics in their categorization. Successful interoperation requires clarity about how the categories of metadata across schemes relate to each other: When do elements have the same meaning? When are elements derivatives, subsets, or variations of each other? When are elements completely unrelated?

• *Structural interoperability*—Each metadata record expresses a set of values for the categories described above. Humans are often quite capable of translating between unstructured values; many recognize that "Bill Gates" and "Gates, William H." are the same person. On the other hand, U.S. and British citizens are likely to interpret the date 10-1-99 differently. Computers are even worse at interpreting unstructured values and so require strict definitions of structure. Authority files, described above, have been the primary mechanism in the library community for enforcing structural interoperability.

• *Syntactic interoperability*—Creators of metadata want to store, exchange, and use metadata records from different sources. Such exchange requires common mechanisms for expressing metadata semantics and structure. These common mechanisms include hypertext markup language (HTML), the resource description framework (RDF), and extensible markup language (XML). The MARC record format, described above, has been the primary mechanism in the library community for addressing syntactic interoperability.

The last two areas of metadata interoperability, structural and syntactic, have been and are being addressed in forums such as the W3C and in the various standards agencies, such as the International Organization for Standardization (ISO),[54] the American National Standards Institute

---

[54]See <http://www.iso.ch/>.

(ANSI),[55] and the (U.S.) National Institute of Standards and Technology (NIST).[56]

The first area, semantic interoperability, is the subject of current research activity[57] and the area in which the knowledge organization and classification expertise of the Library, and the library community in general, has the most to offer. Briefly, the problem can be characterized as follows. Various metadata vocabularies are by nature frequently not semantically distinct but overlap and relate to each other in numerous ways. Achieving interoperability between these packages by means of one-to-one "crosswalks"[58] (tables that show the relationship of elements across various schemes) is useful, but this approach does not scale to the many metadata vocabularies that will inevitably develop.

A more scalable solution is to exploit the fact that many entities and relationships for example, people, places, creations, organizations, events, certain relationships, and the like—are so frequently encountered that they do not fall clearly into the domain of any particular metadata vocabulary but apply across all of them. Mechanisms for semantic interoperability could exploit this fact by expressing the relationships between the vocabularies of individual metadata sets and the core concepts (e.g., places and events) using notions such as subtypes, supertypes, or siblings.[59]

Although a number of these concepts in semantic interoperability are still in the early development or even the research stage, they address a critical problem that the Library needs to recognize: metadata vocabularies will proliferate, and methods for interoperability among them must be developed. The committee believes strongly that the Library needs to take an active role in such research areas if it is going to successfully deal with digital materials and information on the Internet. Furthermore, the

---

[55]See <http://www.ansi.org>.

[56]See <http://www.nist.gov/>.

[57]"A Common Model to Support Interoperable Metadata: Progress Report on Reconciling Metadata Requirements from the Dublin Core and INDECS/DOI Communities," by David Bearman et al., in *D-Lib Magazine*, January 1999. Also see *ABC: A Logical Model for Metadata Interoperability*, by D. Brickley, J. Hunter, and Carl Lagoze, 1999, available online at <http://www.ilrt.bris.ac.uk/discovery/harmony/docs/abc/abc_draft.html>.

[58]*Dublin Core/MARC/GILS Crosswalk* (Washington, D.C.: Network Development and MARC Standards Office, Library of Congress, 1997).

[59]This is similar to techniques developed for natural language processing and computation linguistic research. For example, see *WordNet—A Lexical Database for English*, at <http://www.cogsci.princeton.edu/~wn/> or *WordNet: An Electronic Lexical Database*, Christiane Fellbaum, ed. (Cambridge, Mass.: MIT Press, 1998), p. 423. This is also the main focus of XML.ORG.

Library most assuredly has much to add to these research areas. The Library, by virtue of its years of cataloging experience, has a unique understanding of the nature of the entities and relationships that lie at the root of these interoperability mechanisms.

NEW CATALOGING MODELS

Establishing and expressing the relationships among information resources is one of the most difficult aspects of cataloging. These relationships are multidimensional, bidirectional, and many-to-many. Examples of such relationships are translations, versions, editions, transcriptions, and structures (e.g., the issue of hierarchy and the relationship of articles to serials).

In many ways the relationships between information resources are of primary importance in the management, discovery, and accessibility of these resources. Yet, the basic model of the MARC record, whereby cataloging metadata is packaged into discrete records associated with individual information artifacts (that is, MARC records are resource-centric), makes it unwieldy to express the richness and complexity of these relationships.

The importance of relationships among entities has been recognized for a long time in the database and knowledge representation communities.[60] Entity-relationship modeling and E-R diagrams[61] are tools to model information that expresses entity types (e.g., books, serials, agents, events), the permissible relationships between these entity types (e.g., authoring, creating, publishing) and the constraints on these relationships (e.g., an article must be "in" a journal).

Recent work in the international cataloging community recognizes the importance of relationships for formulating accurate descriptions of the resources commonly dealt with by libraries. The Functional Requirements for Bibliographic Records (FRBR),[62] defined by an International Federation of Library Associations[63] task force and contributed to by the Library of Congress, provides a provocative starting point for discussions

---

[60]For example, see *Knowledge Representation: Logical, Philosophical, and Computational Foundations*, by John F. Sowa (Pacific Grove, Calif.: Brooks/Cole, 1999).

[61]For example, see *The Entity-Relationship Approach to Logical Database Design*, by P.P.S. Chen (Wellesley, Mass.: QED Information Sciences, 1991), p. 83, and *Entity-Relationship Approach: The Use of ER Concept in Knowledge Representation*, by P.P.S. Chen (Washington, D.C.: IEEE Computer Society Press, 1985), p. 327.

[62]See *Functional Requirements for Bibliographic Records* (Munich: K.G. Saur for International Federation of Library Associations and Institutions, 1998).

[63]See <http://www.ifla.org>.

on how bibliographic description might more accurately reflect resource relationships. The FRBR presents a model that distinguishes among intellectual ideas ("works"), the forms in which they are realized ("manifestation," for example, a novel), and their availability as physical objects (e.g., as an individual book or an individual performance of a play). These stages in the evolution of intellectual content are connected by distinguishing relationships that affect the description or metadata for the objects. The FRBR is just a start for rethinking the theory behind bibliographic description, but it provides an interesting foundation for the treatment of digital objects whose plasticity will require that considerably more attention be given to issues of relationships than has been required for physical artifacts. (This plasticity poses a serious challenge to AACR2—which is based on describing a specific manifestation of a work—because manifestations can be fleeting in the digital world.)

The importance of relationships in resource description of digital objects is also reflected in the metadata activities on the World Wide Web. The Web has demonstrated, even in its current primitive form, that the linkages (hyperlinks) between information objects are an integral part of their content. RDF incorporates a data model in which relationships, or "properties," play a key role in the description of digital resources.

The committee understands that it will be a tremendous challenge to change the base model for metadata (e.g., from resource-centric to relationship-centric) in a world of widespread data exchanges (the MARC records that are the basis of cooperative cataloging) and reliance on turnkey software (commercial integrated library systems that are based on MARC). However, it is certain that library-type metadata practices will at some point need to be reexamined in the light of a changed world. It is certainly valid to ask when the time will come that there is sufficient understanding of this changed world to undertake such a process. It is not productive to ignore the fact that changes are inevitable and will be dramatic.

SUMMARY

The creation and utilization of metadata are fundamental activities of the Library of Congress. The Library dedicates enormous resources to them, not just in the Cataloging Directorate but also across the curatorial departments, in the NDLP, and in the Copyright Office. High-quality, well-organized tools for finding a collection's resources are fundamental to the functioning of a modern library.

The discussions above describe the traditional strength and leadership of the Library of Congress in the cataloging and metadata arena. However, the committee hopes that the discussions also demonstrate the volatility in this environment today, with the number of metadata initiatives and players growing rapidly. While no one today can say with any certainty the precise directions in which the field will evolve, any knowledgeable observer can with confidence say that it *will* evolve dramatically in the coming years.

The committee has been enormously uneasy about the Library's metadata involvement but has tried to state crisply its concerns and recommendations. The concerns are related to the committee's belief that the current turmoil in metadata has profound implications for libraries and to its understanding of how enormously difficult it is going to be for the library world to evolve in response to these changes. If there is any one institution that could be expected to be pondering these issues and involved in trying to shape the environment as it evolves, it would be the Library of Congress. Both its scale of operations and its traditional leading role in the area create this expectation. However, the committee was unable to detect any sign that the Library considered this to be a strategic set of issues or that it had mounted any substantial initiative to analyze and plan for the changes that are coming.

As mentioned above, the committee is aware of the interconnectedness of the library world in terms of both metadata standards and data itself. The existing environment does not lend itself easily to any single institution devising its own strategies for coping with change in metadata practice. There is an enormous need for educating the library community on the implications of current developments, for creating initiatives to coordinate strategies, and for becoming seriously involved in the key metadata initiatives under way today, to ensure that actions taken are informed by the needs of the library community. This seems an obvious role for the Library, a role largely unfilled insofar as the committee can tell (although the committee applauds the Library's effort to organize a conference in the fall of 2000 on cataloging policy in the digital age).[64]

It should be made clear that it is *not* the committee's finding that the Library lacks any knowledge of or involvement with metadata developments. As mentioned above, the Library has played a role in a number of areas, and the committee found some very knowledgeable staff at the Library who have a sophisticated understanding of current developments. The concern centers, rather, on the level of institutional involvement with the issues. The committee believes that these developments are of overriding importance for the Library and that they require the Library to become much more active in analyzing and planning for change across

---

[64]See "Library of Congress Hosts Conference on Cataloging Policy in the Digital Age November 15-17," News release, February 22, 2000.

the library community and in influencing the evolution of the various metadata initiatives now under way.

> **Finding:** The Library of Congress is heavily involved in the creation and use of metadata and has long been a leader in the establishment of standards and practices.   However, the metadata environment is evolving rapidly. This will have profound implications for libraries and other information providers generally and for the Library of Congress in particular. It is a responsibility of the Library, and indeed of the nation, to offer leadership here for the benefit of the national and worldwide communities of information providers and users.

> **Recommendation:** The Library should treat the development of a richer but more complex metadata environment as a strategic issue, increasing dramatically its level of involvement and planning in this area, and it should be much more actively involved with the library and information community in advancing the evolution of metadata practices. This effort will require the dedication of resources, direct involvement by the Librarian in setting and adjusting expectations, and the strong commitment of a project leader assigned from the Executive Committee of the Library.

> **Recommendation:** The Library should actively encourage and participate in efforts to develop tools for automatically creating metadata. These tools should be integrated in the cataloging work flow.

6
THE LIBRARY OF CONGRESS AND THE WORLD BEYOND ITS WALLS

No library is an island. Even the isolated monastic libraries of the late antique world, clinging to handfuls of books garnered at great cost and effort, knew of a world of books beyond, cautiously lending titles or having copies made, ardently seeking additional titles by famous authorities.[1] The notion of institutional collaboration was, to be sure, still weak, but its seeds are visible nonetheless. Books are meant to be read at a distance from the author's own social setting and are meant to live beyond the moment in which they are written. Libraries exist to give homes to books as visitors to places where their authors never visited and to preserve them for readers still to arrive. Libraries extend the power of the word over time and over space.

The Library of Congress (LC) looms as a totemic giant in the mythology of libraries.[2] The world over, it is emblematic of the largest and most complete collection of written materials. But all know and agree that even LC is incomplete, incomplete in a thousand ways. It holds millions of titles but has no precise idea of how many books in the world it does *not* hold, although the number is certainly large. The greatness of the Library of Congress since the Second World War lies in the fact that it has devel-

---

[1] See *An Introduction to Divine and Human Readings*, Book One, by Cassiodorus Senator (New York: Columbia University Press, 1946) for an early example of lists of library desiderata.

[2] As described in *Avatars of the Word: From Papyrus to Cyberspace*, by James J. O'Donnell (Cambridge, Mass.: Harvard University Press, 1998), p. 30.

oped its own collection at the same time as it has facilitated the growth and interdependency of the worldwide collection of the treasures of human creativity. It is evidently impossible that copies of *everything* should ever be found in a single place—it takes an Alexandrian monarch[3] or an Argentinian poet[4] to imagine such things. But it is far from impossible that collections great and small will one day be so tightly interlinked by the exchange of data about their holdings that we will eventually know where and how to find a vastly larger percentage of the materials held in them. The last two generations have already seen huge progress in this regard, going back to LC's epochal agreement to disseminate cataloging information from its holdings and now leveraged to a wider world by such widely accessible catalogs as the Research Library Group's (RLG's) Eureka or the Online Computer Library Center's (OCLC's) WorldCat.

All of these real achievements pale by comparison with what can be imagined for the world of cyberspace. Far more information from far more sources can be brought together in nearly real time. The floods of new, increasingly available electronic information can be drawn together, sorted, filtered, and made usefully accessible. Such a possibility is easy to evoke but difficult to achieve. The question of achieving it strikes at the heart of the way in which the Library of Congress goes about its business.

A further prefatory remark is needed here to understand the possibilities for LC. As is brought out in the preceding chapters, the materials that LC embraces are many and various and growing in diversity. For a long time, traditional library materials have formed only a part of the collection: beyond books and journals and maps, LC has been collecting advertising materials, motion pictures, and baseball cards. What all of those materials have in common, however, is their physicality, their collectibility as physical artifacts. The grandeur of LC rests on the size, variety, and value of the physical artifacts gathered there.

Today, at least three additional categories of information material challenge LC's traditional practices. This brief outline resumes some of the discussion of earlier chapters, taking care not to recommend *what* LC should be collecting but emphasizing the decisions and strategies required no matter what the decisions on content may be. The categories of material are as follows:

- *Born-digital*—Under this heading fall materials containing socially valuable and interesting information created in electronic form. Typi-

---

[3]For an elaboration, see *The Vanished Library*, by L. Canfora (Berkeley, Calif: University of California Press, 1989). The dream of Alexandria resurfaces in the contemporary project to build a new, ambitious (but conceptually questionable) library on or near the ancient site.

[4]For an elaboration, see "The Library of Babel," by J. Borges, in his *Ficciones* (New York: Grove Press, 1962), pp. 79-88.

cally, we regard such materials as necessary either because they have no corresponding print form or, if they have one, they possess significant individuality in electronic form to merit inclusion in a serious library collection. Born-digital materials in turn fall into two categories:

—*Artifactual*: These are digital information materials that are published and distributed in ways that depend on particular physical media and artifacts—floppy disks, CD-ROMs, laser video disks, and the like.

—*Nonartifactual*: Increasingly, digital information does not appear in forms that lend themselves to physical collection by libraries. Web sites increase the number of sources where information of the highest social value may be found, but it is often functionally impossible to "acquire" a Web site—even if one copied all the public pages of a site, substantial additional bodies of material that lie behind it (e.g., databases that are accessed by commands issued from the Web pages) would not be publicly available. The quantity and quality of material available in this form can only be expected to grow in the coming years.[5]

• *Turned digital*—By this phrase is meant materials that were originally created in a traditional artifactual form (usually print) but have been converted to digital media for reasons of preservation and/or access. There is already a history of cooperative activity surrounding preservation decisions (that is, decisions to change the media of presentation in order to preserve the content of the original), but this movement must now be accelerated, for two reasons:

—The use of electronic media for preservation has advantages in cost and accessibility over many other media (though electronic media may introduce new preservation problems of their own).

—Digital representations of print materials and other physical artifacts are increasingly popular when the purpose is not only preservation but also a concomitant increase in ease of access and use, particularly for rare or fragile materials.

For digital materials, both "born" and "turned," there is a nationwide and worldwide need for coordination and communication so that expensive and time-consuming projects do not duplicate other efforts. Furthermore, the results of digital preservation efforts can and should be widely shared, and for that reason turned-digital materials will quickly begin to

---

[5]The two categories often blur into each other, as when material is deliberately published on both CD-ROM and the Web.

behave just as born-digital materials do. A library such as LC will presumably first digitize treasures of its own but will then wish to have access to those of other libraries (just as it makes its own available in digital form). All of the categories of cooperation and collaboration outlined above for materials born digital will thus apply here.

The discussions here of collection, preservation, and cataloging all point to this end. In the world of print materials, LC's strategy was straightforward: to leverage its statutory rights of collection (through copyright deposit) to achieve physical collections of unparalleled size and quality. In the digital realms, LC starts with many fewer advantages. The digitization of its own existing collections can give it, to be sure, tremendously rich and exciting materials for a new digital collection. But no matter how aggressively LC collects digital materials, achieving a truly universal collection will now increasingly mean recognizing that not everything can be collected, because the volume of digital information is so great. Also, many publishers and distributors of material of high value will produce material in a form that must be consulted remotely and cannot be physically added to the working collections of the Library. When physical possession is not possible or desirable, it will be all the more important that firm and secure links between LC and other stakeholders in the information community are established. If LC possesses a physical book, it can take its own steps to ensure preservation and accessibility—or even, if appropriate, to practice relative neglect—thereby making it possible for a book to be usable generations after its creation. (Some medieval manuscripts lay neglected, literally on top of storage cabinets, for as long as centuries, but they were still immediately readable on rediscovery.) Where LC possesses the original source files or identical copies, preservation will be a demanding chore. Where LC does not possess the digital source files, assurance of preservation and access will require coordination of a complicated social, legal, and economic strategy.

THE LIBRARY OF CONGRESS—
ROLES FOR THE NEW MILLENNIUM

The Library as Convenor, Coordinator, Partner, Collaborator, and Leader

No library in the world has the prestige or the influence of the Library of Congress, if LC will only use it. Over the last two decades, the Library has been too little visible on the national and international stage, particularly in the digital arena. Too many of the stunning achievements of LC leadership and collaboration are now receding into the hallowed past. Moreover, it has been the case that projects and/or exhibitions of great significance have not always been consistently institutionalized as ongoing services. The committee's contacts with librarians here and abroad and with publishers have repeatedly uncovered the desire to see LC take a more active role in bringing together stakeholders in the rapidly changing world of print publishing (particularly with regard to materials whose primary consumers are not-for-profit organizations such as universities and libraries and whose primary producers are for-profit publishers) and in the emerging world of digital information (especially where not-for-profit users have a large stake in the use of the material). Indeed, the committee believes that LC's inward focus during the past two decades has resulted in a decline of trust and confidence in the research library community in the United States.

At the same time, it is important to be clear about the kind of role that LC can and should take. The vast size of its collections and its national importance to the United States do not elevate it—or any other player—above the rest of the library community. The Library should see itself as a particularly privileged, and therefore particularly responsible, partner in a wide range of conversations. The committee spoke above of the important role LC could play in establishing standards for a wide variety of infrastructural elements of the library of the future, just as it did in the past when it created the MARC record. But LC cannot dictate the outcomes of such a process to others. Rather, its true value would be to bring stakeholders together in a collaborative process that begins by identifying issues and needs that cut across broad swathes of the information community. Having done so, it should then focus on the specialized needs of less-privileged sectors of the information community and, finally, motivate that community to achieve solutions and resolutions that are fair, economical, and functional for all parties.

Examples of such processes in other domains include the Congress of Vienna in 1815 and, in our own day, G7 summits. While LC and all of the other stakeholders are sobered by the realization that the outcomes of high-level summits are always debatable and never last forever (although the Congress of Vienna saw its work last almost 100 years), they can take heart from knowing that LC would participate in such conversations not as one of several hostile parties seeking influence but rather as the genuine representative of a common public good that can advance the interests of other participants in the process. A genuinely broad vision and a determined insistence on turning that vision into reality must be accompanied by a collegial, humble manner that seeks the broadest possible common good for both the users and the producers of information.

The Library must recognize and genuinely respect other senior partners in these undertakings. Over the last three decades, both RLG and OCLC have emerged as serious and respected players in advancing broad and reliable access to library materials. Relations among these three organizations have at times been no better than cool. RLG's and OCLC's joint representations to the committee suggested that they see the value and necessity of working with each other in productive ways and with LC.[6] Collaboration of this sort may not prove easy for LC, because decisions taken two decades ago led to the creation of a highly successful system whereby OCLC distributes catalog records to a wide variety of libraries, and these records include the very substantial body of cataloging created by LC. The results for users have been overwhelmingly positive, however, and the cost savings to the library community extraordinary.[7] Great things have been achieved by LC, OCLC, and RLG, and it is time to look to the future in a trusting and collaborative spirit.

The committee also recommends that the Library reverse its tendency to become isolated and that it participate more actively in the library research community. The experience of installing the new Integrated Library System in 1999 (discussed in detail in Chapter 8) shows that even when the Library waits until a technology is well established and in use at other libraries, its size and scope make it hard to tailor the technology to the Library's needs. The Library should look for ways to influence the technologies it will use earlier in their development cycle, ensuring that both library technology research and product development address issues of scale early on.

The Library of Congress Made Visible

In order to succeed, it is necessary for LC and its leaders to be seen and heard widely in the library community in the United States and abroad. It is unfortunate, although understandable, that none of the three senior officers of the Library has chosen to dedicate time to becoming heavily involved with the library community. An influential group of national librarians meets privately at the annual meeting of the International Federation of Library Associations, but the Librarian of Congress seldom attends these meetings, and his absence attracts wistful comment.

---

[6]As presented to the committee in open session at its September 1999 meeting. OCLC and RLG have since made progress in working together by beginning to collaborate on two working documents to establish best practices for digital archiving. See the news release "RLG and OCLC Explore Digital Archiving," March 10, 2000, at <http://www.rlg.org/pr/pr2000-oclc.html>.

[7]This cost savings is estimated at $268 million annually (from the Statement of James H. Billington, The Librarian of Congress, before the Subcommittee on Legislative Appropriations, Committee on Appropriations, U.S. House of Representatives, Fiscal 2001 Budget Request, January 27, 2000).

The Association of Research Libraries is a respected national coordination and advocacy group headquartered in Washington, D.C., and physically proximate to the Council on Library and Information Resources, renowned for its efforts in preservation, funding, research and, now, for addressing the issues that libraries face in the digital environment. The Library needs to partner with these groups if it is seriously to advance important national information agendas. The National Science Foundation distributed funds through the 1990s for its Digital Libraries Initiative (DLI). The inclusion of LC as a partner of DLI is a promising step in the right direction, but more substantive involvement in the DLI and engagement in other, comparable initiatives need to be pursued aggressively. The Library is at a disadvantage owing to its lack of a research capability and its inability to provide significant funding for research by others, for even when it sees an opportunity it has only modest means to exert influence. Still, LC could provide small research grants to be used for cooperative efforts with others, or it could develop other means to support the needed research (e.g., sponsor visiting research fellows at LC, if such a program were in place).[8]

The Library of Congress must seek out, generate, and empower leaders who will be visible and influential as spokespersons for the library community and the interests of a broad range of information users. Such leadership could be credible and effective at creating the connections that the future of libraries requires.[9]

While the committee cannot provide an exhaustive list of specific actions that the Library should initiate, it would like to suggest one such action. The Library has a prime location on Capitol Hill—an attractive site for a speaker series (perhaps monthly) on various aspects of digital libraries. Such an event would be promoted to interested stakeholders in the Washington metropolitan area, from federal agencies and congressional staff to the library community and industry associations, which would include local information industry people and researchers. The committee is suggesting not that LC totally neglects such outreach initiatives (for its bicentennial in the year 2000, it planned a number of such

---

[8]See *Making IT Better: Expanding Information Technology Research to Meet Society's Needs*, by the Computer Science and Telecommunications Board, National Research Council (Washington, D.C.: National Academy Press, 2000) for a discussion of federal agencies with significant IT needs that have very limited internal resources to support research. *Making IT Better* recommends that such agencies should work more closely with the IT research community to find solutions to the problems they face.

[9]One relatively economical way to enhance Library influence and authority would involve being more generous in providing travel funds to its professional librarians to participate fully in their national associations and in ongoing collaborative initiatives such as DLI.

BOX 6.1
Some Areas Calling for Initiative and Leadership by the Library of Congress

- Defining the subset of digital materials for which LC will assume long-term curatorial responsibility, thereby encouraging other institutions to make similar statements
- Supporting and promoting research and development efforts in digital preservation
- Supporting legislation to revise the copyright law so that the copying and migrating of digital information for preservation purposes become legal
- Encouraging the involvement of key participants from outside the traditional library and information science community in developing information management standards
- Coordinating metadata standards for digital materials so that cooperative cataloging is extended and transformed in the Internet context
- Working with authors and publishers directly to obtain metadata, so as to acquire greater coverage
- Representing the U.S. library community, in cooperation with other major U.S. libraries, in the international library community.[1]

---

[1]One reviewer of this report wisely suggested that the meeting of the International Federation of Library Associations in Boston in August 2001 would provide an unusual opportunity for LC to raise its profile and show its leadership internationally.

events) but that such initiatives need to become a more frequent and routine part of LC's digital future.[10] See Box 6.1 for some areas that call for initiative or leadership by the Library of Congress.

The Library of Congress Is Not the "National Library"

By U.S. law, the Library of Congress is only Congress's library, not the nation's. The Library's role and function thus differ significantly from those of counterpart libraries in other countries. The argument over whether the mission of LC should be adjusted to make it more nearly a national library will continue and is beyond the scope of this report. It is important, however, to understand that a number of the Library's func-

---

[10]Another promising development was the Library's high profile at the spring and fall 2000 meetings of the Coalition for Networked Information Task Force in Washington, D.C., and San Antonio, Tex., respectively.

tions are characteristic of the functions of a national library. These include but are not limited to the following:

- It serves as the national (copyright) depository library with a mission to assemble a comprehensive national collection.
- It is the authoritative national source of cataloging information.
- It de facto represents the United States in bodies and organizations where the other participants represent the national libraries of their countries.

Moreover, the committee believes it is important to call attention to the way in which there will be increasing pressure for LC to function as though it could fulfill such a role. There are models elsewhere (notably the National Library of Medicine and the National Library of Canada) of information coordinated by a consortium, where a single national institution undertakes, on defined terms, to be a library of last resort and at the same time works closely with other institutions to articulate and manage a system that sends users efficiently to the physical collection most convenient to them as often as possible. If LC wishes to avoid criticism for not serving as a library of last resort, it should engage in conversations within the American and global library communities to pursue more aggressively ways and means of building catalogs and finding aids that will support the information needs of American readers and readers around the world without putting undue stress on LC.

The Library of Congress and Other U.S. "National Libraries"

At least three other highly respected organizations share in the functions of a national library for the United States. The National Agricultural Library (NAL) has its own domain, while the National Library of Medicine (NLM) not only takes responsibility for a significant body of the nation's information management, but also has an extraordinary track record in its field for precisely the kind of coordination and technical innovation that the committee identifies in this report as lacking for LC (see Box 6.2). Finally, the National Archives and Records Administration (NARA) incorporates a crucial dimension, "the American Memory," the archival record of American government and some of the nation's most precious national treasures. As the committee explored the contributions that these other organizations make to the virtual national library, it was struck that the formal relations between these organizations had not resulted in more cooperation and cross-organizational learning. NAL, NLM, and NARA have important issues in common, and together they embody a national commitment to the nation's and the world's cultural heritage and scientific present. Yet, subsidiary issues combine to leave them communicating too little with each other. In particular, the reporting line of LC is to the Congress and not to the executive branch, a fact with critical implications for how LC must be managed. This reporting line is allowed to loom too large in the thoughts of those who run these organizations. The committee recommends a regular working relationship between LC and these other organizations at multiple management levels: the organizations should not be in competition with one another.

Findings and Recommendations

Finding: The current transition to digital content calls for extraordinary, unprecedented collaboration and coordination. In most aspects of its work, however, the Library of Congress functions too much in isolation from its clients and peers.

Recommendation: Each major unit of the Library should create an advisory council comprising members from the library, user, and service provider communities, including the private sector. The council for the Library Services unit, for example, should include scholars, general readers, research librarians, public librarians, computer service providers, and publishers. Other units would benefit as well from consultation in this form. Different units of the Library will naturally lend themselves to different configurations of advisory council. Even the Congressional Research Service, which has the closest relationship with a defined community, would benefit from such an arrangement.

Finding: The Library has been too little visible on the national and international stages, particularly in the digital arena.

Recommendation: The Library needs to be more proactive in bringing together stakeholders as partners in digital publishing and digital library research and development (such as the Digital Libraries Initiative). Box 6.1 articulates some specific areas in which LC should take the initiative and/or play a leading role.

Recommendation: The Library of Congress needs to improve its relationships with the Online Computer Library Center and the Research Libraries Group to facilitate the collaborations that will need to take place. Regular executive meetings supplemented by ongoing staff contacts (e.g., a middle management working council) will be necessary to build cooperation.

BOX 6.2
Coordination and Technological Innovation at the National Library of Medicine

A number of the policies and practices that the National Library of Medicine (NLM) uses to foster engagement and technological innovation within the professional community could be profitably employed by the Library of Congress and other libraries as well.[1] The committee suggests not that all of the policies and practices outlined below are entirely absent at LC [2] but rather that LC should carefully consider how NLM conducts business and how NLM policies and practices could be adapted for the benefit of LC.

Senior-Level Oversight. A board of regents, appointed by the secretary of Health and Human Services, functions as the de facto board of directors. The board advises on all important aspects of policy relating to the NLM and is the final review body for NLM's extramural grant programs.

In-House Research and Development. NLM has two main research and development operations, the Lister Hill National Center for Biomedical Communications (LHNCBC) and the National Center for Biotechnology Information (NCBI). In addition, NLM's Systems Reinvention Lab speeds the transition from legacy systems to more modern computer and communications architectures and responds to customer needs with improved library products and services.

Extramural Grants. The extramural programs of NLM fund projects to support research in the management and use of biomedical information. NLM also provides grants designed to improve the infrastructure essential to the modern management of biomedical information, to support training a national pool of scientists to resolve medical informatics issues (support comes as formal programs and individual fellowships), and to support the publication of important scientific information that is not commercially viable.

Outside Technical Advice. Each of the two major research and development operations, LHNCBC and NCBI, has a board of scientific counselors. There is also an initial review group for extramural grants, the Biomedical Library Review Committee. For the Library Operations Division, the Literature Selection Technical Review Committee provides advice about the kinds of journals that should be incorporated into MEDLINE.

Recommendation: The Library of Congress needs to develop a regular working relationship at the senior policy level with federal institutions such as the National Library of Medicine, the National Agricultural Library, the National Archives and Records Administration, and the Smithsonian Institution. Other federal agencies with related missions (such as the

Coordinated System of Libraries. NLM is responsible for eight regional libraries (which generally reside in medical schools) that coordinate library and information services for their geographical areas, interlibrary loan, and outreach, including outreach to public libraries. NLM also serves as the hub of the National Network of Libraries of Medicine. The eight regional libraries, 125 resource libraries, and 4,000 hospital and local libraries are connected in a collaborative fashion.[3]

Independent Outreach. The Friends of the National Library of Medicine, a not-for-profit organization, aims to promote the use and awareness of the NLM.[4] Among its activities, the Friends sponsors an annual conference on health information infrastructure.

Human Resources. The NLM employs a variety of mechanisms to obtain the expertise that it needs. In addition to hiring within the federal system, NLM hosts international visitors and predoctoral and postdoctoral fellows, employs commissioned officers of the U.S. Public Health Service, and uses personal service contracts and other contracting mechanisms extensively, especially for difficult-to-hire expertise. NLM operates the Library Associates Program to recruit new graduates of targeted advanced-degree programs. NLM senior staff reported to the committee that NLM's cutting-edge research and development program is an important asset in attracting quality applicants, given that NLM is often unable to compete on a salary basis with private-sector employers.

SOURCE: Testimony presented at the committee's May 1999 plenary meeting, materials submitted to the committee by the NLM and information at the NLM Web site.

[1]Additional information about the National Library of Medicine may be found at <http://www.nlm.nih.gov>.

[2]For example, there is the organization Friends of the Law Library of Congress. See "Among Friends: Law Library Group Holds Fall Meeting," by Anne Mercer, in *Information Bulletin*, December 1999, p. 297. The Geography and Map Division has the Philip Lee Phillips Society, established to develop, enhance, and promote the collections of the division. See <http://lcweb.loc.gov/rr/geogmap/phillips.html>.

[3]This network was established by the Medical Library Assistance Act of 1965.

[4]See <http://www.fnlm.org> for more information.

National Science Foundation and the Department of Education) might also be included.

FUNDING FOR THE LIBRARY OF CONGRESS

For several important reasons, the committee has delayed a discussion of the funding strategies and realities of LC until just this point. It was necessary to outline the directions LC ought to take, the content it needs to collect, the infrastructure it must support, and the role it must play on the national and world stages before moving to issues of funding. Too often, the tendency in managing a large federal agency is to move in the other direction: to start from the realities of funding and then to move to strategy and management questions. The committee believes that budgetary issues have loomed too large in LC's funding strategies in recent years. Most of LC's funding comes from annual congressional appropriation. Such appropriation typically falls in two parts: continuation of the preceding year's funding, with some approved increment to cover ordinary expenses and mandated salary adjustments, as well as programmatic enhancements in response to specific requests. The Library is also authorized to retain its receipts from copyright registration and other services. (There are statutory restrictions on how far LC can go in generating revenue from, for example, sales in the Library bookshop. These restrictions may need to be revisited as new opportunities emerge.) The committee could not form a clear picture of how much of the conservatism inherent in the annual budget exercise is mandated by government policy and how much is a feature of LC's management style.

There are tensions. Congress is well aware that LC is Congress's library, but the public image of LC has little to do with its congressional service role. The Congressional Research Service arm of LC is professional, well-staffed, and highly responsive to congressional needs. For all that, CRS makes relatively little direct use of the "Library" (i.e., the resources managed by Library Services and the Law Library). Congress continued to support LC generously through the 1990s, at a time when not all federal agencies with cultural missions enjoyed such support. Inevitably there is some friction between the demands of the institution and Congress's keenly felt need to keep its own budget down.[11] Today, LC is fortunate in its patrons on the Hill, but they are few. Shorter Washington careers and myriad demands on congressional attention leave less time and attention for an institution with no clear and vocal constituency. Given, moreover, the imperatives to bring the congressional budget under control, LC's most outspoken supporters cannot responsibly call on their colleagues to write a blank check. Funding, and in particular funding increases, must be made compelling in terms that a broad range of representatives and senators can understand.

The clear choice of LC's present administration has been to support

---

[11]"Generously" is a relative term. The Library falls under the legislative branch's budget in the appropriations process. Because of the desire of the Congress to limit severely its own budget increases, even securing increases to cover inflation is an accomplishment. One such struggle is being played out as this report goes to press at the end of 2000.

the great collections and the new digital initiatives required by emphasizing outreach of several kinds: outreach to the House and Senate through targeted services, outreach to other cultures (Dr. Billington's own scholarly eminence has led to some remarkable joint programs with other countries),[12] and outreach to the broadest American educational public, the K-12 sector. In 2000, LC is benefiting from a generous allocation from the Advertising Council to publicize the Library's 200th birthday in terms that a broad public can appreciate and support. The National Digital Library Program, discussed above, has been frank and direct in making American schoolteachers and students the primary audience.

The committee views these pragmatic priorities with mixed feelings. On the one hand, it would be hard to reject the results that this political insight and acumen, this focus on certain "markets," have won for LC in Congress. In a decade of austerities in federal agencies, LC has done remarkably well in keeping the funding it needs for core services, managing even to innovate creditably at the margins. Dr. Billington and his administration deserve high praise for these successes. In the committee's judgment, the Library's good reputation in the Congress (and its relative success in the appropriations process) is a direct result of Dr. Billington's relationship building. In addition, Dr. Billington was the driving force in making fund raising an important function at LC (e.g., the Madison Council was established in 1989 and the profile and staffing of the Development Office have increased substantially during Dr. Billington's tenure).

At the same time, much is at risk in this strategy. The riches of the Library of Congress are arguably of interest to the broadest American public. However, the committee was struck—in its conversations with, for example, schoolteachers—by the way in which LC is seen as only one of many, many players in the K-12 environment, and not an especially favored one. If LC owns or creates useful material and someone—a teacher, in this example—knows about it, the material will be used. But the LC "brand name" is not yet one to conjure with in cyberspace. The

---

[12]For example, the Russian Leadership Program was established in May 1999 to enable young, emerging leaders of the Russian Federation to see firsthand how a democratic society works at the grass roots. The 1999 program brought 2,200 Russians to 530 U.S. communities. The Congress has renewed the program for 2000. For additional information, see "Leadership Program Funded for 2000," *Information Bulletin*, January 2000, p. 5. Another example is the agreement between LC and the National Library of Spain to collaborate on "Spain, the United States, and the American Frontier: Historias Paralelas (Parallel Histories)." Some of the most important materials relating to the history of Spanish expansion into North America will be made available on the Internet (see LC's press release 00-20, "Library of Congress and National Library of Spain Sign Agreement to Collaborate on Internet Project," February 24, 2000).

distinctiveness of LC and the vital contribution it has made to the American nation lie elsewhere. The committee is concerned that if the realities of the search for funding are allowed too much influence over policy, there will be insufficient attention to two areas in particular:

- *Access to and use of collections by scholars*—If schoolteachers or other members of the public consider LC's materials to be interesting but interchangeable with those of many other sources, research scholars often consider them to be utterly unique, irreplaceable, and priceless. It is safe to say that material for tens of thousands of vital and engaging research projects possessed by LC is traditionally and necessarily difficult to access. The books and papers of LC need to be physically consulted in Washington, D.C.—a challenge for even the most fortunate of scholars and beyond the means of most. Digital technologies can and should make such materials more widely known and accessible well beyond the walls of the building where the originals are kept. But the American Memory project has emphatically and purposely not addressed the scholarly user. At most, a scholarly user will get from that project a sense of what *might* be worth pursuing in the collections, but the digital collections are not themselves useful as scholarly instruments. The committee believes that future digitization must keep the needs of the researcher squarely in mind. This also means using electronic tools for indexing and finding materials, especially when digitization of the primary materials is uneconomical.

- *Metadata and preservation for digital content*—The discussion of infrastructure issues in this report makes clear where there is real and unique value in LC's participation in the digital future. Building and maintaining a consensus around standards for cataloging and other forms of metadata—the surrogates that help librarians and users alike find their way through the welter of materials a great library contains—are tasks of the greatest importance to the world of learning and indeed to all who would use library and archival materials in a creative and timely way. The archiving and preservation of digital content deserve LC's most serious attention. But metadata and cataloging lack pizzazz, and digital preservation is scarcely better off. This is unfortunate.

The committee strongly urges the Library of Congress to address the tasks it is best positioned to address, particularly those that can only be done with public funding or that arise out of its statutory responsibilities (e.g., copyright depository, support for Congress). The committee's understanding of the mission enunciated by the Library (and as described in detail in Chapters 2 to 5) suggests that congressional funding for the

Library of Congress must be continued at a level that enables LC to do the following:

- Carry out the work of Congress as required and requested;
- Maintain the precious collections already in LC's possession and make them available to users, especially scholars;
- Build those collections with both analog and digital materials; and
- Lead in the definition of digital standards and acquire, catalog, archive, and preserve the digital works that fall within the LC charter.

No one should have any illusions about the price tag for this mission. There is today no easy replacement of paper with digital materials, and comparatively few cost-saving benefits will be reaped from automation per se: those days are largely over.[13] (Where opportunities now arise, they go beyond the walls of any single institution, comprising, as they do, the aggressive use of networked technology to—for example—acquire goods and services online in a business-to-business setting.) We live in a time when libraries will see their missions expanded as they continue to collect and preserve analog materials while at the same time participating wholeheartedly in the digital revolution. The users of libraries—from senators to ordinary citizens to research scholars—will demand (and deserve) no less. The committee does suggest that Congress encourage LC to focus its attention on the resources and services that make it unique, even if this means making the subtler and less populist case for funding outlined above, and to put an appeal to a mass audience in second place. The committee believes that a more collaborative and interconnected Library of Congress, with partner libraries and organizations around the country actively sharing in the adventure of the digital age, would have a better claim on congressional attention for the kinds of projects recommended by the committee. Similarly, efforts to build a consensus with a broad coalition of institutions of higher education, publishers, and other stakeholders would result in better service to users and create a stronger, broader constituency.

That said, congressional funding cannot be the limit of what LC needs and seeks. In the last decade there have been signal successes in private fund raising, for the National Digital Library Program in particular. The committee views those successes with both admiration and caution. How far should such fund raising compete with that of other not-for-profit

---

[13]However, process rationalization (which would include some "automation") might result in nontrivial cost savings at LC.

institutions that do not have the federal treasury behind them? Should LC approach corporations as donors or—perhaps better—as partners? The Library owns precious content that many publishers and entertainment industry producers would be happy to develop. It has reservations, however, for it has had some negative experiences with such partners.

These reservations are understandable, but they should transmute not into suspicion but into a strategy for partnership. How can LC work together with the private sector to develop and communicate the riches of the Library? Insofar as LC remains committed to the business of disseminating its collections to a broad public, and in particular to schoolchildren, it should look for neither a core congressional allocation nor charitable contributions to support that commitment. Rather, LC should seek to disseminate its collections to a wider public by means of a mutually beneficial partnership with the private sector—a partnership that goes beyond the contribution of funds or equipment by using the partnership to develop the technical and marketing expertise of the Library (i.e., to effect technology transfer). To the extent that there are legal and practical restrictions on such partnerships, the committee strongly urges Congress to respond by facilitating the creative exploitation of a cultural treasure. In the end, of course, LC's collections belong to the nation, and that fact sets limits to the rights that LC can assign to its prospective partners and thus, inevitably, to the degree of exploitation that is possible.

Mission should drive funding strategy. To the extent that funding tactics begin to impinge on the basic missions of the LC, a grave risk is run, that of losing focus. If LC concentrates on what it does best and what is most important, then indeed it can afford to do some other things as well. At the moment, it appears that the Library's language of appeal to a mass audience has created confusion, both within the organization and outside it. This cannot go on.

Traditional processes can also be facilitated through the use of information technology to improve access for clients and to increase revenue. For example, the Photoduplication Service might sell its products through the Web.[14] There are surely other strategic opportunities of a nontraditional kind, for example, with "portals" that would let the portals' customers link more effectively to LC, while LC would find in such (presumably nonexclusive) arrangements an effective and essentially cost-free marketing strategy.

---

[14]Currently, products may be ordered in person, by mail, or by fax.

Findings and Recommendations

Finding: The Library of Congress is constrained in what it can do by its dependence on congressional funding as well as by other constraints on the ways in which its precious materials can be made better known and be more widely used by the world at large.

Recommendation: The Library of Congress should address the agendas that it is best positioned to address, especially those that are likely to be achieved with public funding. The committee points out two agendas in particular: (1) developing digital collections to address the needs of researchers and (2) facilitating progress on digital preservation and metadata.

Recommendation: Limitations on the Library's ability to generate revenue from its activities should be revisited and restrictions eased, where possible, in order to facilitate mutually beneficial relationships with outside entities. It is unlikely and undesirable that such activity would become a major source of funding—and the committee cannot emphasize too strongly that such revenues should never be taken as an excuse for limiting or reducing government funding for the core missions of the Library—but room must be made for experimentation and partnership.

Finding: Year-to-year operating funds and traditional capital funds will be inadequate sources of funding for new Library initiatives for the foreseeable future because the initiatives are not likely to result in significant cost savings and may well require increased funding—for instance, the National Digital Library Program adds costs and does not result in any savings because the capabilities being developed are new and do not replace any existing processes.

Recommendation: Fund-raising successes with the National Digital Library Program and the Madison Council should be extended to give greater direct support for the Library's core strategy areas. Potential funders include traditional philanthropic givers, corporate partnerships, and newly established high-tech corporations (the "dot-coms") with an interest in the activities supported.

These initiatives and the enhanced relationships with traditional and nontraditional audiences alike would increase the focus and relevance of each LC unit and make LC more important to all outside organizations and the general population. External relations must be geared to more than simply raising money and generating revenue, although in the medium to long term, substantial revenues could be generated for LC even as the partners develop their businesses because of the partnership with LC.

7

MANAGEMENT ISSUES

Throughout its explorations of the Library of Congress (LC), the committee has repeatedly seen the acting out of an important principle: the wise application of information technology to organizational tasks is far more often a question of management than of technology. In this chapter, the committee outlines its findings and recommendations insofar as they affect the practices and vision of management at the Library.

The fundamental management resource of the Library is people. This is an organization with 4,000 staff members ranging from highly specialized professionals, through dedicated clerical and technical staff supporting professional tasks, to a broad range of other support personnel. The committee members were deeply impressed by the loyalty and professionalism of everyone they met but were at the same time distressed by the obstacles that exist to effective management of these human resources. The source of the committee's greatest fear—and the subject of its most anxious deliberations—has been the uncertainty about whether any amount of goodwill, planning, and structured intent can achieve the necessary change, given the constraints of funding and procedure that are imposed on LC from above and without.

Most pervasive is the culture of civil service human resources (HR) practices as implemented at LC. It is beyond the scope of this report to examine closely the boundary between what is necessary (because of statute and other controlling forces outside LC) and what is contingent (the result of LC decisions and practices), and the committee welcomes the HR21 effort (see below) that seeks to get a better handle on what is susceptible to control. Here the committee simply observes that the collection of these practices makes it harder to recruit, hire, train, and retain staff than is generally the case in the commercial and academic sectors and in particular makes it extremely difficult to attract and retain IT staff.

In the 1970s, a group of LC employees filed a class-action case against the Library alleging racial discrimination. Known as "the Cook case" (see Box 7.1), the case was settled in the mid-1990s with a consent decree that adds several layers of court-ordered procedural steps to all hiring and review of personnel. The resources of LC have been focused as never before on achieving a more diverse workforce with greater equality of opportunity. That remains and should remain a central institutional priority. In an environment of limited resources (in terms of both dollars and management attention), however, one undeniable effect of this decree has been to divert attention from other institutional priorities. In the short term, hiring has become slower and more cumbersome, just at a moment when technical staff particularly are pursued with increasing speed and agility by virtually every other sector of the economy. The committee has been encouraged to think that both sides in the case may be nearing the point where they can agree under court direction to terminate the consent decree and move toward hiring practices that are more flexible and that at the same time more effectively build opportunity for all. Achievement of this goal would have a positive effect on morale, productivity, and management throughout the Library.

The Library is in many respects an aging institution with long-established practices. The committee was surprised that information technology initiatives are still spoken of at LC as exercises in "automation," in a way that is seldom heard elsewhere. There are many reasons to leave that language and that habit of thought behind, not least because it is suggestive of outmoded management practices that are rightly held in low esteem by staff representatives. Civil service regulations and the Cook case may explain partly, but cannot account for completely, why LC continues with management practices that are redolent of old, assembly-line methods. Reinventing the processes will mean reinventing the work, an effort that will in turn require close collaboration between LC management and the unions.[1] They must find and share a common vision of a workforce that is more highly skilled and more highly paid and then seek a strategy to approach that vision in a way that maximizes opportunity for all those

---

[1]The Library of Congress has four labor unions: AFSCME 2477 (representing nonprofessional staff), AFSCME 2910 (representing professional staff), the Congressional Research Employees Association (representing all employees of CRS), and the Fraternal Order of Police (representing all of the police officers at LC).

BOX 7.1
The Cook Case

In 1982, Howard Cook and a number of other LC employees filed a discrimination suit in U.S. District Court (the case is commonly referred to simply as "the Cook case") after having had their initial claim rejected by the Library. Cook and the others claimed that LC discriminated against African-American employees and applicants for employment in its hiring and promotional processes. Two years later, the court certified a group of black employees as a class, and in 1987 the Library admitted to liability on the group's claims. However, in December 1988, Judge Norma Holloway Johnson expanded the class to include claims by all black employees, including those qualified for professional and administrative positions from 1975 to the present.

In August 1992, Judge Johnson granted the plaintiffs' motion for a partial summary judgment, finding the Library's three-stage personnel selection process to be so subjective as to discriminate against black applicants for administrative and professional positions. Nearly 2 years later, in April 1994, the attorneys for both sides of the case reached tentative agreement on a settlement that provided for a total of $8.5 million in back pay, 40 promotions, and 10 reassignments. The agreement represents the "greatest monetary relief ever awarded by the federal government to settle a race discrimination case."

Despite protests by several plaintiffs and their supporters, Judge Johnson gave her tentative approval to the agreement in August 1994 and scheduled a fairness hearing for May 1995. Following this hearing, after listening to approximately 200 objections regarding the distribution of the money, promotions, and reassignments, as well as three requests to opt out of the class action suit, Judge Johnson issued the final order approving the settlement agreement in September 1995. She insisted, however, on retaining jurisdiction over the case until December 1, 2000, to oversee (1) implementation of a revised hiring process, (2) reporting requirements related to the hiring process, and (3) competitive and noncompetitive selection decisions.

In 1998, the plaintiffs challenged the Library's implementation of its obligations under the agreement, and the parties are working toward resolving the issues related to the plaintiffs' challenge. During the period of time that the agreement is effective, LC's hiring and promotion practices for professional, administrative, and supervisory technical employees must be accomplished according to a process agreed to by both LC and the plaintiffs' counsel. Any exceptions to the hiring process that occur with special programs, such as the Leadership Development Program or the Selective Placement Program for the Disabled, must also be agreed to by the plaintiffs' counsel.

SOURCE: Text derived largely from "Cook Case Chronology," *The Gazette: Weekly Newspaper for the Library Staff*, November 29, 1996, pp. 12-13. See also "Court Clears Way for Cook Case Payout," by Gail Fineberg, in *Library of Congress Information Bulletin*, November 18, 1996, available online at <gopher://marvel.loc.gov:70/00/loc/pubs/lcib/1996/vol55.no20/1>.

who now work at LC. Information technology is most powerful in organizations where it is seen as bringing opportunity to all.

HUMAN RESOURCES

The Library of Congress has a number of unique strengths that make it an attractive place to work. Its low turnover[2] is a source of pride and an indicator of job satisfaction. People at all levels independently remarked that the most satisfying parts of their job relate to the variety of materials they get to handle, view, and work with. From mailroom clerk to senior manager, many enjoy their access to beautiful or unusual or obscure books, maps, images, and recordings. Another appeal is working for LC on Capitol Hill in support of the national government. Several segments of the LC population (particularly the Congressional Research Service and the senior staff) can contribute directly to the running of the United States government on a regular basis, a role that is highly valued by some employees.

Library of Congress Challenges

Recruitment and Retention

The Library has a number of formidable management challenges that make it difficult to hire new staff and to keep staff with skills in areas that are in high demand. Libraries are increasingly operating in an environment of rapid change, but federal hiring and procurement constraints can impede certain kinds of change (see Box 7.2). To the eye of those on the committee who deal with hiring and management of IT personnel, the federal salaries and grades for IT professionals seem to be desperately below what the market offers. To be sure, the National Library of Medicine seems to be more successful than LC with its IT hiring: even though NLM has the same federal constraints, it can offer as an incentive a more research-oriented environment (see Box 6.2 in Chapter 6). IT organizations in particular need a steady stream of fresh talent to stay current.

It is practically impossible for the Library to hire new college graduates in computer science because of the salary differential between entry-grade government hires and what industry can pay. There are market imbalances everywhere between skilled technology workers and what employers offer, which must make whatever pressures there are on the LC staff in general that much greater for IT staff. LC is able to pay only 60

---

[2]As reported to the committee at its first plenary meeting in February 1999, turnover at the Library is only 2 or 3 percent per year.

percent of the going salaries for IT workers. The differential in total compensation closes at the more senior levels, where the steadiness of federal service, regular work hours, and the assured benefits package also have increased appeal. Indeed, LC reports that hiring senior people is not as problematic as hiring junior IT people. Hiring graduates from new schools of information (such as those at the University of California at Berkeley or the University of Michigan) is also difficult, in part because these graduates have many career options in corporations, universities, and other settings.[3] In general, the Library is able to fill its vacancies for librarians, but the question unanswerable by any outsider is how far the current structure of incentives achieves the right mix of talent for the organization.

Thirty to forty percent of the LC staff will be eligible for retirement by the year 2004.[4] The Library's management sees this as a particular concern in areas where the necessary skill sets are hard to come by (such as certain foreign languages) or require extensive time on the job to acquire (such as a knowledge of collections with large arrearages). For example, CRS staff members who had worked on the Nixon impeachment analyses were able to bring their experience to bear during the Clinton presidential impeachment process. In the committee's view, the upcoming transition in LC's staff can and should be made an opportunity to rethink and redesign jobs and bring fresh talent and viewpoints into the Library. The committee expects that 10 years from now there will be fewer traditional librarian positions in LC and more positions for IT-savvy librarians, although many of the latter may well be filled (if the committee's remarks below about a culture of training are heeded) by persons now filling librarian positions. The changes in technology and infrastructure in the late 1990s and thereafter—for example, the Integrated Library System (ILS)—and the lack of incentive to learn these new ways of doing business may cause those eligible to retire to do so.[5] The committee's sense has been that candidates with prior government service (including retiring military personnel) have loomed large in candidate pools for LC positions. That population is unlikely to have the professional and technical skills needed by the LC of the future, and the committee recommends that

---

[3] See "Libraries Compete for Staff with Dot-coms Seeking Information Managers," *Wall Street Journal*, May 4, 2000, p. A1.

[4] Of course, the actual number of retirees by any given date is likely to be far lower than the total number of those eligible to retire, so the transition is likely to be less dramatic than those numbers imply.

[5] The committee believes staff could be given incentives to learn; for example, goals could be set in annual performance reviews. It believes that ways should be found to tie successful completion and application of the expanded staff development recommended by this report with salary increases or recognition awards.

BOX 7.2
Hiring Employees in the Federal Government

Although the federal government became more flexible in its hiring practices over the past decade, it remains much more rigid than the private sector and more encumbered by strict rules and regulations. This rigidity, which often extends to the work environment, is blamed in part for the "people crisis" faced by the federal government. With a wave of retirements and other staff departures expected throughout the federal government in the next 5 years, it is not clear where fresh talent will be found, because many young people do not see the federal government as offering the high starting pay, casual work environment, and other advantages that they want.[1] Some critics argue that needless layers of bureaucracy and convoluted career paths prevent the federal government from offering the challenging work sought by talented Americans.[2]

The federal hiring process is an important reason that the government cannot compete with private and nonprofit competitors. The process includes special requirements, such as the required advertising of jobs even if a manager already knows of someone who would be highly qualified (some of these requirements are intended to ensure fairness in the hiring process). Indeed, few managers even go recruiting, leaving it to personnel and administrative officers, and most ads for job openings are nondescript.[3] Resumes must be highly structured and go into greater detail than the typical private-sector resume. Certain applicants, such as veterans and the disabled, are favored in the federal hiring process, whereas nepotism (the practice of officials appointing, promoting, or recommending their relatives) is specifically prohibited. Men born after 1959 must have registered with the Selective Service System or have an exemption.[4] Background investigations of prospective employees are routine. Not surprisingly, it can take 3 to 6 months to hire a government employee,[5,6] whereas in the private sector, new employees can be hired virtually overnight.

Perhaps the greatest handicap associated with the federal hiring process, especially in the high-tech field, is rigid pay scales. For example, in the year 2000 a graduate with a bachelor of science in computer or information science would typically become a GS-7 in the federal pay scale, earning just $28,000 to $30,000, whereas the same person could get a job at a high-tech company for as much as twice that salary. The greatest difficulties in hiring are expected in the computer

LC's Human Resources Services Directorate review hiring practices to make sure that job descriptions are written to appeal to applicants outside of the government. The retirements, if and as they happen, should become an opportunity to staff in areas of librarianship and technology needed to meet the digital challenge.

Speed and Flexibility

The need for workforce flexibility in the digital age is in direct conflict

field. By 2006, the government will need to replace 32,315 technology workers because of retirements and other factors and hire 4,600 additional workers to fill newly created computer jobs, according to the latest estimates.[7]

Some agencies are attempting to offer improved compensation and benefits and to streamline the hiring process. For example, in 1999, the Department of State launched two major initiatives targeted at the recruitment and retention of IT professionals: the payment of recruitment bonuses for new federal employees with critical IT skills and retention allowances for current employees with those same skills or for doing Y2K work.[8] The Office of Personnel Management (OPM) has launched a pilot program with 11 federal agencies to help OPM develop new IT job titles, adjust salaries, tweak benefit packages, and accelerate the hiring process.[9] The Bureau of Alcohol, Tobacco and Firearms, an agency of the Treasury Department, has adopted a pay banding system to attract IT workers.[10]

---

[1]"Retirement Wave Creates Vacuum," by Stephen Barr, in *Washington Post*, May 7, 2000, p. A1.

[2]*The New Public Service*, by Paul C. Light (Washington, D.C.: Brookings Institution Press, 1999).

[3]See Barr above.

[4]Office of Personnel Management (OPM), "Applying for a Federal Job," OF 510 (Washington, D.C.: U.S. Government Printing Office, 1995).

[5]Excerpts from *The Book of U.S. Government Jobs*, by Dennis V. Damp, 1999, available online at <http://federaljobs.net>.

[6]At the Library, processes that were introduced as a result of the Cook case can often cause the hiring process to extend beyond 6 months.

[7]See Barr above.

[8]See "Investing in Human Capital—An Organizational Priority," a publication of the Chief Information Officers Council, available online at <http://www.cio.gov/docs/investinginhuman capital.htm>.

[9]See "E-recruitment," by Heather Harreld, in *Federal Computer Week*, May 1, 2000, available online at <http://www.fcw.com/fcw/articles/2000/0501/cov-box2-05-01-00.asp>.

[10]See "ATF Uses Banding System to Lift IT Pay," by Shruti Date, *Government Computer News*, June 12, 2000, available online at <http://www.gcn.com/vol19_no15/community/2196-1.html>.

---

with rigid HR rules at the Library of Congress. The Library's ability to be speedy and to be flexible in writing job descriptions so that it can hire worthy candidates who cross job categories has been further impaired by virtue of its having been adjudged (under the Cook decision) discriminatory in its hiring and promotion practices. This ruling has caused the organization to be even more attentive to procedure in the hiring processes, from writing job descriptions to selecting and screening candidates to interviewing and offering employment packages. This care and deliberateness may satisfy the need to demonstrate fairness and an effective commitment to diversity, but other solutions must be found if the Library is to compete with private-sector firms that also need skilled technical staff. The committee urges that the contract employment model widespread in private industry and among nonprofit organizations be used more often.

Staff Development

Implementing the ILS means that much of the hardware and software in daily use is changing. People who have been accustomed to the mainframe-dumb terminal interface have been given some encouragement to become proficient users of PC hardware and software. The ILS project has addressed that issue by offering 60 or more hours of training. However, this training does not really address the fact that few of the staff have a workable mental model of what is on their own machine, how to store things on a server, and what is a reasonable user interface. Some of the pockets of staff inexperience at LC in mid-1999 were astonishing to members of the committee.

The ILS will support different and more effective processing flows than were possible with the Library's old stand-alone applications. Such revised processes will, however, require procedural and organizational changes likely to be found threatening and uncomfortable by many managers and staff members of the Library. This reorganization and rethinking of business processes will be even more difficult than the technical implementation of the Voyager ILS.

It is sobering to realize that the Library of Congress encourages as little professional development as it does. The committee judges that most professional and technical staff have had far too little opportunity for professional training, continuing education, or development in recent years. Employees regularly reported that they have not been encouraged to explore technology that is not directly applicable to their current job. This makes them less adaptable. The low level of worker exposure to modern technology and the introduction of the ILS have necessitated classes in basic computer skills like using a mouse. But a cataloger who gains a certificate indicating proficiency with a mouse does not necessarily have the ability to mount the shared reference documents from a server or to find what is needed within the LC network, nor will a professional trained in library work necessarily be able to use the library-like resources—such as databases—online or on the World Wide Web.

Training, an important source of current ideas, is underbudgeted (see Box 7.3). Internal training cannot make up all of the difference because it cannot, for example, impart cutting-edge technical skills. While it may be that some employees are not interested in learning (they "just want to

---

BOX 7.3
Training at the Library of Congress

A number of units at the Library are responsible for formal training. The Library-wide directorate for training is the Internal University (IU). The charter of the IU is to provide (usually by procuring outside services) training that is pertinent for the entire institution. Courses such as time management and office automation (e.g., training on word processing packages) are offered, as is a seminar on facilitative leadership, which is taught by LC managers. In addition, the IU coordinates training activities throughout the institution through its Training and Development Advisory Board, which includes representatives from major organizations within LC; coordinates a mentoring program; and initiated LearnITonline, a pilot computer training program.

The major service units also conduct training. The Technical Processing and Automation Instruction Office (TPAIO) offers courses in subjects such as cataloging, acquisitions, and the Integrated Library System, as well as general courses in online public access cataloging, searching, and word processing. TPAIO also coordinates registration for IU courses within Library Services. Information Technology Services provides courses on the use of various software packages, including Microsoft Office and Corel WordPerfect Office. Other units within the Library, such as the Congressional Research Service, also have training programs.

---

push buttons and think of going to Disney World," is how some employees were characterized), there is little support for those who are. Even though a number of training courses are available, there is no evidence of a culture of learning in the organization. There is, for example, very little encouragement for, and even some discouragement of, professional travel for conferences, nor is there sufficient use of temporary project assignments as training opportunities.[6] Creating such a culture requires strong pressure from Human Resources Services, the Internal University, and HR units throughout the Library, but the effort can succeed only if promoted by senior management and supported by managers throughout the organization.

Physical Work Environment

Staff at LC report that among the least satisfying aspects of the LC workplace are the physical spaces. Several people let committee mem-

---

[6]Although it is not in the area of information technology, the Affirmative Action Detail Program that began in mid-2000 is a step in the right direction within the realm of administrative and managerial work. See "Detail Program Provides Career Opportunities," by Dorothy Coley, in *The Gazette*, April 7, 2000, p. 5.

bers know that the Madison Building, while attractive to visitors, was engineered to house books, not offices. In addition, space on Capitol Hill in general is precious, making it even more difficult to provide offices and other rooms with adequate space. The committee saw a mix of settings that often bore out the complaints. Unsatisfactory lighting, desks, and chairs strain eyes, arms, and backs. Crowded workspaces make it a challenge to find a flat work surface on which to lay a book. Posters remind workers to address posture and placement of furniture to avoid injury, but the actual circumstances of work and the furniture available often do not allow good ergonomic choices.[7]

The pathology of obsolete workflows is evident in a variety of places in LC. Many tasks are repetitive ones, differentiated by degree of difficulty. This leads to competition for the easy tasks when the reward system emphasizes the volume of work accomplished but not the difficulty of the problems solved. Union rules and agreements on this and other issues would need to be renegotiated to bring about changes great and small. The committee sees this pathology as both symptom and opportunity. Mechanically and mentally repetitive tasks represent opportunities for technological enhancement, but their continued practice in jumbles of dysfunctional space is a sign that management has not acquired the habit of thinking through such symptoms to the opportunities that lie beyond.

Similarly, within a particular work group, the tasks are often narrowly defined and managed, following an older industrial model of work. Each worker moves materials from one status to another. Workers handle batches of materials held together with one kind of clip, band, or folder and move them to processed status with a different kind of clip, band, or folder. Physical manipulation of these batches shows how the work is progressing. However, not all of the batching techniques make for stable stacking. The threat of the objects of work spilling out of order is constant in some departments. The apparently ad hoc status of the physical binding leads to equally ad hoc solutions for storing excess clips, binders, and folders. Clearly, there is an opportunity to reappraise work and the workflow, to use technology judiciously, and to empower workers to make their jobs more interesting and productive. If the committee may extract a principle from these observations, it is that technology is most often introduced at LC "from the technology in" rather than "from the

---

[7]One person reported buying her own ergonomic keyboard because the red tape involved in getting an approval from management would have caused a delay of several months at least. This employee believed that such a delay would have turned her wrist injury from a minor aggravation into a major disability. Pockets of management responsiveness have been found, but there remain problems.

work out." In the absence of any vision of how technology could improve processes and leverage investments, technology arrives when it has been suitably hyped and imposed on the organization from outside, most often for high-profile tasks or tasks performed in common across many kinds of organizations and hence discussed widely outside LC. It is precisely the most idiosyncratic LC tasks that remain mired in assembly-line piece-work management and practice.[8]

Lessons Learned from Library Projects

A vital sign of successful management is its flair for learning and for facilitating internal technology transfer from one successful project into other settings. Signs of such flair at LC are few but hopeful.

The National Digital Library Program (NDLP) was established with ambitious goals. In order to accomplish them, the program took an unusual (for the Library) shape. A separate department, independent of existing structures and largely without LC organizational constraints, was established. Both management and staff were brought in from outside the Library. By many reports this was a very successful model. The NDLP staff have been nimble and creative and have earned great respect for their productivity and competence. The committee frequently heard the observation, "It could never have been accomplished through the normal channels." It is worth noting that with its clear mission and energetic management, the NDLP has succeeded in attracting an excellent and effective technical staff. The hiring of contractors with special skills necessary for this project was accomplished in record time, particularly given the hiring constraints listed above. A small number of regular employees transferred into the project, even without guaranteed return to their former jobs or employment status (the NDLP positions were typically temporary appointments—NTE, "not to exceed"). The hiring of staff for this special project demonstrates that LC can, when pressed, hire individuals with the technical skills needed to do more than the day-to-day LC operations.

Another instructive project at the Library was the effort to adopt whole-book cataloging. Until 1992, cataloging was organized linearly, with descriptive cataloging (describing the specific characteristics of items) and subject and classification cataloging (adding access points and placing the item in Library of Congress and Dewey classification schemes)

---

[8]During the summer of 1999, several committee members visited the Copyright Office and the Cataloging Directorate to observe work processes. These visits included meetings with line managers as well as informal discussions with staff.

being separate activities carried out by different groups of catalogers. An item passed through a number of different catalogers before it was cataloged fully, and the entire process usually took several months. The Whole-Book Pilot Program tested the concept of having a single cataloger (or single team) catalog an item from the beginning to the end. The success of this effort resulted in a 1992 reorganization of the Cataloging Directorate along whole-book lines. The pilot project was deemed to be a success for a number of reasons:[9]

- It was a good concept.
- Most of the participants volunteered.
- The participants felt like pioneers doing something new and different.
- The people participating in the pilot project were more adventuresome than their colleagues, and they received support from management for that.
- There was ongoing communication among participants.
- The reorganization broke down walls between subject and descriptive catalogers and between catalogers and technicians.
- The teams felt responsible for a finished product.

A number of lessons were also learned from the implementation of the ILS; these are discussed in Chapter 8. The challenge for LC management, at best sporadically met in the past, is to take what can be learned from these experiences and generalize them to the whole of LC.

Human Resources Processes and HR21

The Library has already recognized the difficulties in its human resources (HR) processes and has begun to address some of them in its plans. *HR21: Our Vision for the Future—The Library of Congress Human Resources Strategic Plan, FY 2000-2005* (November 1999) lays out the organization's goals and objectives for the next 5 years (see Box 7.4).

The five goals of HR21 cover some, but not all, of the issues raised above. Moreover, the detailed objectives listed under the HR21 goals do not go as far or as fast as the committee would recommend. According to the document, research shows that Human Resources Services (HRS) Directorate professionals cannot in one step go from being bureaucratic administrators to becoming partners in achieving the goals of the func-

---

[9]As reported to the committee during a site visit to the Library in July 1999.

BOX 7.4
The HR21 Plan—Goals and Objectives

Goal 1—We will compete successfully for highly qualified staff.
Objective 1.1—We will acquire the right competencies at the right time.

Goal 2—We will retain high performers and reward excellence and innovation.
Objective 2.1—We will create an environment that rewards individuals and/ or teams for the achievement of the desired results.

Goal 3—We will train and manage staff to achieve the Library's mission in a changing environment.
Objective 3.1—We will develop management and staff ability to deal with change and give them the skills to succeed in their jobs.
Objective 3.2—We will enhance the capabilities of our current and future leaders to lead change.

Goal 4—We will promote fairness, equal opportunity, and respect for diversity at all levels and in all parts of the Library.
Objective 4.1—We will strengthen and utilize diversity to accomplish our goals.

Goal 5—We will make personnel and administration responsive, efficient, and effective.
Objective 5.1—We will get human resources basics right and align human resources processes to support the Library's mission and goals.

---

tional units. The committee recommends that the Human Resources Services Directorate be more aggressive in pursuit of exactly that goal, that it set its sights on being an agent of change and a business partner, and that it begin drafting goals and plans to that effect immediately, with deadlines for seeing change in some small number of months, not years. While this approach is aggressive and risky, HR experience in industry indicates that it can be done. The goal is for HRS Directorate staff to be judged, and to be seen to be judged, not by their ability to perform HR tasks but by their contribution to achieving the goals of the institution.

Such an effort will require ongoing support from the highest levels of management. The Human Resources Services Directorate needs to be a source of innovation and an active catalyst for change, within both the directorate and the larger Library. It needs to make a compelling business case, which it has done in its HR21 plan, where it outlines some of the milestones toward change. Of course, any such plans coming from an HR organization must expect to be greeted with long-suffering skepticism, and the Human Resources Services Directorate must expect to be judged by its ability to dissolve that skepticism.

In the area of recruitment, the HRS Directorate needs more radical strategies. One example would be to increase the pool of highly qualified candidates—by, for example, implementing processes such as internship. CRS has had good success with its Grad Recruit program, in which graduate students compete for summer positions, which then become the basis for recruitment to permanent positions. This strategy may be effective for both professional librarians and technical staff. The HRS's performance targets for this goal rightly address the long lag time from identified need to employment offer. Its performance target of fewer than 30 calendar days from job order to offer is dead-on,[10] but implementation cannot wait until September 2002 (as is currently anticipated).

The HRS Directorate's objective of retaining and rewarding high performers is an excellent one and will create an environment that rewards results. The commitment to evaluating alternative rewards is clearly necessary, but there is no deadline or performance target for that. Now is the time to outline strategies for creating a culture of risk taking, starting with learning from the risk taking that occurred in the NDLP. Those lessons should be documented in a few weeks, discussed, and the first changes implemented directly afterward.

The strategies for achieving the training goal extend to all categories of Library employees. However, the critical need here is funding, which must be addressed immediately and creatively, not only by requests for congressional funding but also by efforts to find money from salary savings or other sources in the meantime. Training for employees with initiative should be made available as soon as the funding is available. The HRS Directorate, the Internal University, and the training departments around the Library need to make a strong business case to obtain funding for external classes and for travel to conferences and other meetings. Also, in addition to managers being trained to lead change (objective 3.2), they must be catalysts for change now. That will provide training by example and start the process of change immediately.

The HRS Directorate's experience with the issue of diversity shows in

---

[10]Measures of time-to-hire varied sharply according to source, and the committee has not been able to reconcile all the data it gathered. Perception is also important, and it observes that managers and staff alike perceived substantially longer delays than were reported by HRS management. But whether the average time from approval of position to hire is 4 months (the optimistic report of some senior managers) or 6 (a fairly consistent report of line managers and staff), the delay is much too long for a competitive organization.

its strategies and performance targets for goal 4. Yet even here, HRS can do more. It could mine communities that are typically underrepresented during recruitment, merging goal 1 and goal 4, by reaching highly qualified candidates overlooked by other, competing interests.

Findings and Recommendations

Finding: A nimble Library would be positioned to recruit the best and brightest and to keep up with changes in areas affecting its digital future (technology, library professionals).

Recommendation: As Library employees retire, the automatic hiring of replacements with similar skills should be resisted. Retirements should instead be viewed as opportunities to hire staff with the qualifications in librarianship and technology needed to meet the digital challenge, and reengineering should be rewarded when senior management allocates staff positions to units.

Finding: The National Digital Library Program has managed to attract an excellent and effective technical staff. The hiring of temporary "not to exceed" staff and contractors with special skills necessary for NDLP was accomplished rapidly.

Recommendation: The idea of greater reliance on outsourcing and contract employees should be pursued. This initiative must be driven by senior LC management and led jointly by the Human Resources Services Directorate and the heads of the Library's major service units.

Recommendation: Current staff of the National Digital Library Program should be aggressively recruited for retention and assimilation into the broader Library staff.

Finding: The long tenure of many LC employees means that new skills and ideas are less likely to come to the Library through new employees who bring them along from other employers or schools. Instead, innovation must be fostered by the development of existing staff. Thus, training for Library employees is even more important than for the employees of most private-sector organizations.

Finding: Employees of the Library who might be expected to want to develop their professional skills have few opportunities and receive little encouragement. As a result, they have little interest in or motivation for learning.

Recommendation: The Library needs to provide more training opportunities for staff. Professional development, outside technical training, and practice in using the training are all crucial. Congress should be asked to increase the Library's training budget by a significant amount. This increase should be more than an incremental one—it should be on the order of a doubling or tripling in the next budget (for FY02) submitted to the Congress.

Recommendation: The Library must increase the number of junior- and senior-level staff involved in professional association activities. Such involvement can be a source of learning as well as of networking, which can lead to more effective recruitment. It must also increase its training and travel budget to encourage staffers to participate in and assume leadership roles within the Library and in the professional community.

Finding: Additional learning opportunities for LC staff could come through internships at other organizations and through linkages to professionals in every part of the Library. Opportunities for learning could also be created by rotating personnel out for temporary duty in congruent government agencies.

Recommendation: Extending Library internships to both graduate and undergraduate students from professional schools and other academic institutions appears to have been successful and should be used more widely.

Recommendation: The Library of Congress leadership must encourage a culture of innovation and learning in the Library. Actively nurturing the development of staff to take on the next generation of responsibilities is a vital but neglected area of management in LC.

Recommendation: Teams of persons with unlike skills should be created, whereby those with more technical prowess are encouraged to help those with less. Such teams should be responsible for a real product or function and should have an identifiable audience or customer. The Whole-Book Pilot Program exemplifies an approach that should be adapted for other contexts.

Recommendation: A formal assessment and report of lessons learned from the Integrated Library System implementation should be prepared and completed by January 1, 2001, with an emphasis on findings that can guide future projects.

Recommendation: Human resources staff—both in the Human Resources Services Directorate and within the major service units—should become agents of change and business partners more rapidly than is foreseen in the HR21 plan.

COORDINATION OF INFORMATION TECHNOLOGY VISION, STRATEGY, AND STANDARDS

The committee's charge raised fundamental questions about how decisions on the application of information technology to the Library's mission are framed and made. The committee was particularly charged to review the recommendation of an earlier consultant report[11] that the Library appoint a chief information officer (CIO).

Present Situation

The present director of the Information Technology Services (ITS) Directorate conceives of his role as that of a CIO. Others in the Library have mixed opinions on this point, with perhaps the majority holding that there is no one in such a role at the present time, a view shared by the committee. The 1996 Booz-Allen & Hamilton study recommended that a CIO be appointed.

What is clear is that IT decision making is neither transparent nor strategic. The ITS Directorate has a substantial technology budget, which it apportions according to its estimate of Library priorities. That estimate is influenced by decisions of the Library's Executive Committee (EC), but the director of ITS has a rotating rather than a permanent seat on the Executive Committee, and the EC does not oversee or review the ITS

---

[11]In December 1995, the Government Accounting Office, at the request of the Senate Appropriations Committee, contracted with the consulting firm Booz-Allen & Hamilton to review LC's management of its operations and to deliver a report within 6 months. That report was delivered in May 1996. It is available, along with relevant congressional testimony and an accompanying Price Waterhouse financial statement, online at <http://www.gao.gov/special.pubs/loc.htm>.

budget, though it may occasionally give specific direction regarding one project or another.

In addition, an unspecified amount of money is spent in virtually all LC units on information technology equipment, support, and services. These expenditures are under the control of the individual units and are not necessarily coordinated across the LC as a whole. Shadow systems and duplication are the inevitable outcome of such arrangements. There has been no comprehensive financial accounting for IT.

What strikes the committee most forcibly is that the lines distinguishing central responsibility from unit responsibility are poorly drawn and seem to have come about as a result of precedent rather than deliberate planning. To a considerable extent, moreover, the ITS budget is a black box to management beyond ITS. Senior LC managers complain that they do not receive information from ITS in a form that they can understand. Priority setting within ITS is thus significantly free of review by senior management. A fundamental lever for management of the institution as a whole is thus disabled.

Accordingly, decision making about Library priorities and decision making about IT priorities are coordinated mainly by the force of will of senior managers inside and outside ITS, with inevitable frustrations. Inevitably, the goodwill, competence, and integrity of managers come into question, creating an atmosphere of mistrust.

The difficulties are compounded by a culture of separation across LC units. For example, the Law Library goes separately to ITS to seek resources to support its GLIN project. The committee does not see any programmatic vision in LC as a whole that is capable of looking at GLIN and seeing the strong connections between that worthy but underfunded digitization project and ways to link it with activities in other units, such as Library Services, CRS, or the NDLP, to the mutual advantage of all. As long as each unit stands isolated, either providing for itself or begging resources from ITS, these inefficiencies will be perpetuated. The recommendations of the committee for changes in technology management must be assessed in the long run by the impact they have on this endemic and crippling problem. The committee has particularly wished that the technological innovativeness and flexibility of CRS could more directly benefit other units of LC, particularly (but not only) its colleagues in the Law Library. With the right breadth of management vision, it would be possible to fund initiatives in individual units from central funding explicitly because the lessons learned would redound to the benefit of other units or of the Library as a whole: the committee has not seen that perspective taken as often as it should be.

One other observation. The committee was very much struck in meeting and talking with the staff of LC by a de facto endogamy that hampers the organization. Both librarians and IT staff tend to be professionals of long standing with LC; if they have worked elsewhere, it is with other U.S. government agencies, not elsewhere in the library world. Senior people occasionally depart for positions elsewhere in the library profession, but few ever come to LC at that level.[12] One consequence of this has been the growing isolation of the LC community from its natural colleagues nationally and from the technology world in general. The committee believes strongly that the flow of information and ideas from the library and technology sectors *into* LC needs to be enhanced in a variety of ways.

The Chief Information Officer Function

That the question of appointing a CIO has remained in the air for several years at LC is itself a sign of weakness. Adding a title and an office to the organization chart without carefully considering the underlying organizational principles is a recipe for more confusion, not clarification; remaining undecided for several years about whether to do so or not only compounds the confusion. A new CIO would have to be given a clear mandate for management and direction and would add a layer of management to an organization that few think of as lean. But if a clear mandate were in hand today, it is far from certain that anyone would think a CIO was the answer to LC's problems.

Given restrictions on salary within the civil service and the allure of the dot-com world, the experience of other federal agencies in recruiting and retaining appropriate CIOs has been mixed at best.[13] Organizations of similar size in the not-for-profit sector typically pay two-thirds to twice again as much for a CIO as LC can pay, and the private sector pays much more.

Most strikingly, libraries typically do not have chief information officers. They use IT as an instrument for managing their business (as a widget factory would) at the same time as they are mainly in the business

---

[12]The role of the senior managers in the Office of the Librarian—the librarian, deputy librarian, and chief of staff—is discussed in the section titled "Executive Management."

[13]See "CIOs on the Go," by Nancy Ferris, in *Government Executive*, March 1999, pp. 18-34, which reports as follows: "It has been less than 3 years since Congress directed major federal agencies to appoint chief informational [sic] officers, but already more than half of the original CIOs have left their jobs and have been replaced." Also see "VA Official's Departure Emphasizes Technological Brain Drain," by Stephen Barr, in the *Washington Post*, June 4, 2000, p. C2, available online at <http://washingtonpost.com/wp-dyn/articles/A58595-2000Jun3.html>, and "Making a Federal Case of IT," *CIO Magazine*, July 1, 1999, available online at <http://www.cio.com/archive/070199_government.html>.

of providing information. Decisions about IT use in a library are not marginal in any way—they are core business decisions of the institution.

Vision and Implementation

Once the provision of services and budgeting are rationalized, there remain the questions of vision and direction. How shall LC conceive and enact its technological future? The committee believes that LC's technological future is so intimately bound up in its whole institutional future that it is inappropriate to separate decision making on technology from fundamental policy. Accordingly, in the next section of this report the committee makes recommendations on the structure and role of the highest management in LC. For the moment, it simply emphasizes one need that has become very clear to it—the need for transparent and accountable decision making. The committee rarely found cases of indefensible decisions made about technology or budgets, but it found many cases where suspicion and resentment flourish in an atmosphere of uncollegial decisions taken without full openness and accountability. This approach to decision making has led over time to the erosion of trust and the rise of duplicate systems ("if they can't do it for us, we'll do it ourselves"). The committee is not in a position to estimate the costs of this pathology to the system as a whole, but they are real and substantial.

In sum, technology decisions need to be made centrally and openly, with priorities clearly set by the line managers of the Library. Technology professionals should provide expertise and deliver service, not set policy or priorities.

More specifically, the Library of Congress needs an in-house technology group to evaluate Library-wide information and technology needs and provide guidance to the service units. This group must have the resources and talent to understand needs throughout the Library and to anticipate problems. Technical innovation is becoming increasingly information based: that is, more and more about how to create, find, and share information. For example, there is no overall plan to manage and disseminate online content. Various component organizations have pilot projects. The NDLP has an architecture for its own projects—online delivery of digital reproductions. But the NDLP finding aids are digital works in their own right, and that part of NDLP needs to be integrated with the ILS. The Library has not seriously considered a systemwide approach for collecting, archiving, and disseminating online documents.

No one within the Library is explicitly looking at technology and technical trends, envisioning where technology will be 5 years out. No one is bringing that vision to the major service units and content innovators and saying to them, "This is what IT could bring to you in 5 years;

how would you use it?" Being reactive and merely prioritizing scarce resources will not answer these longer-term questions.

The Information Technology Services (ITS) Directorate is chartered to provide a service to the rest of the Library. It is not chartered or budgeted to generate ideas about the Library's future, even as that future relates to technology. Even for shorter-term technical matters, such as online content delivery, there is no organized plan for the Library as a whole. The THOMAS initiative to distribute congressional material publicly came from the Speaker of the House of Representatives, not from LC.

The current ITS Directorate and staff are not well suited to provide technical vision, strategy, or technical leadership for the Library. These roles require an outward-looking organization that participates in national and international library initiatives. No other part of the Library is providing technical leadership either. There is no indication that current initiatives like the Planning, Programming, Budgeting, Evaluation, Executing, and Evaluation System (PPBEEES) will change this.[14] Other parts of the Library naturally emphasize their core business and focus on the short-term technical issues needed to meet their goals. Expectations of ITS seem unrealistically inflated and unrealistically cynical at the same time. ITS was initially excluded from full participation in the Digital Futures Group, and it played a subsidiary role in decision making during the ILS process.

The Digital Futures Group evolved during the time it took to prepare and write this report, and it continues to evolve. The committee's sense is that it represents strategic "adhocracy": that is, a gathering of people and units chosen because of their interest and willingness to participate, not because they represent the right mix of authority and responsibility across the Library. Their mission has been to institutionalize some of the NDLP project in the Library, but it has been conceived too narrowly and too tactically. This temporary alliance of some, but not all, of the relevant managers is no substitute for strategic management.

Given that the Library needs technical leadership, and given that the ITS Directorate is not structured or staffed to provide that leadership, the committee proposes instead that the Library needs a new organization to provide the needed leadership—call it, say, the IT vision, strategy, research, and planning (ITVSRP) group. This group would be chartered to lead the Library of Congress, and the national and world libraries, into

---

[14]PPBEEES is an initiative of the Planning, Management, and Evaluation Directorate, which is discussed in the "Executive Management" section.

the digital age. It would also provide strategic technical thinking for the Library. Members of the ITVSRP group would have a good grasp of current technologies, be effective communicators and diplomats both within LC and without (to help build bridges to industry and academia), and have some grasp of how LC works today. (See below for the committee's recommendation for the leader of this group.) The ITVSRP group would be an ongoing working group of leaders from across the Library and the authority to which every unit of the Library would have to go to get approval for significant technology investments. It would have a small full-time staff.

One important role of the ITVSRP group would be to pull together the best technical workers and visionaries from all sections of the Library and to foster cross-fertilization among technicians, librarians, and researchers, both within the Library and on the national and international stages.

When the committee reviewed (Chapter 2) the several divisions of LC that deal with specific formats of material (maps, prints/photographs, and so on), it asked whether it would be better to expand the scope of the divisions or to create another division for digital artifacts. The committee remains cautious on this topic. On the one hand, there is expertise in, say, the Geography and Map Division that can and should be extended to deal with all forms of cartography, from manuscript to digital. On the other hand, there are cross-organizational advantages to standardizing technologies and thinking about the specific features of digital artifacts. In the end, the committee expects that digital versions of analog artifacts can and should be housed and managed in the units that would manage the items if they were analog. But this will create the specific challenge of building cross-organizational conversation and learning to ensure that digital management is carried out in the most efficient and effective ways. This is not a technological question, and it would not be appropriate for the existing ITS organization to take the primary responsibility in this area. The proposed ITVSRP group would be the natural locus for such engagement.

Outside Expertise

Elsewhere in this report the committee considers some areas in which LC can and should consider outsourcing parts of its technology support. This is most appropriate where existing federal HR, salary, and procurement policies make it difficult or impossible for LC to acquire goods and services economically on its own.

The same analysis can and should be applied to the acquisition of technical expertise. Given the limitations on LC's ability to hire and retain top professional staff and given the striking lack of mobility of staff—both librarians and technologists—within the Library, it is appropriate and necessary that LC use its position and prestige to invite the advice and expertise of a broad range of experts from the for-profit, not-for-profit, and public sectors, including representative users of LC's collections and services. The committee recommends the creation of an external technical advisory board (TAB), under a distinguished outside chair, to sit on a semiannual basis formally with the Executive Committee of the Library. The TAB would (1) advise the Executive Committee of developments and directions in information technology that the TAB thinks will be relevant to the Library's future and (2) offer specific advice on initiatives and enterprises that the library has in hand with the ITVSRP group. In a way, this ongoing TAB would carry on and institutionalize the work of the Committee on an Information Technology Strategy for the Library of Congress. A single report by the committee can—one hopes—have value, but that value is limited. To be able to consult a body of experts on an ongoing basis would continually refresh LC's thinking and direction. The TAB should include librarians from the United States and abroad with a broad vision of the future of libraries, as well as technology specialists with expertise in relevant areas. The prestige and position of LC should make it relatively easy to recruit new members for this body on a continuous basis. The committee further recommends that the technology awareness of LC be enhanced by creating a limited number of visiting research positions within LC for experts (junior to mid-career level) from around the country and the world. These individuals would come to LC for, say, 6 months or a year to work on projects from which they would create work of value to the library profession as a whole, develop their own careers, and, by interacting with appropriate LC staff, catalyze the technology thinking and practice of the organization.[15]

Findings and Recommendations

Finding: Current decision making at the Library regarding information technology is neither transparent nor strategic. In

---

[15]Comparable programs in other parts of the federal government could inform the parameters of a program at the Library: White House fellows, congressional fellows, and rotating program directors at the National Science Foundation and the Defense Advanced Research Projects Agency. Examples of more senior positions include the chief economist and chief technologist positions at the Federal Communications Commission. It should be acknowledged that LC has taken some initiative to bring outsiders to the Library for limited terms (e.g., NDLP's American Memory fellows and the newly created fellowships in conservation).

particular, the lines distinguishing central responsibility from service unit responsibility are unclear.

Finding: Priority setting within the Information Technology Services Directorate is largely free from review by senior management.

Finding: The current level of attention to technical vision and strategy within the Library is not adequate, and the flow of information and ideas from the library community and the information technology sector at large into the Library needs to be enhanced.

Recommendation: The Library should establish an information technology vision, strategy, research, and planning (ITVSRP) group.

Recommendation: The Library should establish an external technical advisory board (TAB).

Recommendation: The Library should not appoint a chief information officer at this time.

Recommendation: The Library should create a limited number of visiting research positions in areas such as digital libraries and digital archiving and preservation.

EXECUTIVE MANAGEMENT

It is no longer possible, if it ever was, for senior management of large organizations to regard information technology as a black box to be controlled and managed by technologists. Certainly a library, the core of whose business is the storage and preservation of information, needs to integrate strategic and tactical thinking about information technology into every level of its management vision. One reason for the committee's reluctance to recommend the creation of a chief information officer position is its belief that to do so in the present environment would have the effect of continuing to defer the day when the core of LC's management takes up its full responsibility in this area.

There are four places in LC today where broad strategic management occurs. In each of the four, however, there are defects that impede the achievement of LC's mission.

In day-to-day bureaucratic terms, the recently founded Planning,

Management and Evaluation Directorate (PMED) office theoretically con-
solidates planning and strategic direction for the Library as a whole. The
PPBEEES process that PMED has initiated is intended to integrate planning and to support decision making. Creation of such a capability is
long overdue, but the committee believes that there has been a fundamental failure of imagination in the way that organization was created. It
seems to treat all units of the Library as functionally similar and to see
itself as merely an honest broker in managing the flow of paper and in
encouraging people to think farther ahead than before. There can be
value to such management, but it is apparent to the committee that it is
precisely in the most volatile areas of the Library's strategic future (ITS,
Library Services) that this initiative is being greeted with the greatest
skepticism and will make the least difference.

One factor here is that PMED is staffed by individuals who have no
experience with LC or with libraries generally but, rather, bring their
government sector managerial expertise to bear on in-house procedures.
The committee has some reservations about whether the government sector is the *only* place to look for external management expertise—LC was
notably successful with two of its relatively recent senior management
appointments precisely because it went outside the government sector—
but regardless of those reservations, this office will clearly add a layer of
bureaucracy and will have little of substantive strategic value to offer.
The PMED office will be challenged to demonstrate that it adds value
congruent with the direct and indirect costs it imposes (indirect costs:
time and effort spent by other Library units in complying with PMED
procedures), and there remains a need to create strategic planning capability in LC that offers the right mix of information gathering and knowledge management, R&D management, and strategic insight.

The committee believes and recommends that the best way forward
for LC at present is to address this need by appointing a second deputy
librarian. This individual would be responsible for overall strategic planning for the Library, would supervise ITS, would chair the ITVSRP group,
would manage the relationship with the external TAB, and would sit with
the librarian, the deputy librarian, and the chief of staff at the highest level
of the organization. This individual would not in any way be a traditional
CIO but would act at a level one step higher in the strategic structure of
the organization. She or he would include information technology and its
implications in a broad view of the institution's strategic needs but would
focus first of all on those strategic needs.

If distinction of title is necessary and useful, then the committee would
suggest that the two relevant offices be deputy librarian (Operations)—
the position now in place—and deputy librarian (Strategic Initiatives).
The committee believes that it would be easier to recruit a highly quali-

fied individual for this position than for the CIO position and that the holder of the position would add more directly and substantively than a CIO to the integration of technology into every aspect of the central planning and management of the organization. The committee's recommendations in Chapter 3—for example, regarding the closer relationship that is needed between the Copyright Office and Library Services (including the NDLP)—need to be pursued and managed at the highest level: such an individual could do that. (The committee believes that such an arrangement would quickly expose opportunities for further integration and cross-organizational learning throughout LC. Many of the individuals inside and outside LC with whom the committee spoke returned repeatedly to the relative lack of integration among the several components of the whole organization.)

A second place where strategic management should occur in LC is the Executive Committee. This group meets regularly with the librarian and is the highest policy body in the organization. For example, it signs off on the final budget request to Congress. The committee has not attended the regular meetings of that group, but based on its discussions with LC staff throughout the study it has the sense that:

- The deliberations are mainly tactical rather than strategic, operational rather than visionary, and event-driven rather than proactive.
- There are significant political tensions within the organization that are played out in that group, reducing its effectiveness as a management team. Put another way, participants in that group come to the room representing their organizations and fight their battles there on those terms, but they are not seen in their organizations as representing the Executive Committee or its decisions.
- The director of ITS has only a rotating seat on the Executive Committee, so for substantial periods of time, ITS's interests and capabilities are unrepresented in that group. Given that the technology budget of the whole Library is held and managed largely by the director of ITS, this is a crucial disconnect. The director of ITS should sit as a permanent member of the Executive Committee.

At the Executive Committee retreat on October 31 and November 1, 1999, the Operations Committee was formed, to be chaired by the deputy librarian; it replaced the Senior Management Reporting Group and is intended to serve as a forum for senior programmatic and infrastructure managers to solve problems and share information. The Executive Committee delegated operational decisions directly to the Operations Committee. This plan by the EC to delegate tactical authority is a promising development.

The third locus of strategic management in LC today has grown up very recently to fill the gaps left by the existing management structures. The Digital Futures Group is largely a partnership between the National Digital Library and Library Services, with participation from ITS. It has been the source of significant new budgetary recommendations for FY01 and is clearly seen as the locus of vision for the digital future of the Library. However, the group is also based on the premise that the digital future is somehow separable and distinct from the future of libraries generally—a fatal premise at this date.[16] The committee hopes that in recommending (1) the creation of the ITVSRP group and (2) the appointment of a new deputy librarian, it can show the way both to generalizing IT vision, planning, and accountability across the Library and to integrating such planning into the broadest decision making of the organization.

The Office of the Librarian

Finally, the Office of the Librarian can and must be the locus of strategic direction for the Library. At this moment in history, that office labors under two disadvantages:

- None of the three most senior members of Library-wide administration (the librarian, the deputy librarian, the chief of staff) had a background in library administration before taking up his or her present appointment. The librarian will always be a political appointment and hence chosen for qualities above and beyond those for which a CEO in a private-sector organization would be chosen. The deputy librarian and the chief of staff were appointed, moreover, to address specific organizational issues of high priority—a limited focus was accepted in return for the specific, substantive contributions they could make and have made. The committee is recommending a second deputy librarian position in just that spirit, to address the burning need of the Library for this decade—specific expertise in strategic thinking and information technology and the ability to build collaborations with the library community and information industry at the highest level in the Library. (The committee observes also that during the tenure of the present librarian, links between LC and the rest of the national and international library community have been forged at and below the level of major service unit heads, for example, at the Library Services or Law Library level. The strategic heart of

---

[16]In particular, the committee believes that the Law Library, the Copyright Office, and CRS all have an important stake in the same "digital future" that is addressed by the Digital Futures Group.

the Library, however, has become relatively isolated from and innocent of contemporary library practice and thinking.

• None of the three senior officers has any specific background or special competence in the field of information technology.

The net effect of these two disadvantages is that the ultimate decision-making power in the Library is underinformed and underqualified to think strategically about the future of the Library and its adoption of information technology in support of its missions at this time. This report can point out directions and validating concepts. But in the end, there is no substitute for leadership that understands the issues directly and that is proactive in leading the process of analysis and planning. What is seen is an administration that is technologically more reactive than proactive and far too inclined to make modest (although accurate) demurrals when faced with questions of the kind this report addresses. In the future, appointments within the Office of the Librarian must seek individuals who have the authority and the experience to lead rather than follow in matters that require technological understanding and to make judgments that will have weight in the Library and beyond. Until such appointments begin to be made, LC will be seen as technologically reactive and will be perceived as a follower rather than a leader in the world of libraries.

Finally, the Office of the Librarian serves best when it is a source of vision for the Library as a whole, a vision that must now expand to embrace the range of technological innovation and possibility that both directly affects the Library and transforms the social setting within which the Library does its work. Similarly, the Office of the Librarian functions best as the recipient and manager of information coming up from all across the Library about what is happening and what is possible. An easy and effective flow of communication about IT initiatives and possibilities from the Office of the Librarian to the whole of the senior management team and to the Library beyond is vital, but the communication must be bidirectional and must be a constantly reinforcing source of new ideas, clarified vision, and refined application of technology in the service of LC's users.

New Tasks for Executive Management

The transformation of libraries everywhere by the onrush of information technology is inevitable. But unless major changes occur, bureaucratic fossilization can and will persist, reducing the effectiveness and increasing the cost of new ideas and projects. A vital part of effective management is not simply to acquire the new or automate the old but to look broadly at processes to see what can and should be changed to take full advantage of new opportunities.

Many operations at LC would benefit from systematic and complete review. Such review should look at all steps of an operation to assess efficiency. More important, and more difficult to answer, is the question, Need this be done at all? Many individual steps seem unnecessary. Merely automating manual operations is not enough to ensure efficiency.

The Copyright Office's charge, for instance, produces scenes reminiscent of the struggles of the sorcerer's apprentice. The sheer mass of what there is to contend with using a mechanism like none other in the world (i.e., created especially and only for Copyright) overwhelms those who might otherwise think of new solutions. Merely to automate what is there now is a mistake. The selection of the ILS has been guided by the need to resolve and integrate all of the existing cataloging tools—SCORPIO, MUMS, etc.—rather than by consideration of future needs (and indeed, integrated library systems tend to be retrospective tools in any event).

Another example is the relatively low level of workflow rationalization in the Library. Many operations are done with paper forms that involve many steps. This costs time and money, as information is transferred from one form to another. The second phase of the ILS implementation expects to reengineer the core Library Services functions; however, that phase not only should involve attention to the processes directly affected by the ILS but also should be considered an opportunity for institution-wide reengineering.

Many of the workflows of the Library could profitably be investigated. The committee was told, for example, that it takes at least a week and six signatures on a paper form to assign a new employee an electronic mailbox. In most organizations, this task is accomplished via an e-mail message from the employee's supervisor. Wherever it looked at the actual workflow affecting individuals, the committee found such tales of redundancy and waste. The ILS implementation office has been a successful and exemplary model of cross-organizational coordination and cooperation.[17] The model needs to be studied and taken as a basis for an even more ambitious study of existing business processes: how they may be improved by the application of information technology and—equally important—how they may be reduced or eliminated by astute management informed by the possibilities of information technology.

Even more important are the fundamental transformations of thinking about what the Library is and how it functions, as outlined in the

---

[17]The ILS implementation is discussed at length in Chapter 8.

earlier chapters. In the end, the success or failure of the Library in the digital age will be marked chiefly by its ability to rethink and reinvent (along with comparable institutions around the world) the way collecting and cataloging are done, whether the artifacts are digital or analog. If this report has a single central message, it is this one.

Findings and Recommendations

Finding: The future of libraries and the future of information technology are inseparable.

Finding: The Planning, Management, and Evaluation Directorate might assist usefully with the process of strategic planning, but there remains a need for improved substantive input into the strategic planning process.

Finding: Before taking up their present appointments, the three senior-most members of Library-wide administration (the librarian, deputy librarian, and chief of staff) did not have particular expertise or experience in library administration or information technology.

Recommendation: The committee recommends appointment of a new deputy librarian (Strategic Initiatives) to supplement the strengths and capabilities of the three members of the Library-wide administration now in place.

Finding: Much of the workflow of the Library is manually based. There seems to be much opportunity for workflow automation. However, the approach should not be to use information technology to automate existing processes but rather to examine the processes themselves and rationalize them across unit boundaries before new information systems are designed and developed or acquired. The Whole-Book Cataloging Pilot Program of some years ago shows how such reengineering can be piloted in limited areas and then extended to a broader range of Library operations. The Copyright Office and the interface between it and Library Services is the first place that deserves attention.

Recommendation: The committee recommends that the Library publish, by January 1, 2001, its own review of this report and an outline of the agenda that the Library will pursue.

8

INFORMATION TECHNOLOGY INFRASTRUCTURE

The information technology (IT) infrastructure and the work of the major service units have long been considered to be orthogonal at the Library of Congress, but that is becoming less and less true because of the movement toward a digital infrastructure for information acquisition, preservation, and access. In addition, current trends in technology and its future uses will continue to suggest and enable new services and new information sources for the Library.

This chapter looks at how the Library of Congress (LC) provides and uses information technology today and offers guidance for the future. Although the chapter occasionally makes specific observations about the organization, it is not a traditional review of information technology within an organization as it might be performed by a management consulting team. Instead, the focus is on the way the Library uses IT as a whole and how key technologies such as IT security, networking, database management, and multimedia are being used, with the aim of learning how IT supports the missions of the Library.

It is not an accident, however, that this particular chapter comes toward the end of the report. Infrastructure choices can and must be made with a full understanding of the institutional mission and the tactical choices made to achieve that mission. One tendency the committee has seen in LC (and one familiar elsewhere in society) is the willingness to be persuaded that a technology that is new and well spoken of elsewhere must be good for something and, more particularly, that a technology or a product that LC can get either at a discount or at no cost is preferable to other products.

Additionally, vision and direction must be set clearly before making technological choices, because it is so difficult to change technologies at the Library. For example, the Library is still affected by the decision made years ago to standardize around OS/2, which led to the truly bizarre situation of needing to install (in 1999) desktop machines that would be able to "dual boot" (i.e., run either as OS/2 machines for certain legacy applications created during the reign of OS/2 or as Windows 95 machines).

THE INFORMATION TECHNOLOGY SERVICES DIRECTORATE

The Information Technology Services (ITS) Directorate is the computer and communication systems and services group for the Library of Congress. It acquires, supports, and maintains the computer, networking, and telephone systems for LC. ITS does most of the in-house programming, handles much of the computer-systems training, and monitors contracts with software and hardware vendors. It has a staff of approximately 200 people (see Figure 8.1).

The ITS Directorate also manages many small to medium-size development projects involving 1 to 10 people for between 3 months and 2 years. Projects generally start with a request from a service organization. ITS works with the client organization to scope the project and to write a requirements document. The project then gets approved in a fairly informal way by consultation among the senior ITS staff and the client organization. Once the project is approved, ITS staff work with the client using a spiral development methodology to manage their work. When the projects are deployed, ITS administers and evolves the applications.

ITS produces substantial and serviceable high-level architectural documents on topics such as storage and retrieval of digital content, centrally supported systems infrastructure, and telecommunications.[1] Its server and storage architectures meet its customers' needs.

Although it is not what in industry would be seen as an exceptionally responsive or cutting-edge technical organization, given the many con-

---

[1]See "Technology Architecture for Storage and Retrieval of Digital Content at the Library of Congress" (ITS, February 1999); "Technology Architecture for the Centrally Supported Systems Infrastructure at the Library of Congress (ITS, February 1999); and "Telecommunications Architecture at the Library of Congress" (ITS, January 1999). All of these are unpublished, internal planning documents.

195

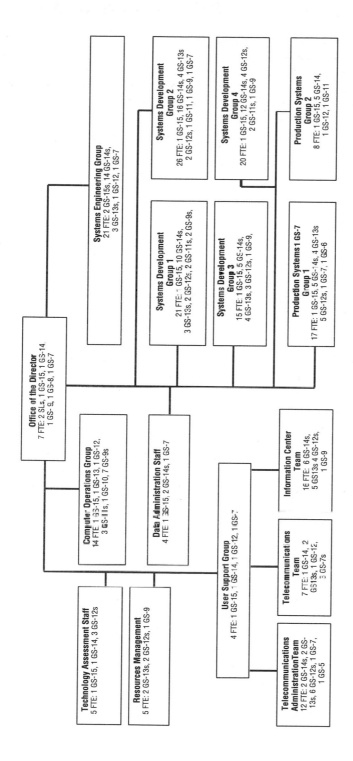

FIGURE 8.1 Organizational structure for the Information Technology Services Directorate. FTE, full-time equivalent(s); GS, general scale; SL, senior level. SOURCE: Unpublished ITS organizational chart and information provided to the committee in 2000.

straints of its environment, ITS adequately provides basic services. The Library of Congress systems work and people get their jobs done, even though—as is true in other organizations—they want more services than the central organization can possibly deliver within budget constraints. The ITS organization at LC operates under unusually difficult hiring constraints (discussed in Chapter 7). These constraints exacerbate the difficulty of attracting talented IT workers, which is a problem that is shared throughout the economy.

The middle-level management cadre seems to be hard-working and competent. They are making the best of limited budgets and limited flexibility with staffing in terms of day-to-day support. They prudently managed the deployment of 5,000 desktop PCs and the transition to systems that addressed the Y2K problem.

ITS staff do not, however, have the technical depth to meet the current challenges. They cannot keep current in areas like networks, security, middleware, and databases (the topics the committee discussed with them) because the Library of Congress does not budget adequate time or money for their continuing education or attendance at professional conferences. Nor is there a budget for members of the ITS staff to spend time investigating new technology. Broader participation in strategic Library initiatives by ITS staff could also be a learning experience for them, allowing them to understand end-user issues and concerns and—probably—inspiring them to consider more innovative technical solutions to the Library's mid- to long-term issues. As a result of the constraints mentioned, the Library lacks a central repository of knowledge about emerging technologies and a capability for experimenting with them. This causes gaps and inefficiencies when these technologies are deployed. The ITS organization also does not have the bench strength to assess critical technology issues from multiple viewpoints or to withstand key personnel departures (this is a particular example of the human resources difficulties described in depth in Chapter 7).

Outsourcing

Historically, ITS did most systems development in-house using ITS staff. Over the last 8 years, the Library has increasingly used third-party software to meet its needs. The primary example of this is the Voyager system from Endeavor Software that forms the basis for the new Integrated Library System (ILS). Similarly, the Copyright Office has contracted with a third party to build the CORDS system, and the Human Resources Services Directorate is using PeopleSoft software. This shift to outsourcing has changed the ITS skills mix: increasingly, ITS staff are acting as contract monitors and administrators rather than developers.

They spend an increasing proportion of their time writing requirements documents, negotiating contracts, managing contractors, and acting as liaison between the vendors and the Library's service organizations.

Outsourcing obviates the need to have large quantities of in-house, low-level technical expertise—the requisite talent can be hired on demand. It may well be that the Library could outsource many of the development, support, and operations tasks performed by the ITS organization; this option has not been sufficiently explored. However, outsourcing also increases the need for people who have a deep understanding of both LC requirements and information technology and who can plan what to outsource and can select, negotiate with, and supervise outside vendors. Application service providers claim that they can perform such functions more economically than in-house organizations. There are, of course, numerous vendors that provide systems in fairly standardized domains such as human resources (and indeed, LC is using commercial off-the-shelf software for this directorate). However, even for areas that may appear to be unique at first glance, existing applications elsewhere might be adapted for LC use. For example, copyright registration is not completely unrelated to other registration processes—those for property deeds, cars, patents, and so on—so it should not be assumed that because the Copyright Office is a unique institution, it must necessarily need custom software. The Library gained experience with out-sourcing in two large projects: the apparently successful ILS (see below for a discussion) and the incomplete and uncertain CORDS project, discussed in detail in Chapters 2 and 3.

The committee believes that the Library will increasingly outsource its IT tasks but will continue to need a strong in-house IT organization to perform some in-house development, training, support, and operations and to review and monitor the outside contracts as well as provide technical feedback on proposed contracts. ITS will need to develop skills and processes for producing useful and timely contract reviews.

The Integrated Library System as a Textbook Case of Outsourcing

The scope and timing of the Integrated Library System make it the outsourcing project for which the most useful information is available. If the Library is to undergo a transformation in the born-digital area, then the ILS project is one of the best guides to its potential success, since it touches a huge part of the organization and is a major IT initiative.

A Library-wide ILS program office involving staff from each of the Library's units managed the acquisition and deployment of the ILS. The requirements came from the end users. Having the users select the system forced them to make the hard decisions about what would be included and what was out. Going to an outside vendor and buying a turnkey system largely defined what was possible (or affordable). This process worked. If the users had gone to ITS for a home-grown system it would have had every feature imaginable and would probably have taken an inordinate amount of time to develop. There is a feeling in ITS that deficiencies in the ILS would not have been acceptable in a custom-built ITS system.

The budget for ILS was a separate line item, under the associate librarian for Library Services and the deputy librarian ($5.5 million to start and $16 million over 7 years to complete the project). The original request for proposals covered acquisitions, cataloging, serials check-in, circulation, and an online public catalog. This system replaces a suite of in-house mainframe applications developed by LC over the last 30 years. The ILS database has 12 million bibliographic entries, nearly 5 million authority records, over 12 million holdings records, approximately 26,000 patron records, over 30,000 vendor records, and more than 60,000 order records. The application supports 3,000 simultaneous users, including members of the public making requests via the LC Web site. The Library selected Endeavor Information Systems' client/server Voyager system. Voyager supports Windows clients accessing a large Sun/Solaris backend server system (SUN E10000 with 56 processors and 64 gigabytes of memory) running Voyager on an Oracle database. A SUN E3500 is the Web server and a SUN E4500 is the test server.

The Library does not have source code access to Voyager. Endeavor fixes bugs and provides new releases periodically. (Since installation of the system, Endeavor Information Systems has been acquired by Reed Elsevier PLC, one of the largest scientific publishers in the world. It is unclear how this development will affect libraries that use the product.)

The ILS program office worked with implementation teams and with ITS and other organizations. ITS managed the hardware and software installations on the servers and is operating the ILS system. ITS also worked with Endeavor via the ILS program office, although clearly Library Services personnel were in charge. If such arrangements are to become increasingly commonplace at LC, then the ITS staff will need training in contract management to further develop their ability to supervise contracts.

The ILS implementation involved 82 teams comprising more than 500 people. There are a small number of ILS technical groups (three) compared to the number of policy groups (nine). The three ILS technical groups address host, workstations, and user support. This echoes what is going on within LC: technology is underemphasized by groups other than ITS, even in major technical undertakings. For example, the first large deployment problem for ILS was technical (the multiprocessor problem discussed below). The committee cannot tell yet if large problems in other areas, such as training staff to use the system, were successfully solved. That particular problem is less of an issue in ITS-developed systems because they are designed specifically to meet Library of Congress user requirements.

The ILS was first rolled out for operational use in the autumn of 1999. The early trials, in the spring of 1999, were promising. Problems were identified, but overall, the team was optimistic. Benchmark tests at the hardware vendor site in the spring indicated that more memory was required—and the Library complied. Early deployments in August and completion of deployment by October 1, 1999, went well but exposed some more performance problems. ITS continues to work with Endeavor, Oracle, and Sun to address these problems.

The ILS reduced cataloging productivity during the transition and training periods. Training staff for the transition to the ILS involved delicate negotiations with the unions to reduce the required productivity level during the transition period. Productivity may be even lower because Voyager is not tuned to the unique characteristics of the Library of Congress. The Library staff had, moreover, been using the old system for 20 years, and they knew it inside out. Switching to the new system (with the old workflow) is bound to be slower for a while, although the ILS program leadership expects this productivity decline to be a temporary one. Designing a new workflow based on the ILS should yield productivity benefits. That reengineering effort, begun in 2000, includes business process improvements and continuation of the conversion of the manual processes (shelf-list and serials).

The ILS replaces a number of manual and automated systems. Its integration provides inventory control that can help improve physical security, an ongoing issue at the Library, and that substantially reduces the number of steps necessary to track down a copy of a book requested by a Congressperson. By integrating a number of functions under one project, ILS can realize the kinds of synergies and savings that could be realized on an even larger scale if ITS or an organization involving ITS were tasked with reviewing and monitoring systems and infrastructure development across the Library.

In summary, the committee sees ILS as a success story. The Library built the cross-functional organization that coordinated both the technical and organizational issues. It is unlikely that ITS could have built such an ambitious system in-house. The system is operational, and the Library is poised to reengineer the workflows, which may yield substantial productivity improvements.

This example also demonstrates some other lessons and raises a few issues. It can be hard for LC to buy off-the-shelf software for library-specific applications, because the Library is often many times larger than the next largest institution (indeed, accommodating LC's size was a challenge for the ILS implementation). Things that work for others may not scale up to LC needs. In the specific area of integrated library systems, LC is following rather than leading the large university libraries. The Library's size and variety of offerings alone are a challenge to the vendors. In a different world, the Library of Congress might have led the transition to an integrated library system. As it happened, the Library did not have the skill or organization to develop an ILS, so it is just an observer (and a very large customer) on the new scene. The fact that LC was slow to adopt an ILS reflects the enormity of the task, some budget issues, and the fact that the old system was actually working. The Y2K issue provided the additional motivation for the Congress and the Library to act.

How will the Library participate (*if* it participates) in the development of next-generation automated library systems? The original case for the ILS mentioned better integration with digital library efforts. The intent was to gain built-in Web browsing capability and connections to Web sites, including its own. It is now time to look beyond the initial installation of the ILS.

The Information Technology Services Directorate As a Service Organization

Organizational units served by ITS express frustration about the difficulty of getting staff time and other resources from ITS, although they generally understand the difficulties of serving a variety of organizational units, each with its own priorities, from a single pool of people and budget. The committee believes this frustration comes from two basic flaws in the ITS Directorate: ITS does not act like a service organization, and its services are free.

The ITS Directorate has no explicit service-level agreements[2] with its clients and indeed has few performance metrics, either for internal use or for reporting to ITS clients. With no regular or public measures of system performance and availability and no support metrics, there is no way for organizational units to compare the actual usefulness of ITS services with the potential usefulness of decentralized IT support units. In fact, since

---

[2]See *Complete Guide to IT Service Level Agreements: Matching Service Quality to Business Needs*, by Andrew Hiles and Philip Jan Rothstein (Brookfield, Conn.: Rothstein Associates, 1999). Also see <http://www.amdahl.com/aplus/servlevel/contents.html>.

there are so few metrics, ITS cannot even evaluate its own performance or measure internal improvements.

The lack of ITS reporting is related to the fact that ITS services are obtained by persuasion rather than by paying for them. There is not even any direct way to determine, after the fact, how much a particular project costs. ITS is not a budget line item for service units, yet IT expenses and staff account for nearly 10 percent of the total budget. Better accounting for IT costs would facilitate better overall management. The Library's management needs to rationalize roles, authority, and responsibilities within the organization as a whole. There needs to be clear definition of the role of the individual units and the role of ITS. ITS itself should function as a service bureau for LC as a whole. Funding should come to it through its clients, the various service units. Those units should have the option of using or refusing to use ITS services within broad limits, short of causing outright financial or technical inefficiency for the Library. That is, individual units should be able to contract for services outside or perform them within their own units or agree with other units of LC on joint ventures or contract with ITS.[3] In return, the information technology vision, strategy, research, and planning (ITVSRP) group discussed in Chapter 7 and, ultimately, the new deputy librarian should sit in judgment on cases where allowing decentralized or external service provision would be uneconomical or technically unsound for the Library as a whole. For example, the Library needs a resource that can provide technical advice on contracts and recommendations about current and future technology. ITS should not be the only unit making those decisions, though obviously both ITS and other units will make recommendations according to their best professional judgment.

If these steps are taken (and for this it would probably be best to engage an outside management consulting firm with experience in this area for a short time during the restructuring under the new deputy librarian), then the cost of ITS will be more clearly understood. A unit with an IT project will see the full costs identified in its budget and know how much it is paying ITS and how much it is spending internally. With such clear information, it will be better able to make judgments about priorities and the relative value of upgrades and replacements. ITS then becomes a market-based service unit existing to meet the needs of customers who pay the bills for services rendered. That market discipline would go a

---

[3]For additional discussion of the merits of outsourcing versus in-house support, see "IT Outsourcing: Maximize Flexibility and Control," by Mary C. Lacity, Leslie P. Willcocks, and David F. Feeny, in *Harvard Business Review*, May/June 1995, pp. 57-81.

long way toward resolving the continuing disputes about resource levels, scheduling, and general relations with users.

Information Technology Support Beyond the ITS Organization

Besides ITS staff, approximately 200 people in the individual service units perform IT-related functions such as frontline support or dedicated IT development for their service unit. Some organizations (e.g., the Congressional Research Service) have built their own IT group to avoid having to compete for ITS's attention for some projects (although large-scale initiatives such as the Inquiry Status Information System (ISIS) and the Legislative Information System (LIS) involve partnering with ITS). This in effect assigns a cost to the ITS services—CRS can now do a project in-house or contract it to ITS. ITS can argue that as a larger and broader service organization, it provides better service. Certainly, CRS continues to rely on ITS for phone, network, e-mail, and Internet services, infrastructure that is best supported by a central IT organization. However, CRS staff are increasingly developing their own small applications with their local IT staff. The decision by CRS to spend its own money rather than try to make use of the nominally free service provided by ITS indicates strongly that the system for budgeting and setting priorities for ITS activities is not functioning adequately.

Findings and Recommendations

Finding: As the Library increasingly outsources its information technology tasks, it will continue to need a strong in-house information technology organization to perform some in-house development, training, support, and operations and to review and monitor these outside contracts as well as to provide technical feedback on proposed contracts.[4]

Finding: The Library is underinvesting in the continuing education of its Information Technology Services Directorate staff in technical development and in new skills such as contract management.

---

[4]Or, as was done with NDLP, a relatively autonomous team formed within the Library. This strategy of formalized skunk works has been very effective in other industries. Notable examples are IBM's PC business unit in the early 1980s and HP's Ink Jet business unit in the late 1980s. In general, any initiative that addresses "disruptive technologies" (see *The Innovator's Dilemma*, by Clayton Christensen (Cambridge, Mass.: Harvard Business School Press, 1997) could be handled this way.

Recommendation: The Library should budget much more of each technical staff member's time for continuing education and participation at professional conferences and should allocate more funds to cover travel and registration expenses.

Recommendation: A practice and a budget should be established to partner members of the Information Technology Services Directorate staff who are interested in exploring a particular new technology with staff in the service units or with outside institutions that are interested in working on a pilot project applicable to the Library's needs.

Finding: The ITS Directorate lacks measurement and reporting systems and a cost-accounting system that would allow it and its clients to make trade-offs among implementation alternatives and to evaluate the quality of the ITS Directorate's service.

Recommendation: Together, the Library's service organizations and its Information Technology Services Directorate should institute service-level agreements based on metrics of system availability, performance, and support requests. These metrics should be used to track ITS Directorate process improvements. Developing and implementing service-level agreements should be a high priority for the new deputy librarian (Strategic Initiatives) and the information technology vision, strategy, research, and planning group.

Recommendation: Wherever possible, services provided by the Information Technology Services Directorate should be charged against the budgets of the client organization within the Library. This would allow comparing the costs and benefits of servicing from within the client organization, outsourcing to the ITS Directorate, or outsourcing outside the Library.

HARDWARE AND SOFTWARE

The Library IT infrastructure is undergoing a major transformation as this report is being written. First, the desktop PCs have all been upgraded, from a variety of machines to a fairly uniform collection of 5,000 desktop Intel Pentium II processors running Windows 95, Corel Office, and Netscape Navigator. ITS is phasing out the use of OS/2 and Windows 3.1.

The upgrade of several thousand desktop PCs and the training of the staff on the "new" (Windows 95) user interface went fairly smoothly. About 150 people throughout the Library do most of the frontline support. There is one IT support person for every 25 desktop PCs (counting staff in ITS and staff in the service units), which is typical of well-supported organizations. The choice of the 5-year-old Windows 95 over Windows 98 or NT4 reflects the Library's conservatism. ITS plans to automate desktop software deployment using Tivoli, although the committee did not find anyone knowledgeable about this plan, nor is there a resource plan. Today, the process is manual and based on sneaker net.

As discussed in the preceding section, many of the IBM mainframe services were replaced by the ILS. This deployment went as smoothly as could be expected, given the scope of the project and the extreme time pressure to meet the Y2K deadline.

The Library has standardized on IBM AIX and SUN Solaris servers. It is also standardizing on Windows NT4 servers for file and print, phasing out various Netware file and print servers. The Library has contracted with EMC Corporation to provide 42 terabytes of storage to support ILS and other projects over the next several years. The Library has some Sybase databases but has largely standardized on Oracle for its database system and PeopleSoft for human resources applications. Client programming is generally done in Visual Basic and Access, using browsers as client interfaces, although some interfaces have been developed with Powerbuilder. Overall, there is a trend to the Web-based model, including increased use of Java.

For a large organization that relies on IT, it is surprising to find that e-mail is not yet a universal capability within the Library. For example, the LC police force is not connected to e-mail or to some other LC communication systems. It would be an ideal group for wireless communication, either cell phones or pagers with alphanumeric two-way communication. The committee was troubled to find that during a fire emergency, the guards were unaware of the alarm in another LC building.

ITS and the Library of Congress did a good job with respect to Y2K. They had a contingency plan in case deployment of the ILS was delayed, and they executed well in upgrading existing systems, replacing them where necessary.

Information Technology Security

By far the most serious infrastructure problem seen at LC was the lack of IT security. This problem needs urgent attention.[5] The current secu-

---

[5]The Library is not unaware of the importance of IT security and, indeed, has commissioned a number of reports on the subject, which were shared with the committee.

rity policy is driven piecemeal by outside forces, mostly auditors. Auditor input has been valuable when it has focused on a particular area of security and the auditors have followed up to check on the status of specific vulnerabilities. However, audits can also lead to unproductive actions. For example, LC installed a firewall because it was told to do so, without understanding just what it should or could do. This configuration placed the public reading room systems on the inside of the firewall, giving outsiders easy access to the systems the firewall was supposed to protect. On the plus side, previous audits focused on host/operating system security, so that improvements continue to be made to solve the specific vulnerabilities discovered and IT staff have a clear picture of their stand-alone host security and vulnerabilities. They now need to develop an understanding of distributed security issues and skills to deal with them. This is particularly pressing since enhanced connectivity to the Library will provide more and more opportunities for attacks using the network or distributed applications such as the Web, and the Library is a highly visible, attractive target for would-be perpetrators.

The chief security officer has given considerable attention to organizational and human resource issues (such as education and process). However, there is evidence to suggest that organizational issues still require attention—the vulnerability that enabled the THOMAS break-in in January 2000 was understood before the break-in, but LC did not implement an effective defensive measure in a timely fashion. Nor have the technical challenges of distributed security been tackled, and the committee saw no evidence of any plan to do so. As discussed above, concentrating on tactical responses can delay the advent of strategic and sweeping architectural solutions.

For example, many of the different systems rely on passwords for user authentication, with the usual result that users find they must have as many passwords as there are systems they use. To reduce the confusion, LC is using Tivoli to propagate passwords among systems, a typical tactical response but one that does not address fundamental weaknesses. In demonstrations, the committee observed that important passwords were clearly too short and were being sent over the network unencrypted. Work is under way to implement a virtual private network to protect accesses from foreign offices, but more work is needed to protect all distributed logins.

A strategic plan for this area would instead set a goal of moving as quickly as possible (perhaps in small steps) toward a modern, distributed authentication technology, sometimes called "single login" or "network login." Several such schemes are now available using, for example, encrypted telnet, IPSec, X.509 certificates, and Kerberos; they would address the confusion that password propagation is trying to reduce and at the same time eliminate many other alarming security exposures, such as sending passwords over the network in the clear. While the committee heard several organizations mention the need for such technologies, it found no real movement in that direction.

Resources should be devoted immediately to understanding the Library's distributed security needs and concerns. A series of audits targeted at issues such as network access, distributed authentication, access control, and Web security would be the first step in getting specific professional advice on the topics (much as the National Security Agency's review of CRS systems impelled CRS to secure its part of the network). A series of audits might provide the impetus for fixing the security problems identified in the audits; follow-through support from all levels in the organization will be necessary to ensure change. In parallel, a member of the ITS staff with expertise in both security and networks should become knowledgeable about common distributed security errors so as to ensure that the Library does not make them. The completion of this task may necessitate external technical training or consulting services. This person should then perform continuous internal security audits.

One example of the sort of vulnerabilities that an informed audit should catch is unnecessary listeners on TCP ports, which should be shut down. An audit should also address what is perhaps the largest overlooked area of computer security at the Library: auditing and logging. Until recently, since LC staff did not know what information was logged, they did not know if a nonobvious break-in had occurred. As a result of the THOMAS break-in,[6] staff now monitor a subset of their static files for unauthorized changes. It is possible that other logging information exists that they should be viewing. Finally, it is hard—indeed impossible—to enforce security policies with Windows 95; Microsoft recommends NT4 or Windows 2000 for business users. This discussion of security problems merely touches on the problems the committee identified during its discussions with the ITS staff on security issues.

The Library needs to set its own security goals thoughtfully. If it wants to be perceived as a reliable source of information on the Web, it must consider that the lack of security allows alterations to the information it publishes on the Web. The break-in to THOMAS damaged that site's reputation for providing information of high integrity and showed that the THOMAS system and other parts of the LC Web site are vulnerable to attack. In this case, the attack was fairly benign, since it changed data in a more or less obvious manner. But Web disinformation is becom-

---

6 "Hackers Deface Library of Congress Site," by Diane Frank, in *Federal Computer Week*, January 19, 2000, available online at <http://www.fcw.com/fcw/articles/2000/0117/web-lochack-01-19-00.asp>.

ing more sophisticated. Stock traders are increasingly leery of postings to their newsgroups and other sites, for example. An attack on THOMAS could cause a Congress member's constituency to misconstrue a bill and press for a vote that would in fact be counter to its interests.

The Library's future stewardship of digital materials will place further demands on its security infrastructure. As the Library begins to offer controlled access to digital materials, it will need to deploy a more flexible system for their protection. Examples of the restrictions LC may need to honor include copyright and licensing and contractual restrictions such as those that accompany the work of the Shoah Foundation (discussed in Box 1.1). The storage system will need to associate with an item metadata indicating who has access to that item. In addition, it will need to identify its users or their key attributes with confidence in order to apply properly the rules associated with that metadata. As discussed in the *Digital Dilemma,*[7] there are still many outstanding issues, both technical and socioeconomic, including the need to control who can view the contents of an item, what can be copied or referenced from an item, and even how searches and indexing can be supported over all items while still honoring the heterogeneous restrictions involved.

The ITS Data Center Disaster Recovery Strategies and other planning documents outline LC's proposed approach to anticipating a variety of potential disasters that could compromise or destroy LC's unique collections or make its resources unavailable to the Congress and the nation. Unfortunately, Congress did not fund the disaster recovery mechanisms requested by the Library in past years. This is a false economy. As it stands, the LC's digital assets are all stored on Capitol Hill. Most agencies and corporations store their data and programs in two or more locations, so that a disaster at one site would be unlikely to destroy the data at other sites. There should be a complete and current copy of the Library's digital assets at one or more sites, preferably far from Washington, D.C.

Networking

After security problems, computer networking is the next infrastructure issue that needs urgent attention for both current and future needs.

---

[7] For additional discussion on copyright and digital preservation, see Chapter 3 of *The Digital Dilemma,* by the Computer Science and Telecommunications Board, National Research Council (Washington, D.C.: National Academy Press, 2000); "Digital Preservation Needs and Requirements in RLG Member Institutions," by Margaret Hedstrom and Sheon Montgomery, Research Libraries Group, available online at <http://www.rlg.org/preserv/digpres.html>; and the film "Into the Future," by the Council on Library and Information Resources, description available online at <http://www.clir.org/pubs/film/film.html#future>.

The network is underpowered. The Library currently supports approximately 80 percent of staff workstations with token ring network connections. These networks are linked in a collapsed star topology through Cisco routers interconnected via a 155 megabit/second asynchronous transfer mode (ATM) backbone. The token rings are being upgraded to 100 megabit/second Ethernets on an as-needed basis (or as funds are available; as of June 2000, approximately 900 workstations had 100 megabit/second connections). There are several identifiable problems with this structure and plan.

ATM switches are designed to switch digitized telephone traffic; they are a second-best choice for Internet applications because they are more costly and complex than alternatives such as a gigabit Ethernet switch. Also, to avoid massive disruptions during an overload they must be configured either with private virtual circuits (which forfeit the opportunity to take advantage of traffic burstiness) or to begin dropping data when operating well below their rated capacity.[8] This latter concern regarding overload does not currently affect the LC network, presumably because the aggregate load on the ATM switch is being limited by the low-speed token rings. As those token rings are replaced with 100 megabit/second Ethernets and the routers are upgraded for higher data rates, it is likely that the shortcomings of the ATM switch will become more apparent.

As for as-needed local network upgrades, ITS has a poor track record of identifying need in an accurate and timely fashion. For example, the National Digital Library's scanning contractor generates 4 to 5 gigabytes/hour and reports that the network is the bottleneck in getting this data to Library Services. Similarly, the Geography and Map Division creates 300-megabyte files at the rate of 1 to 2 gigabytes/hour, and then wavelet compresses them. The network is the bottleneck. ITS staff did not seem to understand that they needed to upgrade the network to support video, Web access, and future multimedia applications and information transfer everywhere. They should have upgraded the network when the PCs were upgraded rather than getting PCs with antiquated token-ring network cards.

These upgrades should allow continuous data gathering as well as monitoring the use of both the backbone network and the Internet access links, so that the Library can keep ahead of what will undoubtedly be a rapidly rising load. (In industry, a current standard rule for sizing Internet

---

[8]For additional discussion, see "Frames Reaffirmed at ATM's Expense," by Kevin Tolly, in *Network Magazine*, September 1998, pp. 60-64, available online at <http://www.tolly.com/KT/NetworkMagazine/framesreaffirmed9809.htm>, and "Optical Internets and Their Role in Future Telecommunications Systems," (draft) by Andrew K. Bjerring and Bill St. Arnaud, undated, available online at <http://www.canet3.net/frames/papers.html>.

links is to provide capacity for twice the load observed during the busy hours of the day.) As far as the committee could tell, there is no instrumentation in place to measure the security or the performance of the network. It did not get the sense that LC staff understand current and future network demands. This situation is just one aspect of the poor or nonexistent ITS metrics. Indeed, some ITS staff told the committee that they thought network bandwidth was adequate—completely contradicting the calls for more bandwidth.

Databases and Storage

The Library is creating databases (Oracle, Sybase, and so on) at the rate of four per year. Each of these databases and the associated applications will require long-term care and feeding such as backup and restore, security management, system upgrades, and reorganization, even when the database itself is of modest size. To meet its goals, ITS needs to have a clear, long-term plan to ensure adequate database administration and application support in the future. As it stands, ITS faces a substantial maintenance burden for each of these applications.

The Library made a storage estimate[9] of 43 petabytes (thousands of terabytes) to digitize the Motion Picture, Broadcasting, and Recorded Sound Division and 5 petabytes for the Geography and Map Division. These estimates are for preservation-quality digitizations that do not take into effect compression, which might save space by a factor of 10 to 100. Still, the committee believes that the Library would need several petabytes of storage to store preservation-quality digital images of all its assets. For access quality, perhaps 1 petabyte would be adequate. No matter how the storage needs of the Library of Congress are measured they will be huge in the coming years.

In light of these huge demands, the committee has some concerns about the current storage pool and storage area network solution. LC recently spent $10 million on a solid, cutting edge technology: a 42-terabyte storage area network based on EMC/FiberChannel, which includes backup and restore functions. That amounts to $240 million per petabyte—not an affordable approach for LC. The current storage architecture and estimates do not make a clear distinction between storage for access and storage for preservation. In addition, the estimates do not clearly identify whether the amount of storage being discussed is before

---

[9]Information provided to the committee in a Library document entitled "Digital Storage Analysis," March 31, 1999.

or after replication for reliability, nor do they address the fact that the fraction of data modified in a given year is negligible (virtually all changes are additions). This specific access pattern allows alternative storage solutions (see below).

If the Library's storage needs are as massive as the committee suspects (several thousand terabytes), the Library should consider a lower-cost strategy for storage systems, like that adopted by the Internet Archive and others. The Library's hierarchical storage management system (a tape management system) was installed based on the assumption that disk storage is very expensive. Now that disk prices are approaching the price of nearline tape, LC should reevaluate its archiving strategy. The goals of maintaining current, authoritative information very reliably and keeping track of older material that is no longer current have become muddled into a single tape backup system. For an application like this, where changes are additions, it would make sense to send newly added files across a network to two or three geographically distant sites that maintain replicas rather than to use redundant arrays of independent disks, which can provide (probably unnecessarily) high performance and good protection against individual disk failures, but little or no protection against site disasters. Since many data items are rarely accessed, the system requires only modest access performance.

Information Retrieval

The Library of Congress was once a leader in the development of information retrieval technology. Library staff created software to provide online access to their catalogs at a time when online catalogs were a novelty. Like many other organizations, the Library has found it difficult to keep up with the pace of change in retrieval software and is making increased use of retrieval packages provided by third parties. The retrieval software provided with the ILS will be used for most catalog access. Applications with a larger full-text component (e.g., THOMAS) make use of other third-party software (primarily InQuery). Given the rate at which IR technology is evolving, the shift to third-party software is appropriate—relatively few organizations can now afford to build their own retrieval software.

Information retrieval technology has become much more visible with the popularity of Web searching. Once the purview of trained searchers, today's retrieval software allows novice users to find information on the Web, a collection that is huge by the standards of a few years ago. Retrieval software is evolving in several ways: the ability to search the full text of documents in many different languages; support for images, sound, and other media; user aids to help searchers formulate better queries; performance improvements to allow very large collections to be searched more quickly; feedback techniques to allow searchers to find documents similar to a known document; machine learning techniques to provide recommendations based on a history of use; and document summarization to extract relevant portions of a long document or to combine information from several documents.

The rapid evolution of retrieval software provides real benefits for users, but it complicates the task of system integration for organizations like the Library of Congress that have rich and varied collections and a heterogeneous user population. Clearly, the Library needs a strategy for dealing with information retrieval issues. Information retrieval is currently supported by multiple systems, each with different capabilities and support issues. The InQuery system used in supporting natural language queries to THOMAS and other systems is no longer available from the supplier, and it is unclear whether the product will continue to be supported. The use of PDF to store Global Legal Information Network documents complicates retrieval since there are no good text extractors for PDF. Support for foreign language retrieval, important for applications in the Law Library and Library Services, is weak. Several other retrieval issues have been identified but are not yet being addressed: in particular, the need for access control within the search engines (as discussed in the IT security section above) and the need to provide general support for searching structured documents.

Digital Repository

As discussed in Chapter 4, the Library is experimenting with a repository system (TEAMS) donated by Artesia Technologies, but it is unclear to the committee how much progress has been made in implementing this system. Most of the functioning of repositories depends upon having the appropriate information (metadata) to support the management and preservation of the digital objects deposited. It is unclear whether the Library has been creating such administrative and technical metadata for the American Memory collections. It is imperative that the Library give the implementation of a robust repository very high priority and that it ensure that the metadata needed to manage its digital collections over time and through the process of migration in response to technological change are available for all objects in its digital collection. The committee reviewed the Repository Requirements Report dated September 1998 and found this document to be an excellent general outline specification.[10]

---

[10]The Repository Requirements Report was prepared in 1998 by a small group of LC staff representing ITS, Library Services, the NDLP, and the Copyright Office. It was intended to provide a framework for identifying and analyzing the digital asset repository requirements for LC initiatives and projects.

Findings and Recommendations

Finding: E-mail is not yet universal in the Library.

Recommendation: Infrastructure should be deployed so that all Library employees have easy access to e-mail.

Finding: LC computer and information security competence and policies are seriously inadequate.

Recommendation: The Library should hire or contract with technical experts to examine the current situation and recommend a plan to secure LC information systems. Then, once a plan is in hand, the Library should implement it.

Finding: Although the Library has identified a disaster recovery strategy as a priority, Congress has decided not to fund the implementation of any such strategy.

Recommendation: Congress should provide the funding for a disaster recovery strategy and its implementation for the Library.

Finding: The Library's networking infrastructure needs urgent attention with respect to serving both current and future needs. The Library's current policy is to upgrade to fast Ethernet as needed, which is problematic (it is difficult to identify the need in an accurate and timely fashion). The ATM switch currently used as a backbone is poorly matched to the near-term needs of the Library. Network performance is measured on an ad hoc basis at best, so performance information is generally not available when it is really needed.

Recommendation: The ITS Directorate needs to upgrade all of the Library's local area networks to 100 megabit/second Ethernet on an as-soon-as-possible basis rather than on an as-needed basis. It also needs to replace the ATM switch with Ethernet switches of 1 gigabit or greater and institute continuous performance measurement of internal network usage and Internet access usage. The Congress should provide funding to support these upgrades.

Recommendation: The use of a network firewall as the sole

means of segregating internal from external usage of LC systems needs to be augmented as soon as is feasible in favor of "defense in depth" that incorporates defensive security on the individual computer systems of the Library.

Finding: The Library's storage pool goals of maintaining current, authoritative information very reliably and keeping track of older material are muddled. The current approach, which entails high-priced storage, makes it prohibitively expensive to put most of the Library online. The disaster recovery plan will nearly double the storage requirements.

Recommendation: The Library should establish disk-based storage for online data and for an online disaster recovery facility using low-cost commodity disks. The Library should also experiment with disk mirroring across a network to two or three distant sites that maintain replicas, for availability and reliability of archives, and use tapes exclusively to hold files that are rarely needed. Some of the resources being spent on installing a separate specialized storage area network for disk sharing should instead be spent on a general, high-performance network for those and other needs.

Finding: The implementation of a robust digital repository is needed to support the Library's major digital initiatives. The current rate of progress in implementing such a repository is not adequate.

Recommendation: The Library should place a higher priority on implementing an appropriate repository.

AFTERWORD

Any study of the future of a social institution runs the risk of becoming so attached to analysis of the present state of the institution as to lose sight of the horizon. In these concluding remarks, it is not the committee's purpose to summarize its findings and recommendations (that is done in the Executive Summary), but to encourage readers of this report to take a deep breath and to look out to the horizon.

The Library of Congress would not exist and would not hold so large a place in the imaginative life of our culture unless it embodied powerful ideas. It collects broadly and it gives access to what it has collected. It serves no narrow set of interests but rather the broadest public purposes of a powerful nation. It represents the commitment of the governing bodies of that nation to a strategy of preserving the heritage of the past and making it useful for the future. The vast size of LC's collections is dwarfed only by the ambition of the purposes it serves.

The committee has sought throughout its work on this report to maintain that breadth of vision. Its recommendations are meant to support LC today as it pursues that vision. But the intent is not only to provide solutions for today's problems. If that were so, the last chapter, about the nuts and bolts of information technology, might be several times its present length and minutely detailed. Instead, the committee has come to believe that what LC and its friends need most today is to anchor the struggle with today's problems more firmly than ever to the vision of the future that animates the Library. With the Library and its friends focused

214

on a common vision, it will be easier to take the steps—some small, some large—that need to be taken.

None of this will be cheap. The Library has grown enormously beyond what Congress could have expected in 1800, but Congress and the nation have responded handsomely to the challenges of growth implicit in the missions entrusted to LC. It is the committee's warmest recommendation as it submits this report that the management of LC and its allies in the Congress and elsewhere always remember the formidable magnitude of LC's missions and look upon that responsibility with characteristically American optimism. For what LC is and has been, the future will seem expensive, but for the value it delivers to the nation and the world, the Library is and always has been a bargain. The value it can add if it achieves a vision for the digital age will also make it a bargain in the future. The increases in cost over the next decade may seem steep by traditional budget parameters, but they will still be linear and not geometric—amounting to small-percentage increases every year. And the results will be of immense value: of that the committee is certain.

How should LC begin to pursue that vision? In other words, of all that has been said here, what should LC undertake first and most urgently? The committee would suggest the following priorities:

• First, information technology can, should, and must be taken as a strategic asset of the Library as a whole and managed strategically from the very top. The committee's recommendation that an additional deputy librarian be appointed speaks directly to this urgent, indeed desperate, need.

• Second, some fires must be put out. For example, network and security issues need to be addressed on an urgent basis, before the year 2000 is out.

• Third, within a year, there needs to be serious strategic planning. Concrete projects must be established and undertaken to make real the Library's ability to select, acquire, preserve, and manage digital content. These initiatives must reach across the whole interlinked set of processes from copyright registration through deposit to reader services. The projects must be undertaken, moreover, in the context of worldwide and nationwide consultation and collaboration.

All that the committee has said in this report is embraced by those three priorities. If this report is well received and implemented, then by the end of the summer of 2001, clear and dramatic movement will be visible and LC will be well on its way to reclaiming real leadership in the broad community of libraries.

The Library of Congress must continue to collect the cultural products of the United States and the world on the broadest scale possible and to do so while working with energy and imagination to make those collections available to the broadest possible audience. Libraries may attract our attention with their contents, but they earn our admiration for opening up their treasures to readers. Digital technologies may seem to overwhelm us with their quantity, but they can and should dazzle us by their power for making information accessible on a scale never before imagined.

In the end, then, the committee entrusts to its colleagues at LC its profound sense that the challenges they face can be, should be, and indeed are exhilarating ones. To have responsibility for a great library in this time of dramatic change and opportunity carries both great risk and great opportunity. The risk and the opportunity are unavoidable; wisdom lies in seizing the opportunity.

BIBLIOGRAPHY

GENERAL

Achenbach, Joel. 1999. "The Too-Much-Information Age." *Washington Post*, March 12, p. A1.

Appiah, Anthony. 1997. "Realizing the Virtual Library." *Gateways to Knowledge*, Lawrence Dowler, ed. Cambridge, Mass.: MIT Press.

Arms, Caroline R. 1996. "Historical Collections for the National Digital Library, Part 1: Lessons and Challenges at the Library of Congress." *D-Lib Magazine* (April). Available online at <http://www.dlib.org/dlib/april96/loc/04c-arms.html>.

Arms, Caroline R. 1996. "Historical Collections for the National Digital Library, Part 2: Lessons and Challenges at the Library of Congress." *D-Lib Magazine* (May). Available online at <http://www.dlib.org/dlib/may96/loc/05c-arms.html>.

Association of Research Libraries. Forthcoming. *ARL Supplementary Statistics 1988-99*. Washington, D.C.: Association of Research Libraries.

Baker, T., and Clifford A. Lynch. 1998. "Summary of a Working Group on Metadata." *A Research Agenda for Digital Libraries: Summary Report of the Series of Joint NSF-EU Working Groups on Future Directions for Digital Libraries Research*, P. Schauble and A.F. Smeaton, eds. Paris: European Research Consortium for Informatics and Mathematics.

Bellin, Angela. 1999. "LC Hosts Law Library Workshop." *The Gazette*, July 23, p. 1.

Berkeley Digital Library SunSITE, University of California at Berkeley. 1996. "Digital Library SunSITE Collection and Preservation Policy." Available online at <http://sunsite.berkely.edu/Admin/collection.html>.

Billington, James H. 1994. "The Electronic Library." *Media Studies Journal* (Winter): 109-112.

Billington, James H. 1996. "Libraries, the Library of Congress, and the Information Age." *Daedalus: Journal of the American Academy of Arts and Sciences* (Fall): 54.

Billington, James H. 1996. "Statement of Dr. James H. Billington, the Librarian of Congress, to the Joint Committee on the Library." U.S. Congress, Washington, D.C., May 7.

Billington, James H. 1998. "The Intellectual and Cultural Dimensions of International Relations: Making the Case for the 'Soft Stuff'." Essay prepared for the President's Committee on the Arts and the Humanities, Washington, D.C.

Billington, James H. 1998. "Statement of James H. Billington, the Librarian of Congress, Before the Senate Rules and Administration Committee." U.S. Senate, Washington, D.C.

Billington, James H. 1998. "Statement of James H. Billington, the Librarian of Congress, on the FY 1999 Budget Request Before the House Appropriations Committee, U.S. House of Representatives." Washington, D.C., February 3.

Billington, James H. 1999. "Statement of James H. Billington, the Librarian of Congress, on the Fiscal 2000 Budget Request Before the Subcommittee on Legislative Appropriation, House Appropriations Committee, U.S. House of Representatives." Washington, D.C., February 10.

Billington, James H. 1999. "Statement of James H. Billington, the Librarian of Congress, on the Fiscal 2000 Budget Request Before the Subcommittee on Legislative Branch, Committee on Appropriations, U.S. Senate." Washington, D.C., March 17.

Billington, James H. 2000. "Statement of James H. Billington, the Librarian of Congress, on the Fiscal 2001 Budget Request Before the Subcommittee on Legislative Branch, Committee on Appropriations, U.S. Senate." Washington, D.C., January 27.

Bloch, Howard R., and Carla Hesse, eds. 1995. *Future Libraries*. Berkeley, Calif.: University of California Press. Also in a special issue of the journal *Representations*, Spring 1993.

Borges, Jorge Luis. 1962. *Ficciones*, Anthony Kerrigan, ed. New York: Grove Press.

Bounds, Wendy. 1999. "A Trove of Memorable Moments Goes Online: Time Warner to Open Its Venerable Collection to Rivals, Consumers." *Wall Street Journal*, March 25, p. B1.

Bransten, Lisa. 1999. "NetLibrary Targets an Early Market for e-Books." *Wall Street Journal*, November 4, p. B12.

Canfora, Luciano. 1990. *The Vanished Library*, Martin Ryle, trans. Berkeley: University of California Press.

Carlton, Jim. 2000. "Amazon.com Beats Analysts' Estimates." *Wall Street Journal*, April 27, p. A3.

Cassiodorus, Senator. 1946. *An Introduction to Divine and Human Readings*, Leslie Webber Jones, trans. New York: Columbia University Press.

Christensen, Clayton. 1997. *The Innovator's Dilemma: When New Technologies Cause Great Firms to Fail*. Cambridge, Mass.: Harvard Business School Press.

Clark, Don. 1999. "Digital Books on the Web Move Closer to the Market." *Washington Post*, August 31, p. B1.

Clausing, Jeri. 1999. "Government Moves to Make Data More Accessible." *Capital Technology Dispatch: The New York Times on the Web*, August 17, pp. 1-4. Available online at <http://www.nytimes.com/library/tech/99/08/cyber/capital/17capital.html>.

Cole, John Y. 1993. *Jefferson's Legacy: A Brief History of the Library of Congress*. Washington, D.C.: Library of Congress. Available online at <http://lcweb.loc.gov/loc/legacy/>.

Conaway, James. 2000. *America's Library: The Story of the Library of Congress 1800-2000*. New Haven, Conn.: Yale University Press.

Council on Library and Information Resources. 1999. *Scholarship, Instruction, and Libraries at the Turn of the Century: Results from Five Task Forces Appointed by the American Council of Learned Societies and the Council on Library and Information Resources*. Washington, D.C.: CLIR.

Council on Library and Information Resources. Undated. Discussion of the film *Into the Future*. Washington, D.C.: CLIR. Available online at <http://www.clir.org/pubs/film/film.html#future>.

Crouch, Cameron. 1998. "Corbis Images Build Market Momentum." *M2Presswire*, October 15. Available online at <http://www.corbis.com>.

Crouch, Cameron. 1999. "Corbis Opens Its Art Collection." *PC World Online*, November 17. Available online at <http://www.corbis.com>.

Damp, Dennis V. 1999. *The Book of U.S. Government Jobs: Where They Are, What's Available, and How to Get One*. Moon Township, Pa.: Bookhaven Press.

Dominguez, Patricia Buck, and Luke Swindler. 1993. "Cooperative Collection Development at the Research Triangle University Libraries: A Model for the Nation." *College & Research Libraries* 54 (November): 470-496.

Eco, Umberto. 1996. "Afterword." *The Future of the Book*, G. Nunberg, ed. Berkeley, Calif.: University of California Press, pp. 295-306.

"EarthWeb Launches ITKnowledge: Services Provider Goes Live with Subscription-Based Online Technical Reference Library for IT Professionals." 1998. Available online at <http:// www.internetwire.com/technews/tn/archive/tn981060.htm>.

Fineberg, Gail. 1999. "JHB in Brazil: Librarian Explores International Digital Project." *The Gazette*, October, p. 28.

Fischer, Audrey. 1999. "Digital Is the Library's Future." *The Gazette*, May 7, p. 1.

Furie, B. 1998. *Understanding MARC Bibliographic: Machine-Readable Cataloging*. Washington, D.C.: Cataloging Distribution Service, Library of Congress.

Gadsby, William. 1995. "Status of General Accounting Office Reviews of the Library of Congress." Statement of J. William Gadsby, director, Government Business Operations Issues, General Government Division, U.S. General Accounting Office, Before the Joint Committee on the Library of Congress, U.S. Senate, Washington, D.C., November 29.

Gadsby, J. William, Robert W. Gramling, Joyce C. Doria, and Paul E. Lohneis. 1996. "Testimony Before the Joint Committee on the Library of Congress: Library of Congress, Opportunities to Improve General and Financial Management," with attachments. Washington, D.C.: U.S. General Accounting Office, May 7.

Gazette, The. 1999. Special Issue on the Russian Leadership Program. October 18.

Gorman, Michael. 1989. *The Concise AACR2, 1988 Revision*. Chicago: American Library Association.

Hafner, Katie. 1999. "Books to Bytes: The Electronic Archive." *The New York Times*, April 8, p. E1.

Hawkins, Brian L. 1996. "The Unsustainability of Traditional Libraries." *Executive Strategies* 2(3): 1-16.

Hedstrom, Margaret, and Sheon Montgomery. Undated. "Digital Preservation Needs and Requirements in RLG Member Institutions." Research Libraries Group. Available online at <http://www.rlg.org/preserv/digpres.html>.

Hilts, Paul. 1999. "Donnelley, Microsoft Team to Expand eBook Business." *Publishers Weekly*, November 8, p. 11.

Hilts, Paul. 2000. "Ebrary.com Offers Web as Serious Research Tool." *Publishers Weekly*, March 27. Available online at <http://www.publishersweekly.com/articles/20000327_85475.asp>.

Hodges, Doug, and Carrol D. Lunau. 1999. "The National Library of Canada's Digital Library Initiatives." *Library Hi Tech* 17(2): 152.

Information Bulletin. 1999. "Digital Distance Education: Copyright Office Releases Study." Vol. 58, No. 7, p. 176.

Information Bulletin. 1999. "Library Opens Learning Center: National Digital Library Learning Center to Serve as Training Facility for Educators." Vol. 58, No. 7, p. 153.

Information Bulletin. 2000. "Leadership Program Funded for 2000." Vol. 59, No. 1, p. 5.

I/O magazine. 2000. "Ebrary Solves a Very Big Problem." Available online at <http://www.iowebsite.com/products/3_1.html>.

Joseph, Linda. 1998. "Cyberbee: Cavalcade of American History." *Multimedia Schools* 5(3). Available online at <http://www.infotoday.com/MMSchools/may98/cybe0598. htm>.

Kane, Margaret. 2000. "Stephen King Rewrites E-book Biz." *ZDnet News*, March 16. Available online at <http://www.zdnet.com/zdnn/stories/news/0,4586,2469310,00.html>.

Kiernan, Vincent. 1999. "An Ambitious Plan to Sell Electronic Books." *Chronicle of Higher Education* 45(32).

Kohl, David F. 1997. "Resource Sharing in a Changing Ohio Environment." *Library Trends* 45 (Winter): 435-437.

Kohl, David F. 1998. "How the Virtual Library Transforms Interlibrary Loans—The OhioLINK Experience." *Interlending & Document Supply* 26(2): 65-69.

Lamolinara, Guy. 1999. "Experts Explore Frontiers of the Mind." *The Gazette*, July 2, p. 1.

Law Library of Congress. 1996. "GLIN Country Membership." Washington, D.C.: Global Legal Information Network (GLIN), Library of Congress, April.

Law Library of Congress. 1996. *Services of the Law Library of Congress.* Washington, D.C.: Library of Congress, December.

Law Library of Congress. 1999. *A Century of Lawmaking for a New Nation. U.S. Congressional Documents and Debates 1774-1873.* Washington, D.C.: Library of Congress. Available online at <http://memory.loc.gov/ammem/amlaw/>.

Law Library of Congress. Undated. "The Law Library of Congress: Some Facts." Washington, D.C.: Library of Congress.

Levy, Steven. 2000. "It's Time to Turn the Last Page." *Newsweek*, January 1, pp. 96-98.

Library of Congress. 1995. "United States Copyright Office: A Brief History and Overview." Washington, D.C.: Library of Congress, September. Available online at <http://lcweb.loc.gov/ copyright/docs/circ1a.html>.

Library of Congress. 1996. *Annual Report of the Librarian of Congress for the Fiscal Year Ending 30 September 1996.* Washington, D.C.: Library of Congress.

Library of Congress. 1997. *Annual Report of the James Madison Council of the Library of Congress, 1997.* Washington, D.C.: Library of Congress.

Library of Congress. 1997. *Annual Report of the Librarian of Congress for the Fiscal Year Ending 30 September 1997.* Washington, D.C.: Library of Congress.

Library of Congress. 1997. *Library of Congress Strategic Plan (1997-2004).* Washington, D.C.: Library of Congress.

Library of Congress. 1997. "The Library of Congress Thomas Jefferson Building." Washington, D.C.: Library of Congress, September.

Library of Congress. 1997. "Modes of Cataloging Employed in the Cataloging Directorate." January 27. Available online at <http://lcweb.loc.gov/catdir/catmodes.html>.

Library of Congress. 1997. *National Digital Library Program of the Library of Congress. Annual Report 1997.* Washington, D.C.: Library of Congress.

Library of Congress. 1997. "Selected Listing of Awards to National Digital Library Program: American Memory, Including Learning Page and Today in History Attachment 4." Washington, D.C.: Library of Congress, November 20.

Library of Congress. 1997. *The State Centers for the Book Handbook.* Washington, D.C.: Library of Congress.

Library of Congress. 1997. "25 Questions Most Frequently Asked by Visitors." Washington, D.C.: Library of Congress.

Library of Congress. 1998. *American Memory, Collections, National Digital Library.* November. Available online at <http://memory.loc.gov/ammem/collections/finder.html>.

Library of Congress. 1998. *Annual Report of the Librarian of Congress for the Fiscal Year Ending 30 September 1998.* Washington, D.C.: Library of Congress.

Library of Congress. 1998. "Cataloging at the Library of Congress." June 26. Available online at <http://lcweb.loc.gov/faq/catfaq.html>.

Library of Congress. 1998. *Cataloging Directorate Annual Report: Fiscal Year 1998*. Available online at <http://lcweb.loc.gov/catdir/annual98.html>.

Library of Congress. 1998. *Financial Statements for Fiscal 1997, Audit Report No. 98-2001, Office of the Inspector General*. Presented to the President of the U.S. Senate and the Speaker of the U.S. House of Representatives by the Library of Congress, Washington, D.C., April 27.

Library of Congress. 1998. "How to Find: Prints & Photographs Division (P&P) Materials Over Internet." Washington, D.C.: Library of Congress, February 25.

Library of Congress. 1998. *Public Services in the Library of Congress*. Washington, D.C.: Library of Congress.

Library of Congress. 1998. *Readings from Around the World: International Perspectives, 1998*. Washington, D.C.: Library of Congress.

Library of Congress. 1999. *Annual Report of the Librarian of Congress: For the Fiscal Year Ending 30 September 1998*. Washington, D.C.: Library of Congress.

Library of Congress. 1999. *Bibliographic Control Workflow*. Washington, D.C.: Library of Congress, June 22.

Library of Congress. 1999. "Facts: National Library Service for the Blind and Physically Handicapped." Washington, D.C.: Library of Congress, January.

Library of Congress. 1999. *Financial Statements for Fiscal 1998, Submitted by James H. Billington, the Librarian of Congress, to the President of the Senate and the Speaker of the House of Representatives, April 1, 1999*. Washington, D.C.: Library of Congress.

Library of Congress. 1999. *Illustrated Book Study*. Joint project with Cornell University, Department of Preservation and Conservation, and Picture Elements, Inc. Washington, D.C.: Library of Congress.

Library of Congress. 1999. "The Library of Congress Bicentennial, 1800-2000." Videotape. Washington, D.C.: Library of Congress, January 21.

Library of Congress. 1999. "Library of Congress Classification Outline." Washington, D.C.: Library of Congress, April 7. Available online at <http://lcweb.loc.gov/catdir/cpso/lcco/lcco.html>.

Library of Congress. 1999. "Library of Congress Organization Chart." Washington, D.C.: Library of Congress.

Library of Congress. 1999. "Library of Congress Pinyin Conversion Project: Table of Contents." May 28. Available online at <http://lcweb.loc.gov/catdir/pinyin/pinyin. html>.

Library of Congress. 1999. "MARC 21 Concise Bibliographic: Introduction." Washington, D.C.: Library of Congress, July 2. Available online at <http://lcweb.loc.gov/marc/bibliographic/ecbdintr.html>.

Library of Congress. 1999. "The Mission and Strategic Priorities of the Library of Congress: 1997-2004." Washington, D.C.: Library of Congress. Available online at <http://lcweb.loc.gov/ndl/mission.html>.

Library of Congress. 1999. "Search Systems Available in the Newspaper and Current Periodical Reading Room." Available online at <http://lcweb.loc.gov/rr/news/ss.html>.

Library of Congress. 1999. "Special Announcement 99-4: Realignment of the Congressional Research Service." Washington, D.C.: Office of the Librarian, February 11.

Library of Congress. 1999. "Technological Strategies for a National Digital Library: Summary of Conference Proceedings Sept. 1-2." Library of Congress Bicentennial 1800-2000 News, press release.

Library of Congress. 1999. *A World of Books: International Perspectives 1999*. Washington, D.C.: Library of Congress.

Library of Congress. 2000. *Annual Report of the Librarian of Congress: For the Fiscal Year Ending 30 September 1999*. Washington, D.C.: Library of Congress.

Library of Congress. 2000. *Financial Statements for Fiscal 1999*. Washington, D.C.: Library of Congress.

Library of Congress. 2000. "Library of Congress and National Library of Spain Sign Agreement to Collaborate on Internet Project." Press release, PR 00-20, February 24. Available online at <http://www.loc.gov/today/pr/2000/00-020.html>.

Library of Congress. 2000. "Library of Congress Hosts Conference on Cataloging Policy in the Digital Age Nov. 15-17." Press release, PR 00-013, February 22. Available online at <http://www.loc.gov/today/pr/2000/00-013.html>.

Library of Congress, Bicentennial Program Office. 1999. "Bicentennial 1800-2000: A Message from the Librarian of Congress." Washington, D.C.: Library of Congress.

Library of Congress, Cataloging Directorate Management Team. 1999. "Library of Congress Leadership in Cataloging." Washington, D.C.: Library of Congress, May 13. Available online at <http://lcweb.loc.gov/catdir/catman.html>.

Library of Congress, Cataloging Distribution Service. 1989. *Library of Congress Rule Interpretations*. Washington, D.C.: Library of Congress.

Library of Congress, Cataloging in Publication Division. 1994. *CIP Publishers Manual*. Washington, D.C.: Library of Congress.

Library of Congress, Cataloging in Publication Division. 1994. *PCN Publishers Manual: Guidelines for the Preassigned Card Number Program*. Washington, D.C.: Library of Congress.

Library of Congress, Center for the Book. 1997. *Building a Nation of Readers*. Washington, D.C.: Library of Congress.

Library of Congress, Financial Services Directorate. 1997. *Annual Report for the Fiscal Year Ending September 30, 1997*. Prepared for the secretary of the Library of Congress Trust Fund Board. Washington, D.C.: Library of Congress.

Library of Congress, Humanities and Social Sciences Division. 1998. *Information for Researchers Using the Library of Congress*. Washington, D.C.: Library of Congress.

Library of Congress, National Digital Library. 1997. "Learning with the Library of Congress." Washington, D.C.: Library of Congress, November.

Library of Congress, National Library Service for the Blind and Physically Handicapped. 1998. *Library Resources for the Blind and Physically Handicapped: A Directory with FY 1997 Statistics on Readership, Circulation, Budget, Staff, and Collections*. Washington, D.C.: Library of Congress, March-April.

Library of Congress, National Library Service for the Blind and Physically Handicapped. 1999. "Braille Book Review." Washington, D.C.: Library of Congress, March-April.

Library of Congress, National Library Service for the Blind and Physically Handicapped. 1999. *Facts: Books for Blind and Physically Handicapped Individuals*. January. Available online at <http://www.loc.gov/nls/reference/facts-books.html>.

Library of Congress, National Library Service for the Blind and Physically Handicapped. 1999. *Talking Book Topics*, 65(2). Washington, D.C.: Library of Congress.

Library of Congress, Public Affairs Office. 1993. "Background and History." Washington, D.C.: Library of Congress.

Library of Congress, Public Affairs Office. 1998. "Facts About the Library of Congress, as of September 30, 1997." Washington, D.C.: Library of Congress, April.

Library of Congress, Public Affairs Office. 1998. "The Library of Congress." Washington, D.C.: Library of Congress, January.

Library of Congress, Regional and Cooperative Cataloging Division. 1998. *Program for Cooperative Cataloging*. Washington, D.C.: Library of Congress.

Library of Congress. Undated. "American Memory Collections Available, National Digital Library." Available online at <http://memory.loc.gov/ammem/dli2/html/collection.html>.

Library of Congress. Undated. "American Treasures of the Library of Congress." Washington, D.C.: Library of Congress.

Library of Congress. Undated. "Asian Reading Room." Washington, D.C.: Library of Congress. Available online at <http://lcweb.loc.gov/rr/asian>.

Library of Congress. Undated. *Cataloging Distribution Service 1999-2000, Bibliographic Products & Services.* Washington, D.C.: Library of Congress.

Library of Congress. Undated. *Challenges to Building an Effective Digital Library.* Washington, D.C.: Library of Congress.

Library of Congress. Undated. "Collections Policy Statement—Electronic Resources." Washington, D.C.: Library of Congress.

Library of Congress. Undated. "Collections Policy Statements—Introduction and Index." Available online at <http://lcweb.loc.gov/acq/devpol/cps.html>.

Library of Congress. Undated. *Databases with Full-Text Magazine and Newspaper Articles* (accessible within the Library of Congress only). Database listing available online at <http://lcweb.loc.gov/rr/news/ftext.html>.

Library of Congress. Undated. *Fulltext Titles on CD-ROM & Microfilm in the Newspaper and Current Periodical Reading Room.* Available online at <http://lcweb.loc.gov/rr/news/full.html>.

Library of Congress. Undated. *Global Resources: The International Collection of the Library of Congress.* Washington, D.C.: Library of Congress.

Library of Congress. Undated. "How to Find a Newspaper in This Reading Room." Washington, D.C.: Library of Congress.

Library of Congress. Undated. "How to Find a United Nations Document or Publication in This Reading Room." Washington, D.C.: Library of Congress.

Library of Congress. Undated. "How to Find a U.S. Government Publication." Washington, D.C.: Library of Congress.

Library of Congress. Undated. "Library of Congress Acquisitions: Transfers of Surplus Library Material from Other Federal Agencies." Washington, D.C.: Library of Congress. Available online at <http://lcweb.loc.gov/acq/fedsur.html>.

Library of Congress. Undated. *Library of Congress Cataloging Directorate Annual Report—Fiscal Year 1998.* Washington, D.C.: Library of Congress. Available online at <http://lcweb.loc.gov/catdir/annual98.html>.

Library of Congress. Undated. "Library of Congress Frequently Asked Questions: Acquisitions FAQ." Washington, D.C.: Library of Congress. Available online at <http://lcweb.loc.gov/faq/acq/fax.html>.

Library of Congress. Undated. "Library of Congress Frequently Asked Questions: Cataloging at the Library of Congress." Washington, D.C.: Library of Congress. Available online at <http://lcweb.loc.gov/faq/acqfaq.html>.

Library of Congress. Undated. "Library of Congress: National Digital Library, Visitor's Film, Memory and Imagination, American Treasures of the Library of Congress." Washington, D.C.: Library of Congress, video.

Library of Congress. Undated. *Library of Congress On-Line Resources.* Washington, D.C.: Library of Congress.

Library of Congress. Undated. "Library of Congress Overseas Offices." Washington, D.C.: Library of Congress. Available online at <http://lcweb.loc.gov/acq/ovop/>.

Library of Congress. Undated. "Modes of Cataloging Employed in the Cataloging Directorate, U.S. Library of Congress, Washington, D.C." Washington, D.C.: Library of Congress. Available online at <http://lcweb.loc.gov/catdir/catmodes.html>.

Library of Congress. Undated. *National Digital Library Program Educational Outreach*. Washington, D.C.: Library of Congress.

Library of Congress. Undated. "Newspaper & Current Periodical Room." General information. Available online at <http://lcweb.loc.gov/global/ncp/ncp.html>.

Library of Congress. Undated. "PCN Preassigned Card Number Program." Washington, D.C.: Library of Congress. Available online at <http://lcweb2.loc.gov/pcn>.

Library of Congress. Undated. *Prints & Photographs (P&P) Online Catalog*. Available online at <http://lcweb.loc.gov/rr/print/catalog.html>.

Library of Congress. Undated. *U.S. Library of Congress, Subchapter A—Copyright Office and Procedures*. Washington, D.C.: Library of Congress.

Light, Paul C. 1999. *The New Public Service*. Washington, D.C.: Brookings Institution Press.

Lindberg, Donald A.B. 1999. "Statement by Donald A.B. Lindberg, M.D., Director, National Library of Medicine, on Fiscal Year 2000 President's Budget Request for the National Library of Medicine, February 25, 1999." Available online at <http://www.senate.gov/~appropriations/old/labor/nlm2_23.htm>.

Line, Maurice B. 1999. "Do National Libraries Have a Future?" *LOGOS* 10(3): 154-159.

Meloan, Steve. 1998. "No Way to Run a Culture." *Wired News*, February 13. Available online at <http://www.wired.com/news/culture/0,1284,10301,00.html>.

Mercer, Anne. 1999. "Among Friends: Law Library Group Holds Fall Meeting." *Information Bulletin*, December, p. 297. Available online at <http://lcweb.loc.gov/loc/lcib/9912/friends.html>.

Microsoft Corporation. 2000. "Microsoft Collaborates with barnesandnoble.com to Accelerate Availability of eBooks." Press release, January 6. Available online at <http://www.microsoft.com/PressPass/features/2000/01-06barnesnoble.asp>.

Mitchell, John. 1999. "Cataloging Forum Focuses on Cooperative Effort." *The Gazette*, January 15, p. 9.

Mulhollan, Daniel P. 1999. *CRS Report for Congress, Annual Report of the Congressional Research Service for Fiscal Year 1998, to the Joint Committee on the Library, March 1999, Pursuant to Section 321, Public Law 91-510*. Washington, D.C.: Congressional Research Service, Library of Congress.

Mulhollan, Daniel P. 1999. "Statement of Daniel P. Mulhollan, director, Congressional Research Service, before the Subcommittee on Legislative Appropriations, Committee on Appropriations, U.S. Senate, on the Fiscal 2000 Budget Request." Washington, D.C., March 17.

Mulhollan, Daniel P. 1999. "Statement on the Fiscal 2000 Budget Request before the Subcommittee on Legislative Appropriations, Committee on Appropriations, U.S. House of Representatives." Washington, D.C., February 10.

News Bulletin of McDowell County [North Carolina]. 1999. "Russian Leadership Program Comes to McDowell." September 1, p. 1.

Nunberg, Geoffrey. 1996. *The Future of the Book*. Berkeley, Calif.: University of California Press.

Nunberg, Geoffrey. 1998. "Will Libraries Survive?" *The American Prospect* 41 (November-December): 16-23. Available online at <http://www.prospect.org/archives/41/41nunb.html>.

O'Donnell, James J. 1998. *Avatars of the Word: From Papyrus to Cyberspace*. Cambridge, Mass.: Harvard University Press.

Oka, Christine K. 2000. "netLibrary.com." *Library Journal Digital*, May 1, review. Available online at <http://www.libraryjournal.com/articles/multimedia/databasedisc/20000501_14497.asp>.

Online Computer Library Center. 1999. "OCLC Research Project Measures Scope of the Web." Press release, September 8. Available online at <http://www.oclc.org/oclc/press/19990908a.htm>.

Peters, Marybeth. 1999. "Statement Before the Subcommittee on Legislative Appropriations, Committee on Appropriations, U.S. House of Representatives, Fiscal 2000 Budget Request." Washington, D.C., February 10.

Peters, Marybeth. 1999. "Statement of Marybeth Peters, Register of Copyrights, Before the Subcommittee on Legislative Branch Appropriations, Committee on Appropriations, U.S. Senate, on the Fiscal Year 2000 Budget Request." Library of Congress. Washington, D.C., March 17.

Price Waterhouse. 1995. *Financial Statement Audit for the Library of Congress for Fiscal Year 1995. Executive Summary of Reports of Independent Accountants, Appendix II.* Arlington, Va.: Price Waterhouse, September 30.

Publishers Weekly. 1999. "Barnes & Noble Buys Stake in On-Demand Press." November 8, p. 10.

Reid, Calvin. 1999. "B&T in On-Demand Pact with Xlibris." *Publishers Weekly,* November 15. Available online at <http://www.publishersweekly.com/articles/19991115_82641.asp>.

Reimers, Barbara DePompa. 2000. "New Technologies Transform Publishing Industry: Production Time and Costs Are Being Cut While Publishers Gain More Flexibility." *Information Week,* March 27. Available online at <http://www.informationweek.com/779/ebooks.htm>.

Research Libraries Group. 2000. "RLG and OCLC Explore Digital Archiving." Press release, Mountain View, Calif., March 10. Available online at <http://www.rlg.org/pr/pr2000-oclc.html>.

Ricks, Mary Kay. 1999. "Chart a Course to the Library of Congress." *Washington Post,* March 18, p. M3.

Rundquist, Paul S. 1995. *CRS Report for Congress, Joint Committee on the Library: Duties and Responsibilities.* Washington, D.C.: Congressional Research Service, Library of Congress.

Rusbridge, Chris. 1998. "Towards the Hybrid Library." *D-Lib Magazine* (July/August). Available online at <http://www.dlib.org/dlib/july98/rusbridge/07rusbridge.html>.

Russian Leadership Program, Library of Congress. 1999. *Open House, Open World, Open Politics.* Washington, D.C.: Library of Congress, Summer.

Samuelson, Pamela. 1994. "Will the Copyright Office Be Obsolete in the Twenty-First Century?" *Cardozo Arts & Entertainment Law Journal* 13(1): 55-67.

Saur, K.G. 1998. *Functional Requirements for Bibliographic Records.* Munich: International Federation of Library Associations and Institutions.

SeyboldReports.com. 2000. "The Editors' Hot Picks: Ebrary.com 1021." Available online at <http://38.241.81.30/SRPS/free/hotpicks/ebooks.html>.

Shapiro, Carl, and Hal R. Varian. 1999. *Information Rules: A Strategic Guide to the Network Economy.* Boston, Mass.: Harvard Business School Press.

Susan Spilka. 1999. "Reference Linking Service to Aid Scientists Conducting Online Research." Press release posted to the liblicense-list <liblicense-l@lists.yale.edu> archive available online at <http://www.library.yale.edu/-llicense/ListArchives>," John Wiley Publishers, New York, November 16.

St. Lifer, Evan, and Michael Rogers. 1996. "Lawmakers Seek Retooled Mission from LC's Billington: But Librarian Strongly Rejects Consultant Recommendation for Alternative Approach; Gingrich Agrees." *Library Journal* (June 1):14.

Survivors of the Shoah Visual History Foundation. 1999. *Who Can Tell Them What Really Happened?* Los Angeles: Survivors of the Shoah Visual History Foundation. Available online at <http://www.vhf.org/>.

Tyler, Christina. 1999. "NDL Learning Center Reopens, Aids Teachers." *The Gazette*, June 25, p. 1.

Tyler, Christina. 1999. "Law Library's NDL Project Gets Award for Website." *The Gazette*, July 30, p. 12.

Urschel, Donna. 1999. "Pact Allows Digital Deposits of Dissertations." *The Gazette* 10(04).

Urschel, Donna. 1999. "Security Plan Requires Preservation Assessments." *The Gazette*, January 15, p. 3.

U.S. General Accounting Office. 1991. *Report to the Librarian of Congress. Financial Audit: First Audit of the Library of Congress Discloses Significant Problems.* Washington, D.C.: GAO, August 22.

U.S. House of Representatives, Committee on House Administration. 1999. "Legislative Reorganization Acts of 1946 (PL 79-601) and 1970 (PL 91-510), House of Representatives Administrative Reform Technical Corrections Act of 1996 (PL 104-186) and Rules of the House of Representatives adopted on January 6, 1999: Committee Jurisdiction." Available online at <http://www.house.gov/cha/jurisdiction/body_jurisdiction.html>.

U.S. Office of Personnel Management. 1995. "Applying for a Federal Job." OF 510. Washington, D.C.: U.S. Government Printing Office.

Van de Sompel, Herbert, and Carl Lagoze. 2000. "The Santa Fe Convention of the Open Archives Initiative." *D-Lib Magazine* 6(2). Available online at <http://www.dlib.org/dlib/february00/ vandesompel-oai/02vandesompel-oai.html>.

Vosper, Robert. Undated. *The Farmington Plan Survey: A Summary of the Separate Studies of 1957-1961.* Champaign, Ill.: University of Illinois Graduate School of Library Science.

Walker, Leslie. 1999. "Data Basics: Federal Sites a Big Hit." *Washington Post,* June 10, p. E7.

Wand, Patricia. 1999. "Statement before the Subcommittee on Legislative Appropriations, Committee on Appropriations, U.S. House of Representatives, Fiscal 2000 Budget Request." Washington, D.C., February 10.

White, Ben. 1999. "Capitol Architect Cited in Library Fire: Investigators Note Office Has History of Safety Violations." *Washington Post*, July 13, p. A17.

White, Ben. 1999. "Clicking on Hill's Experts." *Washington Post*, February 10, p. A21.

Wilgoren, Jodi. 1998. "Education, an Exploration of Ideas, Issues and Trends in Education: Clicking on the Past." *Los Angeles Times*, July 8, p. B2.

Williams, Edwin E. 1961. *Farmington Plan Handbook.* Revised to 1961 and abridged. Ithaca, N.Y.: Association of Research Libraries.

Zeitchik, Steven M. 2000. "Houston Startup Targets Undergrads." *Publishers Weekly*, April 17. Available online at <http://www.publishersweekly.com/articles/20000417_85721. asp>.

Zeitchik, Steven M. 2000. "Microsoft, Bn.com in E-book Deal." *Publishersweekly.com*, January 10. Available online at <http://www.publishersweekly.com/articles/20000110_83924. asp>.

Zolt, Stacey. 1999. "King Papers Deal Stalls: Library May Need to Raise Some Private Funds." *Roll Call: News Scoops*, November 4.

Zolt, Stacey. 1999. "Reading Helpers: Library Program Aids the Blind." *Roll Call: Around The Hill*, February 22.

HUMAN RESOURCES

Archer, Analisa. 1999. "CRS Begins Graduate Recruit Program." *The Gazette*, October 1, p. 1.

Austin, Cortez. 1999. "Meeting Mentors: Library Pilot Program Begins." *The Gazette*, December 10, p. 3.

Barr, Stephen. 1999. "Executives Point to Pay As Problem: Top Managers Difficult to Recruit and Retain." *Washington Post*, June 22, p. A15.

Barr, Stephen. 1999. "Federal Salaries Likely to Rise 4.8%." *Washington Post*, October 10, p. A1.

Barr, Stephen. 1999. "Making a Federal Case of IT." *CIO Magazine*, July 1. Available online at <http://www.cio.com/archive/070199_government.html>.

Barr, Stephen. 2000. "Retirement Wave Creates Vacuum." *Washington Post*, May 7, p. A1.

Barr, Stephen. 2000. "VA Official's Departure Emphasizes Technological Brain Drain." *Washington Post*, June 4, p. C2.

Barr, Stephen, and John F. Harris. 1999. "Clinton Plans New Push to Expand Unions' Role in Agencies' Decisions." *Washington Post*, October 5, p. A15.

Bass, Brad, and L. Scott Tillett. 1999. "Panel: Changes Can Lure IT Labor." *Federal Computer Week*, March 8, p. 1. Available online at <http://www.fcw.com/fcw/articles/1999/FCW_030899_145.asp>.

Bauer, Claude J. 1999. "Government IT Skills Shortage Looms." *Washington Post*, July 11, p. L11.

Billington, James H. 1999. "The Library of Congress Selective Placement Program for Individuals with Disabilities." Office of the Librarian Special Announcement No. 99-15. Washington, D.C.: Library of Congress, October 13.

Black, Kim. 1999. "LC Workplace Ergonomics Program for Working Smarter—Using the Mouse Safely." *The Gazette*, May 7, p. 9.

Blacks in Government, Library of Congress Chapter. 1999. "Library of Congress Moves to Oust Employees Fighting Discrimination." Press release, August 2.

Booz-Allen & Hamilton. 1996. *Management Review of the Library of Congress*. Prepared for the U.S. General Accounting Office, Washington, D.C., May 7.

Bureau of National Affairs Labor Daily. 1992. "Library of Congress Promotion Policies Violate Title VII, District Court Rules." August 26.

Bureau of National Affairs Labor Daily. 1993. "Library of Congress Hiring Plan Defended at House Oversight Hearing." March 22.

Carter, Constance. 1999. "Nation's Reference Librarians Serve All Who Seek Information." *The Gazette*, pp. 6-9.

Causey, Mike. 1999. "At the Library of Congress, Employees Sing for Their Subsidies." *Washington Post*, July 19, p. B7.

Chief Information Officers Council. Undated. "Investing in Human Capital—An Organizational Priority." Washington, D.C.: Chief Information Officers Council. Available online at <http://www.cio.gov/docs/investinginhumancapital.htm>.

Coley, Dorothy. 2000. "Detail Program Provides Career Opportunities." *The Gazette*, April 7, p. 5.

Date, Shruti. 2000. "ATF Uses Banding System to Lift IT Pay." *Government Computer News*, June 12. Available online at <http://www.gcn.com/vol19_no15/community/2196-1.html>.

Ferris, Nancy. 1999. "CIOs on the Go." *Government Executive* 31(3): 18-34.

Fineberg, Gail. 1996. "$8.5 Million Cook Payout Cleared." *The Gazette*, November 29, p. 1.

Fineberg, Gail. 1998. "DLC Assesses Progress, Change at LC." *The Gazette*, June 12, p. 1.

Fineberg, Gail. 1998. "Scott: Staff Ideas Merit Consideration." *The Gazette*, January 9, p. 3.

Fineberg, Gail. 1999. "LC Internal University Trains Teams in Action." *The Gazette,* February 12, p. 11.

Fineberg, Gail. 1999. "Staff Chosen for LC Leadership Development." *The Gazette,* September 17, p. 1.

Fineberg, Gail. 1999. "Strategic Plan: HRS Forms New Partnerships." *The Gazette,* November 19, p. 1.

Gazette, The. 1999. "Judge Considers Cook Dispute." March 5, p. 2.

Gazette, The. 1999. "Smith Takes the Helm at LC HR." June 25, p. 1.

Gazette, The. 1999. "Veteran Auditor Named LC's Inspector General." February 12, p. 6.

George, James. 1999. "Training." *C&L News and Views* 1(June-October): 5.

Harreld, Heather. 1999. "Tight Budgets Pinch Training, CIOs Report." *Federal Computer Week* 13(2): 1. Available online at <http://208.201.97.5/pubs/fcw/1999/jan25/fcw-newstrain-1-25-99.html>.

Harreld, Heather. 2000. "E-recruitment." *Federal Computer Week,* May 1. Available online at <http://www.fcw.com/fcw/articles/2000/0501/cov-box2-05-01-00.asp>.

Keller, Amy. 1999. "Staffer Sues Library for Race Discrimination." *Roll Call: News Scoops,* December 6.

Kelly, JoAnn. 1999. "Library of Congress in Dispute Over Settlement in Bias Case." *The Hill,* April 7, p. 1.

Library of Congress. 1998. *Fairness and Equal Opportunity at the Library of Congress.* Washington, D.C.: Library of Congress.

Library of Congress. 1999. *Library of Congress 1999 Pilot Mentoring Program.* Washington, D.C.: Library of Congress.

Library of Congress. 1999. "Mission-Critical Education and Training Matrix." Washington, D.C.: Library of Congress.

Library of Congress, Communications Task Force. 1996. *Improving Management Employee Relations by Creating Better Internal Communications Processes: Management Improvement Plan Objective 3.1.* Washington, D.C.: Library of Congress, September 30.

Library of Congress. Undated. *Leadership Development Program.* Washington, D.C.: Library of Congress.

National Academy of Public Administration. 1997. *Library of Congress Human Resources Services Study.* Washington, D.C.: Center for Human Resources Management, NAPA, August-September.

National Academy of Public Administration. 1999. *The United States Holocaust Memorial Museum: A Study of Governance and Management, Executive Summary.* Washington, D.C.: NAPA.

Pershing, Ben. 1999. "Library Unions to File Complaint on Fire Systems." *Roll Call,* May 6, p. 12.

Tillett, L. Scott. 1999. "Lugar Looks to Boost USDA CIO Authority." *Federal Computer Week,* May 10, p. 6. Available online at <http://www.fcw.com/fcw/articles/1999/FCW_051099_466.asp>.

Trescott, Jacqueline. 1999. "Holocaust Museum Scrutiny: Report Cites Need for Strengthened Management." *Washington Post,* Aug. 18, p. C1.

Tyler, Christina. 1999. "Program Opens Jobs to Persons with Disabilities." *The Gazette,* October 22, p. 1.

Tyler, Christina. 1999. "Zich Retired, But His Work for LC Isn't Finished." *The Gazette,* October 8, p. 4.

U.S. House of Representatives, Committee on House Administration, Subcommittee on Libraries and Memorials. 1990. *Underrepresentation of Minorities in Supergrade Positions and Above at the Library of Congress, April 26, 1990: Hearing, Testimony, Statements, Letters, Report.*

U.S. House of Representatives, Subcommittee on Libraries and Memorials, Committee on House Administration Jointly with Subcommittee on Oversight and Investigations, Committee on Post Office and Civil Service. 1993. *Library of Congress Personnel Policies and Procedures, March 18, 1993, Joint Hearings.*

U.S. Office of Personnel Management. 1994. "Federal Hiring Process More Direct for Qualified Applicants." Press release, November 16. Available online at <http://www.opm.gov/pressrel/ 1994/PR941116.htm>.

Wall Street Journal. 1999. "Work Week: A Special News Report About Life on the Job—and Trends Taking Shape There." August 31, p. A1.

Wall Street Journal. 2000. "Libraries Compete for Staff with Dot-Coms Seeking Information Managers." May 4, p. A1.

Weeks, Linton. 1995. "The Continuing Hurt of History: Black Library Staff Express Shock at Plantation Exhibit." *Washington Post,* December 22, p. C1.

INFORMATION TECHNOLOGY

Advanced Digital Information Corporation. 1999. *ADIC Data Protection Case Study: Survivors of the Shoah Visual History Foundation.* July. Available online at <http://www.adic.com>.

Allen, J. 1995. *Natural Language Understanding,* 2nd ed. Redwood City, Calif.: Benjamin/Cummings.

Anthes, Gary H. 1991. "GAO Report Lauds FBI System, Pans Library of Congress IS." *ComputerWorld* 25(37): 101.

Baker, James M., and George E. Klechefski. 1998. *Risk Analysis Study for a Representative Magnetic Tape Collection.* Michael K. Hoel, ed. Preservation Research and Testing Series No. 9808. Prepared for the Preservation Directorate, Library of Congress.

Bearman, David, et al. 1999. "A Common Model to Support Interoperable Metadata." *D-Lib Magazine* 5(1). Available online at <http://www.dlib.org/dlib/january99/bearman/01bearman.html>.

Bjerring, Andrew K., and Bill St. Arnaud. Undated. "Optical Internets and Their Role in Future Telecommunications Systems." Draft. Available online at <http://www.canet3.net/frames/papers.html>.

Brickley, Dan, Jane Hunter, and Carl Lagoze. 1999. *ABC: A Logical Model for Metadata Interoperability,* Harmony Discussion Note. Available online at <http://www.ilrt.bris.ac.uk/discovery/harmony/docs/abc/abc_draft.html>.

Chen, Eva, Corinna Fales, and Julie Thompson. 1997. "Digitized Primary Source Documents from the Library of Congress in History and Social Studies Curriculum." *Library Trends* 45(4): 664-675.

Chen, Peter. 1985. *Entity-Relationship Approach: The Use of ER Concept in Knowledge Representation.* Washington, D.C.: IEEE Computer Society Press.

Chen, Peter. 1991. *The Entity-Relationship Approach to Logical Database Design.* Wellesley, Mass.: QED Information Sciences.

Computer Science and Telecommunications Board, National Research Council. 2000. *The Digital Dilemma: Intellectual Property in the Information Age.* Washington, D.C.: National Academy Press.

Computer Science and Telecommunications Board, National Research Council. 2000. *Making IT Better: Expanding the Scope of Information Technology to Meet Society's Needs.* Washington, D.C.: National Academy Press.

Computer Systems Laboratory. 1997. *Report for the Library of Congress: Establishing an Incident Handling Capability.* Gaithersburg, Md.: National Institute of Standards and Technology, May 29.

Congressional Research Service. 1998. *The Legislative Information System: 1999 Objectives and Plans for the Retrieval System*. Washington, D.C.: Library of Congress, November 30.

Croft, W. Bruce, ed. 2000. *Advances in Information Retrieval: Recent Research from the Center for Intelligent Information Retrieval*. Boston: Kluwer Academic Publishers.

Fellbaum, Christiane. *WordNet—An Electronic Lexical Database*. Cambridge, Mass.: MIT Press, p. 423.

Fineberg, Gail. 1999. "Experts Work Nonstop to Fix ILS During This Shakedown Period." *The Gazette*, September 10, p. 1.

Fineberg, Gail. 1999. "LC Celebrates ILS Launch; Thanks Staff." *The Gazette* 10(38): 1.

Fineberg, Gail. 1999. "LC Home Page Redesigned for Wider Appeal." *The Gazette* 10(3): 1.

Fineberg, Gail. 1999. "Library's Manual Shelflist Operation Goes Online with LC ILS." *The Gazette*, July 30, p. 8.

Fineberg, Gail. 1999. "No Small Order, Staff Replaces 2,300 PCs for ILS." *The Gazette*, July 2, p. 1.

Fineberg, Gail. 1999. "Work Begins in LC ILS on Day 1 of Cataloging." *The Gazette*, July 30, p. 1.

Fischer, Audrey. 1999. "Sun Server Lends Bright Future to ILS." *The Gazette*, June 11, p. 1.

Fischer, Audrey. Undated. *Preparing for the 21st Century: Information Technology at the Library of Congress in the 1990s and Beyond*.

Foot, Richard. 1998. "Automating the British Library: A Case Study in Project Implementation." *New Library World* 99(1140): 69-71.

Frank, Diane. 2000. "Hackers Deface Library of Congress Site." *Federal Computer Week*, January 19. Available online at <http://www.fcw.com/fcw/articles/2000/0117/web-lochack-01-19-00.asp>.

Gazette, The. 1999. "LC ILS ADA/Ergonomics Announcement." June 11, p. 11.

Government Accountants Journal, The. 1998. Annual Technology Issue—Preparing for Tomorrow's Way of Doing Business. Vol. 47, No. 2.

Gribben, Jim. 1999. "Information Technology—News You Can Use." *C&L News and Views* 1(5): 4.

Gumbel, Peter. 1999. "Making History: Steven Spielberg's Oral History of Holocaust Survivors Has Videotaped 50,000 Interviews. Now Comes the Hard Part." *Wall Street Journal*, March 22, p. R9.

Hammer, Rhonda, and Douglas Kellner. 1999. "Multimedia Pedagogy for the New Millennium." *Journal of Adolescent & Adult Literacy* 42(7): 522.

Hiles, Andrew. 1999. *Complete Guide to IT Service Level Agreements: Matching Service Quality to Business Needs*. Brookfield, Conn.: Philip Jan Rothstein.

International Federation of Library Associations and Institutions, Study Group on the Functional Requirements for Bibliographic Records. 1998. *Functional Requirements for Bibliographic Records: Final Report*. Munich: K.G. Saur.

International Technology Research Institute, World Technology Division. 1999. *Digital Information Organization in Japan*. Baltimore, Md.: Loyola College in Maryland. Available online at <http://itri.loyola.edu/digilibs/toc.htm>.

Lacity, Mary C., Leslie P. Willcocks, and David F. Feeny. 1995. "IT Outsourcing: Maximize Flexibility and Control." *Harvard Business Review* 73(3): 84-93.

Lagoze, Carl, and S. Payette. 2000. "Metadata: Foundation for Image Management and Use." *Moving Theory into Practice: Digital Imaging for Libraries and Archives*, A.R. Kenney and O.Y. Rieger, eds. Mountain View, Calif.: Research Libraries Group.

Lagoze, Carl, Clifford Lynch, and Ron Daniel, Jr. 1996. "The Warwick Framework: A Container Architecture for Aggregating Sets of Metadata." Cornell Computer Science Technical Report TR96-1593. Ithaca, N.Y.: Cornell University, June. Available online at <http://www.ncstrl.org:80/Dienst/UI/2.0/Describe/ncstrl.cornell/TR96-1593>.

Lawrence, S., and C.G. Giles. 1999. "Search Engines Fall Short." *Science* 285(5426): 295.

Library of Congress. 1993. *Delivering Electronic Information in a Knowledge-Based Democracy: Summary of Conference Proceedings, July 14, 1993.* Washington, D.C.: Library of Congress.

Library of Congress. 1995. *About the Copyright Office Electronic Registration, Recordation and Deposit System (CORDS) via the INTERNET.* SL-11-July 1995. Washington, D.C.: Library of Congress.

Library of Congress. 1995. *Duplication Among Legislative Tracking Systems: Findings.* Report prepared for the House and Senate Appropriations Committees pursuant to House Report 103-517. Washington, D.C.: Library of Congress, July 14.

Library of Congress. 1995. *LCR 1620, Computer Security Policy of the Library of Congress (Computer Security Act of 1987, Public Law 100-235).* Washington, D.C.: Library of Congress, November 22.

Library of Congress. 1996. "Integrated Library System Concept, Library of Congress" [figure]. Washington, D.C.: Library of Congress, December.

Library of Congress. 1996. *A Plan for a New Legislative Information System for the United States Congress, Pursuant to Public Law 104-53.* Washington, D.C.: Library of Congress, February 16.

Library of Congress. 1997. *The Case for an Integrated Library System at the Library of Congress.* Washington, D.C.: Library of Congress, January 17.

Library of Congress. 1997. "Statement of Work—ILS. Section C: Description, Specification, Work Statement (RFP97-12)." Washington, D.C.: Library of Congress.

Library of Congress. 1999. "Library of Congress Launches Web-Braille on the Internet for Blind and Visually Impaired Library Users." Library of Congress Bicentennial 1800-2000 News. Press release, PR 99-147, October 5.

Library of Congress. 1999. *National Digital Library Program File Formats.* Washington, D.C.: Library of Congress.

Library of Congress, ILS Workstation Steering Group. 1999. "Using the Cataloging Macros." June 2.

Library of Congress, National Library Service for the Blind and Physically Handicapped. 1998. *Digital Talking Books: Planning for the Future.* Washington, D.C.: Library of Congress.

Library of Congress, Systems Development Group. 1998. *System Development Life Cycle Methodology for Internet Application Development.* Washington, D.C.: Library of Congress.

Library of Congress. Undated. "Technical Notes on Formats for Digital Reproductions." Available online at <http://memory.loc.gov/ammem/award/html/technical_notes1.html>.

Lohr, Steve, with John Markoff. 1999. "Internet Fuels Revival of Centralized 'Big Iron' Computing." *The New York Times on the Web, Technology,* May 21, pp. 1-9. Available online at <http://www.nytimes.com/library/tech/99/05/biztech/articles/19net.htm>.

Manns, Basil. 1998. *Testing and Monitoring the CD Audio Collection—Part 1: Baseline Report for Natural Aging Study.* Washington, D.C.: Preservation Research and Testing Division, Library of Congress, October.

McKiernan, Gerry. 1999. "Embedded Multimedia in Electronic Journals." *Multimedia Information and Technology* 24(4): 338-343.

McNealy, Scott. 1999. "Why We Don't Want You to Buy Our Software." *The Wall Street Journal,* September 1.

Majeska, Marilyn Lundell. 1988. *Talking Book: Pioneering and Beyond*. Washington, D.C.: National Library Service for the Blind and Physically Handicapped, Library of Congress.

Network Development and MARC Standards Office, Library of Congress. 1999. *Dublin Core/MARC/GILS Crosswalk*. Available online at <http://lcweb.loc.gov/marc/dccross.html>.

Noam, Eli M. 1998. "Will Books Become the Dumb Medium?" *Educom Review* (March/April): 18.

Nugent, William R. 1997. *Digitizing Library Collections for Preservation and Archiving: A Handbook for Curators*. Preservation Research and Testing Series No. 9705. Washington, D.C.: Preservation Directorate, Library of Congress, May.

Ohnemus, Edward. 1996. "LC Plans for Integrated Library System." *The Gazette*, November 29.

Picture Elements, Inc. 1995. "Guidelines for Electronic Preservation of Visual Materials, Part 1." Submitted to the Library of Congress, Washington, D.C., March 2.

Research Libraries Group. 1999. *AMICO Library: This Year, Add the AMICO Library to Your Information Resources*. Mountain View, Calif.: RLG. See also <http://www.rlg.org/amico/>.

Research Libraries Group. 1999. *Archival Resources: Bringing the World's Archives to the Desktop*. Mountain View, Calif.: RLG. Home page available online at <http://www.rlg.org>.

Resnick, Paul. 1997. "Filtering Information on the Internet." *Scientific American* (March): 106-108. Available online at <http://www.sciam.com/0397issue/0397resnick.html>.

Rohrbach, Peter T. 1985. *FIND: Automation at the Library of Congress. The First Twenty-five Years and Beyond*. Washington, D.C.: Library of Congress.

Smith, Abby. 1999. *Why Digitize?* Washington, D.C.: Council on Library and Information Resources.

Sowa, J.F. 2000. *Knowledge Representation: Logical, Philosophical, and Computational Foundations*. Pacific Grove, Calif.: Brooks/Cole.

Sparc-Jones, K., and P. Willett, eds. 1997. *Readings in Information Retrieval*. Los Angeles: Morgan Kaufmann Publishers.

Storm, William D. 1998. *Unified Strategy for the Preservation of Audio and Video Materials, Updated Ed.* Preservation Research and Testing Series No. 9806. Washington, D.C.: Preservation Directorate, Library of Congress.

Thorin, Suzanne E., ed. 1986. "Automation at the Library of Congress: Insider Views." Washington, D.C.: Library of Congress Professional Association.

Tolly, Kevin. 1998. "Frames Reaffirmed at ATM's Expense." *Network Magazine*, September, p. 60-64.

Tyler, Christina. 1999. "CDS Keeps Up with Shift to ILS." *The Gazette*, September 10, p. 3.

Tyler, Christina. 1999. "Digital Scan Center Handles Rare, Fragile Materials for Digital Preservation." *The Gazette*, October 22, p. 6.

Tyler, Christina. 1999. "ILS to Make Book Loans Easier." *The Gazette*, July 30, p. 1.

Tyler, Christina. 1999. "ILS Training Will Not Stop After Start Dates." *The Gazette*, July 23, p. 6.

Urschel, Donna. 1999. "Tillett: ILS 'On Track' for 1999." *The Gazette*, February 5, p. 8.

Williams, Larry. 1999. "Search Engines Not Keeping Up with Torrent of Accessible Info." *Mercury News*, July 7.

ADDITIONAL MATERIAL ON OR FROM THE LIBRARY OF CONGRESS

Arms, Caroline. 1999. "Getting the Picture: Observations from the Library of Congress on Providing Online Access to Pictorial Images." *Library Trends*, 48(2): 379-409. Available online at <http://memory.loc.gov/ammen/techdocs/libt1999/libt1999.html >.

Becker, Herbert S. 1996. "ILS Business Case." Memorandum from Herbert S. Becker, director, Information Technology Services, Library of Congress, Washington, D.C., to Tabb, Tillett, Hayduchok, Wiggins, Zimmerman, Kresh, Webster. Draft, November 27.

Becker, Herbert S. 1999. "Library of Congress Telephone Directory June 1999." Memorandum from Herbert S. Becker, director, Information Technology Services, Library of Congress, to Library staff, August 9.

Billington, James H. 1987. "The Librarian of Congress to Members of the Library Staff." Memorandum, December 22.

Bryant, Thomas. 1999. "Memorandum from Thomas Bryant, director of Planning Management and Evaluation Directorate, Library of Congress, to Participants and Others, Distributing the Minutes of the Strategic Planning Committee Meeting of January 5."

Burke, Michael D. 1999. "Constraints to Progress." Memorandum. Washington, D.C.: U.S. Copyright Office, Library of Congress, March 5.

Campbell, Laura. 1999. "Digital Library Vision Statement from the NDL." Draft statement from Laura Campbell, Library of Congress, to Alan Inouye, Computer Science and Telecommunications Board, National Research Council, Washington, D.C., April 12.

Campbell, Laura. 1999. "National Digital Library: A Presentation by Laura Campbell at the Australian National Library Council." February.

Cohen, Cliff. 1999. "LS Constraints." Memorandum from Cliff Cohen, Library Services, Library of Congress, to Virginia Sorkin, Office of the Librarian, Library of Congress, February 26.

Cohen, Cliff. 1999. "Response to Action #6—Fort Meade, Full Operation of Module MDEP." Memorandum from Cliff Cohen, Library of Congress, Washington, D.C., to Kathy Williams, budget officer, Financial Services Directorate, Library of Congress, September 2.

Cohen, Cliff. 1999. "Response to Action #7—Preventive Preservation." Memorandum from Cliff Cohen, Library of Congress, to Kathy Williams, budget officer, Financial Services Directorate, Library of Congress, September 2.

Cohen, Cliff. 1999. "Response to Action #15 Relating to the Capitalizing on ILS MDEP." Memorandum from Cliff Cohen, Library of Congress, to Kathy Williams, budget officer, Financial Services Directorate, Library of Congress, September 2.

Congressional Research Service. 1996. *Supporting the Legislative Work of the Congress in a Period of Fiscal Constraint.* Washington, D.C.: Library of Congress, February.

Congressional Research Service. 1998. *A Report on the Congressional Legislation Information System Program Plan.* Washington, D.C.: Library of Congress, March 30.

Congressional Research Service. 1999. "Congressional Policy Concerning the Distribution of CRS Written Products to the Public." March 9.

Congressional Research Service. 1999. *Social Security Briefing Book.* Briefing book is updated periodically and is available through the CRS staff-only Web site; for a copy of this briefing book or others, contact CRS or your member of Congress.

Congressional Research Service. 1999. "Summary of CBO Preliminary Worksheet for S.1578 [105th Congress]—CRS Website for Public Use." Washington, D.C.: Library of Congress, March 8.

Congressional Research Service. 1999. *Tobacco Briefing Book.* Briefing book is updated periodically and is available through the CRS staff-only Web site; for a copy of this briefing book or others, contact CRS or your member of Congress.

Congressional Research Service, Office of Information Resources Management. 1999. "CRS Information Hub." Washington, D.C.: Library of Congress, April 12.

Curran, Donald C. 1987. "Memorandum to CAP Members, SISP Project Team, and Department Liaison Group about the Library of Congress Strategic Information System Plan." August 19.

Evans, Angela. 1999. "FY01 AOC MDEP Follow-up Actions on Succession Planning." Memorandum from Angela Evans, deputy director, Congressional Research Service, Library of Congress, Washington, D.C., to Kathy Williams, budget officer, Financial Services Directorate, August 23.

Global Legal Information Network. Undated. *Global Legal Information Network (GLIN), Digital Law Library.* Viewgraph presentation.

Hiring Improvement Process (HIP-2000) Group, Library of Congress. 1999. *Hiring Improvement Process: Final Report, Detailed Recommendations, Technology White Papers.* Draft, September 9.

HR21 Strategic Planning Working Group, Library of Congress. 1999. *HR21: Our Vision for the Future—HR21 Strategic and Integrated Change Plan.* Draft, September 9.

Landergan, Brian. 1998. "JMMB Computer Operations Group, Computer Equipment Information." Library of Congress, Information Technology Services, August 1.

Law Library of Congress. 1999. "NRC Information Technology Strategy for the Library of Congress." Law Library of Congress Briefing, Washington, D.C., April 12.

Law Library of Congress. Undated. *GLIN (Global Legal Information Network), Business Plan (1992-2004).* Washington, D.C.: Library of Congress.

Law Library of Congress. Undated. "Law Library, Constraints to Implementing Information Technology Plans." Washington, D.C.: Library of Congress.

Library of Congress. 1988. *Library of Congress Planning Committee Issues Recommendation: The Library of Congress in the Year 2000: A Vision.* Proposed by the Management and Planning Committee. Washington, D.C.: Library of Congress, June 29.

Library of Congress. 1988. *The Report of the Management and Planning Committee to the Librarian of Congress* [excerpts]. Washington, D.C.: Library of Congress, November 18.

Library of Congress. 1990. *Library of Congress Organization: May 1990.* Washington, D.C.: Library of Congress.

Library of Congress. 1994. "Strategic Directions Toward a Digital Library Coalition (A Working Paper)." October 11.

Library of Congress. 1995. "Electronic Journals Prototype: Results of Phase I." Washington, D.C.: Library of Congress, September 19.

Library of Congress. 1997. "The Case for an Integrated Library System at the Library of Congress." Washington, D.C.: Library of Congress, January 17.

Library of Congress. 1997. "Computer Security Incident Handling Procedures." Memorandum, October 1.

Library of Congress. 1997. "Copyright Office Workflow Chart." Washington, D.C.: Library of Congress.

Library of Congress. 1997. *Financial Statement Audit 9/30/96, Preliminary Notification of Findings and Recommendations of Audit Location: Information Technology Services (ITS), IT General Controls—Systems Development.* Washington, D.C.: Library of Congress.

Library of Congress. 1997. "Human Resources Services (HRS) Automated Systems, Summary from 1997 Retreat." Washington, D.C.: Library of Congress.

Library of Congress. 1997. *Information Technology Services Computer Security Plan.* September 10.

Library of Congress. 1997. *ITS Data Center Disaster Recovery Strategies Alternative Analysis*. October 10.

Library of Congress. 1997. *National Digital Library Program Strategic Plan (NDLP), Mission—National Digital Library Program Goals and Objectives*.

Library of Congress. 1997. *What Is an ILS? The Library of Congress ILS Project—Overview for the Joint Committee on the Library*. Washington, D.C.: Library of Congress, May 8.

Library of Congress. 1998. *Acquisitions by Source, September 30, 1998*, with attachments "General Statistics from the Library Services Staff Home Page" and p. 15 ("Copyright Services") of the *Annual Report of the Librarian of Congress 1998*.

Library of Congress. 1998. *Congressional Research Service Information Technology Development, A Status Report, September 23, 1998*. Washington, D.C.: Library of Congress.

Library of Congress. 1998. *Financial Services Directorate Strategic Plan—Fiscal Years 1999-2004*. Washington, D.C.: Library of Congress, November.

Library of Congress. 1998. *Fiscal 1999 Budget—All Sources*. Washington, D.C.: Library of Congress.

Library of Congress. 1998. *LC Security Milestones, Information Technology Services*. Washington, D.C.: Library of Congress.

Library of Congress. 1998. *Legal Issues Presented by Proposals for the General Release of CRS Products to the Public*. Washington, D.C.: Library of Congress, February 24.

Library of Congress. 1998. *Library of Congress—Information Technology Services Year 2000 Project, Action Plan, December 31, 1998*. Washington, D.C.: Library of Congress.

Library of Congress. 1998. *Monthly Status Reports for September 1998, Information Technology Services (ITS)*. Compiled by ITS. Washington, D.C.: Library of Congress.

Library of Congress. 1998. "Repository Requirements Report." Washington, D.C.: Library of Congress.

Library of Congress. 1998. *Security Plan, Updated and Abridged June 1998*, pp. 1-18. Washington, D.C.: Library of Congress, October 15.

Library of Congress. 1999. "A2: CATWHOL." Bibliographic Workflow Training Documents (Non-Serial Catalogers) 14, 15, 16, 19, 20, 21, and 26. Washington, D.C.: Library of Congress.

Library of Congress. 1999. "Authorities Workflow in LC-ILS." Bibliographic Workflow Training Document 6. Washington, D.C.: Library of Congress, May 18.

Library of Congress. 1999. "Authority Validation." Bibliographic Workflow Training Document 5. Washington, D.C.: Library of Congress, May 25.

Library of Congress. 1999. "Cataloging Policy and Support Office, Federal Library Resources Institute." Washington, D.C.: Library of Congress, July 20.

Library of Congress. 1999. "Cataloging Team Workflow in Voyager, New Work (Printed Monograph) with IBC Record." Bibliographic Workflow Training Document 18. Washington, D.C.: Library of Congress, May 25.

Library of Congress. 1999. "Comprehensive Mailing List System (CMLS)." Washington, D.C.: Library of Congress, April 29.

Library of Congress. 1999. "Electronic Resources—Main Reading Room" [table of electronic resources available in the Main Reading Room]. Washington, D.C.: Library of Congress, January 12.

Library of Congress. 1999. *Fairness and Equal Opportunity at the Library of Congress—Update (October 1, 1998–June 30, 1999)*. Washington, D.C.: Library of Congress, July.

Library of Congress. 1999. *FY 2001 Digital Future Management Decision Package (MDEPs): Summary Level Outcomes*. Washington, D.C.: Library of Congress, September 14.

Library of Congress. 1999. *HR21: Our Vision for the Future—The Library of Congress Human Resources Strategic Plan, FY 2000-2005*. Washington, D.C.: Library of Congress, November.

Library of Congress. 1999. *Information Technology Infrastructure for Creation, Storage and Preservation of Digital Reproductions and Provision of Access through American Memory.* Washington, D.C.: Library of Congress, February 17.

Library of Congress. 1999. *Information Technology Security Plan 1999-2000.* Washington, D.C.: Library of Congress.

Library of Congress. 1999. "Information Technology Strategy Beyond the Year 2000." Presentation to the Computer Science and Telecommunications Board, National Research Council, Washington, D.C., February 18.

Library of Congress. 1999. "Library Services Tracking of Items in Process," Bibliographic Workflow Training Document 10. Washington, D.C.: Library of Congress, May 15.

Library of Congress. 1999. "List of Macros for Cataloging in Voyager." Bibliographic Workflow Training Document 3. Washington, D.C.: Library of Congress, May 22.

Library of Congress. 1999. "Local Processing Field (906): Proposal for Subfields, Their Order, Their Content." Bibliographic Workflow Training Document 8. Washington, D.C.: Library of Congress, May 18.

Library of Congress. 1999. "Mission-Critical Systems Complete (Projected)" [graph]. Washington, D.C.: Library of Congress, February 28.

Library of Congress. 1999. "Order of MARC 21 Fields in LC-ILS Bibliographic Records." Bibliographic Workflow Training Document 13. Washington, D.C.: Library of Congress, May 18.

Library of Congress. 1999. *Planning, Programming, Budgeting, Execution and Evaluation System, Fiscal 2001-2005, Management Decision Package (MDEP) Justification. MDEP Detailed Schedule for Fiscal 2001 Budget Sessions and Fiscal 2001 MDEP Follow up Actions.* Washington, D.C.: Library of Congress.

Library of Congress. 1999. *Planning, Programming, Budgeting, Execution and Evaluation System, Fiscal 2001-2005, Management Decision Package (MDEP) Justification. Title of New Initiative—MDEP: Audit of NLS/BPH Machine-Lending Agencies, Financial Related Audits & Security Audits.* Washington, D.C.: Library of Congress.

Library of Congress. 1999. *Planning, Programming, Budgeting, Execution and Evaluation System, Fiscal 2001-2005, Management Decision Package (MDEP) Justification. Title of New Initiative—MDEP: Base Funding for Police Positions Established Under Public Law 105-277 (Emergency Supplemental Funding for Security Enhancements).* Washington, D.C.: Library of Congress.

Library of Congress. 1999. *Planning, Programming, Budgeting, Execution and Evaluation System, Fiscal 2001-2005, Management Decision Package (MDEP) Justification. Title of New Initiative—MDEP: Coolidge Auditorium (Attachment to MBRS Equipment MDEP).* Washington, D.C.: Library of Congress.

Library of Congress. 1999. *Planning, Programming, Budgeting, Execution and Evaluation System, Fiscal 2001-2005, Management Decision Package (MDEP) Justification. Title of New Initiative—MDEP: Item Level Tracking and Inventory Control Capability.* Washington, D.C.: Library of Congress.

Library of Congress. 1999. *Planning, Programming, Budgeting, Execution and Evaluation System, Fiscal 2001-2005, Management Decision Package (MDEP) Justification. Title of New Initiative—MDEP: Law Library Essential Personnel.* Washington, D.C.: Library of Congress.

Library of Congress. 1999. "Preferences." Bibliographic Workflow Training Document 1. Washington, D.C.: Library of Congress, May 22.

Library of Congress. 1999. "Subject Authorities Workflow in LC-ILS." Bibliographic Workflow Training Document 7. Washington, D.C.: Library of Congress, May 18.

Library of Congress. 1999. *Technology Architecture for Storage and Retrieval of Digital Content at the Library of Congress.* Washington, D.C.: Information Technology Services, Library of Congress, May 4.

Library of Congress. 1999. "Technology Architecture for the Centrally Supported Systems Infrastructure at the Library of Congress." Final draft. Washington, D.C.: Library of Congress, February 9.

Library of Congress. 1999. "Use of the Workflow Overviews." Bibliographic Workflow Training Document 21. Washington, D.C.: Library of Congress, May 2.

Library of Congress, Cataloging Directorate. 1999. *Tactical Plan for FY 1999 and FY 2000—Vision, Mission, Goals.* Washington, D.C.: Library of Congress. Draft, March 12.

Library of Congress, Contracts and Logistics Services. 1997. "Illustrated Book Study—Development of Guidelines for Preservation Scanning of Printed Continuous Tone Images." Contract between Library of Congress and Cornell University—Contract No. 97CLCCT7021.

Library of Congress, Executive Committee. 1999. "Executive Committee Post Retreat Report." Washington, D.C.: Library of Congress, November 5.

Library of Congress, Information Technology Services. 1996. "The Chief Information Officer (CIO) Function at the Library of Congress." Washington, D.C.: Library of Congress, October 29.

Library of Congress, Information Technology Services. 1999. *DRAFT Information Technology Security Plan.* Draft, January 21.

Library of Congress, Information Technology Services. 1999. *Technology Architecture for Storage and Retrieval of Digital Content at the Library of Congress,* Revised. Washington, D.C.: Library of Congress.

Library of Congress, Information Technology Services. 1999. "Telecommunications Architecture at the Library of Congress." January.

Library of Congress, Internet Resources Team. 1995. *Staff Internet Handbook: Providing and Using Electronic Information at the Library of Congress.* September.

Library of Congress, ILS Bibliographic Issues Resolution Group. 1999. "ILS Searching Strategy for Cataloging." Memorandum from ILS Bibliographic Issues Resolution Group to Cataloging Staff, transmitting Bibliographic Workflow Training Document, May 28.

Library of Congress, Management Steering Committee. 1997. *The Library of Congress Electronic Resources Project: Report and Recommendations from the Management Steering Committee.* Washington, D.C.: Library of Congress, December 15.

Library of Congress, National Digital Library Program. 1998. "American Memory Historical Collections from the Library of Congress." Viewgraph presentation. Washington, D.C.: Library of Congress, November 11.

Library of Congress, National Digital Library Program Management Team. 1997. *National Digital Library Program Strategic Plan.* Washington, D.C.: Library of Congress, January 23.

Library of Congress, National Library Service for the Blind and Physically Handicapped. 1999. "National Library Service for the Blind and Physically Handicapped (NLS) Network System (NLSNET)." Washington, D.C.: Library of Congress, April 29.

Library of Congress, National Library Service for the Blind and Physically Handicapped. 1999. "National Library Service for the Blind and Physically Handicapped (NLS) Union Catalog System." Washington, D.C.: Library of Congress, April 29.

Library of Congress. Undated. "CORDS Processing" [flow chart]. Washington, D.C.: Library of Congress.

Library of Congress. Undated. "Evaluation of Work Needs for Better Staffing." Selected responses. Washington, D.C.: Library of Congress.

Library of Congress. Undated. "Information Transfer, Production of Books and Magazines, and Circulation System for Network Libraries" [charts]. Washington, D.C.: Library of Congress.

Library of Congress. Undated. "Key Component of an Integrated Planning and Program Execution Process—Organization Chart." Washington, D.C.: Library of Congress.

Library of Congress. Undated. "Library of Congress Hiring System." Washington, D.C.: Library of Congress.

Library of Congress. Undated. "Library of Congress Human Resource Management." Washington, D.C.: Library of Congress.

Library of Congress. Undated. "RS/6000 User Password Standards and Procedures." Washington, D.C.: Library of Congress.

Library of Congress. Undated. "Summary of CRS Collections." Prepared for the study subcommittees on management and technical infrastructure for visit to LC, Washington, D.C., April 12-13, 1999.

Library of Congress. Undated. "Selection of Copyright Registration Deposits." Washington, D.C.: Library of Congress.

Library of Congress. Undated. "The Legislative Information System of the United States Congress, an Outline: Background, Goals, How It Works Today, The Next Two Years, Future Issues." Prepared for the study subcommittees on management and technical infrastructure for visit to LC, Washington, D.C., April 12-13, 1999.

Library of Congress. Undated. *The Law Library's Global Legal Information Network (GLIN), Business Plan (1992–2004)*. Washington, D.C.: Library of Congress.

Library of Congress. [various dates]. "Cataloging Workflows" [addresses various divisions of cataloging. Materials are dated 1998 and 1999]. Washington, D.C.: Library of Congress.

Mandelbaum, Jane. 1999. "Databases Compiled from Information Provided by Roland Nelson and Tom McCready." Memorandum, May 26.

Miller, Diana Frazier. 1998. "Here Today, Gone Tomorrow? The Archivability of Electronic Records." Presented at AALL Program #A8, Anaheim, Calif., July 12. A Selected List of Sources. Washington, D.C.: Law Library, Library of Congress.

Morris, Susan R. 1999. "ILS Training Documents for NAS Visitors." Memorandum from Susan Morris, Library of Congress, Washington, D.C., to Virginia Sorkin, July 15.

Muccino, Donald J. 1999. "OCLC Cooperative Initiatives for Digital Information—IT Strategy for the Library of Congress." Presentation to Computer Science and Telecommunications Board, National Research Council, Palo Alto, Calif., September 15.

Mulhollan, Daniel P. 1999. "Constraints on Achieving Technology Goals." Memorandum from Daniel P. Mulhollan, director, Congressional Research Service, to JoAnn C. Jenkins, chief of staff, Library of Congress, Washington, D.C., February 26.

Mulhollan, Daniel P. 1999. "Fiscal Year 2000 Staffing Requests." Memorandum from Daniel P. Mulhollan, director, Congressional Research Service, Library of Congress, Washington, D.C., to NRC, July 7.

National Institutes of Health, National Library of Medicine. "NLM Information Technology Personnel Resources." Washington, D.C.: Department of Health and Human Services, NIH.

Peters, Marybeth. 1999. "Problems in Registration Due to Changes in Methods of Distribution—Electronic Commerce." Outline of questions/problems. Washington, D.C.: U.S. Copyright Office, Library of Congress, July 27.

Reddy, Raj, and Michael I. Shamos. 1999. "The Universal Library." Presentation at the University of Michigan, September 21.

Romano Reynolds, Regina. 1999. "E journals information." Memorandum to Virginia Sorkin, Library of Congress, Washington, D.C., April 21.

Roth, Dennis M. 1999. "Contract Language on Technology (Article XL)." Memorandum from Dennis Roth, president, Congressional Research Employees Association, to Alan Inouye, Computer Science and Telecommunications Board, National Research Council, April 22.

Sfeir, George N. 1996. "Country Law Studies—United Arab Emirates: Criminal Law and Procedures." Washington, D.C.: Law Library, Library of Congress, July.

Shelley, Michael H. 1988. "Comments on the Arthur Young Draft Interim Progress Report." Memorandum from Michael Shelley, chief, Shared Cataloging Division, to Declan Murphy, special assistant to the librarian, Library of Congress, Washington, D.C.

Singleton, John W. 1999. "Workplace Violence Prevention Training/Briefing." Memorandum by John W. Singleton, chairman, Workplace Violence Prevention Program, Library of Congress, Washington, D.C., October 27.

Sorkin, Virginia. 1999. "MDEPs as of 9/9/99." Memorandum from Virginia Sorkin, Office of the Librarian, Library of Congress, Washington, D.C., to Alan Inouye, Computer Science and Telecommunications Board, National Research Council, September 10.

Sorkin, Virginia. 1999. Memorandum from Virginia Sorkin, Office of the Librarian, Library of Congress, Washington, D.C., to Diane Kresh about LC serials projects, April 21.

Stork, Judy. 1997. "Computer Security." Memorandum from Judy Stork, deputy director, Information Technology Services, Library of Congress, Washington, D.C., June 2.

Stork, Judy L. 1999. "Assignments from FY01 Budget Sessions and Corrected Audio/Visual MDEP for ITS/PAO Funding." Memorandum and attachments from Judy L. Stork, Information Technology Services, via Herbert S. Becker, director, Information Technology Services, to Kathy Williams, budget officer, Financial Services, Library of Congress, Washington, D.C., August 23.

U.S. Copyright Office. 1996. *U.S. Copyright Office Electronic Registration, Recordation and Deposit System, CORDS Long Range Cost-Benefit Plan FY '98-FY 2004.* Washington, D.C.: Library of Congress, December 6.

Whitlock, Margaret. 1998. "Collections policy statement for electronic resources." Memorandum from Margaret Whitlock, chair, Collections Policy Committee, Law Library of Congress, Washington, D.C., to Winston Tabb, associate librarian for Library Services, December 14.

Zich, Robert. 1998. "The Library of Congress as a Digital Library." Draft, August 12.

OTHER MATERIALS

Agre, Philip E. 1999. "Information and Institutional Change: The Case of Digital Libraries." Draft. To appear in Ann P. Bishop, Barbara P. Buttenfield, and Nancy Van House, eds. 2000. *Digital Library Use: Social Practice in Design and Evaluation.* Cambridge, Mass.: MIT Press. See draft available online at <http://dlis.gseis.ucla.edu/people/pagre/dl.html>.

Canter, Rhoda W. 1988. "Interim Progress Report for Contract J70054, Management Review of the Library of Congress." Washington, D.C.: Arthur Young & Company, September 12.

Canter, Rhoda W. 1989. "Revised Second Interim Progress Report for Contract J70054, Management Review of the Library of Congress." Arthur Young & Company, Washington, D.C., January 26.

DeGlopper, Donald R. 1998. "First Piece on the Law Library for the Proposed 'LC Encyclopedia.'" Draft, July. Prepared for May 1999 mailing of the Computer Science and Telecommunications Board, National Research Council, Washington, D.C.

DeGlopper, Donald R. 1998. "Revised Piece on the Law Library for the Proposed 'LC Encyclopedia.'" John Cole, ed., August. Prepared for May 1999 mailing of the Computer Science and Telecommunications Board, National Research Council, Washington, D.C.

Digital Talking Book Standards Committee. 1998. National Information Standards Organization, December 10.

Peter D. Hart Research Associates, Inc. 1998. *Key Findings from a Nationwide Survey Conducted for the Library of Congress by Peter D. Hart Research Associates.* Set of three presentations about Survey Study #5241 and a slide presentation. Washington, D.C.: Peter D. Hart Research Associates, Inc.

Research Applications, Inc. 1998. *Survey of Employees of the Library of Congress—Report of Results.* Rockville, Md.: Research Applications, Inc., June.

Troy Systems, Inc. 1997. *Final Library of Congress ITS Data Center Risk Assessment Report.* Prepared for the Library of Congress by Troy Systems, Fairfax, Va., April 16.

WheelGroup Corporation. 1998. "Security Design Review and Evaluation of the Library of Congress Network Architecture." Report for the Library of Congress, Washington, D.C.

Wynn, Albert R. 1999. Letter from Albert R. Wynn, U.S. House of Representatives, to James H. Billington, Library of Congress, Washington, D.C., July 12.

Appendixes

A

Biographies of
Committee Members

JAMES J. O'DONNELL, *Chair*, combines expertise in managing a large university computing facility with his academic credentials as a scholar of classical studies. He provides a unique perspective that incorporates an understanding of the collections and mission of the Library of Congress with real-world experience as the vice-provost for information systems and computing at the University of Pennsylvania. He is well recognized as an innovator in the use of information technology in education, a pioneer in electronic publishing, and a strong promoter of the use of computers and networks to support all aspects of the university environment. He chaired the University of Pennsylvania's Task Force to Restructure Computing, which brought about major operational changes in the way computing services were made available on campus. As the vice-provost for information systems and computing, he is responsible for providing the university's technology infrastructure, data administration, systems security, and services to users, as well as developing hardware and software standards for the university. Dr. O'Donnell is the coeditor of *NewJour*, an online index of new electronic journals, and the author of many articles on electronic publishing and teaching with technology; these include "Cost and Value in Electronic Publishing," "Thinking Strategically About Electronic Publishing," "Teaching with Technology and with Students," and "New Tools for Teaching." His book *Avatars of the Word: From Papyrus to Cyberspace* was published in 1998. Dr. O'Donnell received his B.A. from Princeton University in 1972 and his Ph.D. from Yale University in 1975. He received a National Endowment for the Humanities

Fellowship in 1989 and a Guggenheim Fellowship in 1990. Dr. O'Donnell also is the author of articles and several books on the classics and continues to teach classical studies at the University of Pennsylvania. Before his tenure at the University of Pennsylvania, he was on the faculty of Cornell University, Catholic University of America, and Bryn Mawr College.

JAMES BLACKABY has developed collections management programs for the National Trust for Historic Preservation, the Hirshhorn Museum and Sculpture Garden, Historic Hudson Valley, the National Museum of African Art, the Society for the Preservation of New England Antiquities, the Wolfsonian Foundation, and several smaller sites. Mr. Blackaby has worked on a number of extensive imaging projects, including databases for photographic archives at the Smithsonian's African Art Museum and the United States Holocaust Memorial Museum (which offer online access to imagery). Mr. Blackaby has also worked on collections systems that are connected to image databases such as the joint project developed by the Walker Art Center and the Minneapolis Institute of Arts called ArtsConnectEd. He has worked on such Web-based education projects as the Wexner Learning Center of the United States Holocaust Memorial Museum and a children's program for the National Institute of Conservation's Save Outdoor Sculpture program, as well as Internet projects at the Holocaust Museum, the Walker Art Center, and other institutions. Mr. Blackaby's work with the Society for the Preservation of New England Antiquities (SPNEA) over the past 8 years has included projects intended to provide Internet access to the SPNEA's historic properties with walk-through tours, the ability to view details in rooms, a way to compare historic views with modern interpretations, and a mechanism to deliver oral histories. In part, the SPNEA project is spurred by an interest in making its properties accessible to the handicapped through alternative delivery systems. Following through on work at WGBH and working with Microsoft's Accessibility office, Mr. Blackaby has been exploring the use of technology with physically disabled audiences. He completed his B.A. and attended graduate school at the University of Oregon. He serves currently as director of Internet strategies and information services at Mystic Seaport Museum.

ROSS E. BROWN joined Analog Devices on May 10, 1993, as vice president for human resources. He reports to Jerry Fishman, the president and chief executive officer, and is accountable for the management of Analog's worldwide human resources organization. Before joining Analog Devices, Mr. Brown was employed by the Digital Equipment Corporation (DEC) for 11 years. During his career at DEC, he held several positions of progressive responsibility within the human resources organization. In his last position at DEC, Mr. Brown functioned as the director of human resources for the United States. Before joining DEC in 1982, he held various positions within the human resources organizations at Siemens-Allis, Inc., Allis Chalmers Corporation, the Miller Brewing Company, and the General Motors Corporation. He holds a B.S. in political science from Lincoln University of Missouri and a J.D. from the Detroit College of Law at Michigan State University.

GINNIE COOPER has been the director of libraries for the Multnomah County Library in Portland, Oregon, since April 1990. She is the former director of Alameda County Library in Fremont, California, and, earlier, the Kenosha Public Library in Kenosha, Wisconsin. Ms. Cooper has also held positions with the University of Minnesota Medical School, the Washington County Library in Minnesota, the Federal Bureau of Indian Affairs, and the St. Paul Public Schools. She has 28 years of experience in the library profession. She is a former president of the Public Library Association, a division of the American Library Association, and served as an elected member of the governing council of the American Library Association and on the Board of the Urban Library Council. A graduate of South Dakota State University (English and speech education), Ms. Cooper holds an M.A. in Library Science from the University of Minnesota.

DALE FLECKER, associate director for planning and systems at the Harvard University Library, has contributed and/or participated in several research projects and library-related committees. He has been active in the Digital Library Federation and now serves as chairman of the federation's Architecture Committee. Mr. Flecker received a Ph.B. with a concentration in history from Wayne State University in 1965. In 1978, he received an M.A. in library science from the University of Michigan. At the Harvard University Library, Mr. Flecker is responsible for leadership and planning for library-wide information systems. He is extensively involved in planning and implementing information technology campuswide. The department (21 full-time employees and a $3.7-million budget in FY98) is responsible for the development and operation of automated systems for the Harvard libraries. Mr. Flecker initiated, planned, and managed successive phases of development of the HOLLIS system, a basic tool in most areas of library operations. He is a member of the administrative council of the Harvard University Library and represents Harvard at national meetings (Association of Research Libraries, Center for Research Libraries, Council on Library Resources, OCLC research libraries, Coalition for Networked Information, Digital Library Federation).

Mr. Flecker is also extensively involved in the regional and national development of automated library networks (NELINET, OCLC).

NANCY FRISHBERG is the executive director of New Media Centers, a nonprofit consortium of higher education institutions and corporations promoting teaching and learning using new media products and solutions. Dr. Frishberg brings experience from information technology, higher education, and nonprofit organizations to the New Media Centers. At Apple Computer, she supported Newton OS licensing partners in their engineering efforts. At IBM, she held positions in academic marketing, applied research management, and user interface research. Her consulting clients have included government agencies and arts organizations as well as education and business organizations. She earned her doctorate in linguistics from the University of California at San Diego and has held academic appointments at the Rochester Institute of Technology (Rochester, New York), Hampshire College (Amherst, Massachusetts), and New York University (New York City). Dr. Frishberg has served on the technology team of the San Carlos Charter Learning Center, as cochair of demonstrations at CHI'98 (in Los Angeles), on the executive council of the Association of Computers and the Humanities, on the Board of the Association for Software Design, and on the Educational Standards Committee of the Conference of Interpreter Trainers. Over the past 3 years, she has produced and hosted seven video teleconferences focusing on uses of and support for new media technologies in training and education. Her research interests include user interfaces for interactive media, the linguistic structure of sign languages, and human-computer interfaces for sign languages and sign language users.

JAMES GRAY is a specialist in database and transaction processing computer systems at Microsoft Corporation. His research focuses on scaleable computing: building superservers and workgroup systems from commodity software and hardware. Before joining Microsoft, he worked at Digital, Tandem, IBM, and AT&T on database and transaction processing systems, including RDB, ACMS, NonstopSQL, Pathway, System R, SQL/DS, DB2, and IMS-Fast Path. He is editor of the *Performance Handbook for Database and Transaction Processing Systems* and coauthor of *Transaction Processing Concepts and Techniques*. He is a member of the National Academy of Engineering, a fellow of the Association for Computing Machinery (ACM), a member of the President's Information Technology Advisory Committee, a trustee of the VLDB Foundation, and editor of the Morgan Kaufmann series on data management. He has been a McKay Fellow at the University of California at Berkeley. His current activities include research on fault-tolerant, parallel, and distributed database systems. Dr. Gray received his Ph.D. in computer science (1969) from the University of California at Berkeley. He is a former member of the Computer Science and Telecommunications Board (CSTB), and he also served on the CSTB committee that produced *Computing the Future* in 1992. In 1998, Dr. Gray won the ACM's Turing Award.

MARGARET HEDSTROM is an associate professor in the School of Information at the University of Michigan, where she teaches in the areas of archives, electronic records management, and digital preservation. Before joining the faculty at Michigan in 1995, she worked for 10 years at the New York State Archives and Records Administration, where she was chief of state records advisory services and director of the Center for Electronic Records. Dr. Hedstrom earned master's degrees in library science and history and a Ph.D. in history from the University of Wisconsin at Madison. She wrote a dissertation on the history of office automation in the 1950s and 1960s. She is a fellow of the Society of American Archivists and was the first recipient of the annual Award for Excellence in New York State Government Information Services. Dr. Hedstrom is widely published on various aspects of archival management, electronic records, and preservation in digital environments and has served as a consultant to many government archival programs. Her current research interests include digital preservation strategies, the impact of electronic communications on organizational memory and documentation, and remote access to archival materials.

CARL LAGOZE is a digital library scientist in the Computer Science Department at Cornell University. In that capacity, he leads a number of digital library research efforts in the department and across the university, collaborating with the university library and the Office of Information Technology. Mr. Lagoze's research is funded through a number of National Science Foundation and Defense Advanced Research Projects Agency grants and, most notably, a major grant from the multiagency Digital Libraries Initiative Phase 2. In general, this research can be characterized as investigations into the technical and organizational issues in the development and administration of distributed digital libraries. The recent focus of this research is on policy: What are the policies that need to be asserted to ensure the reliability, security, and preservation of content and services in distributed digital libraries, and what are the mechanisms for enforcing those policies? Mr. Lagoze is the coinventor of Dienst, a widely deployed protocol and architecture for distributed document libraries. He is also the coauthor of the Warwick Framework, a modular metadata model for digital content, which is a conceptual basis for the Resource Description Framework (RDF), now a World Wide Web metadata standard. Mr. Lagoze's professional activities include serving on the advisory committee of the Dublin Core Metadata Initiative, serving on the program committee of U.S. and international digital library conferences, and giving numerous talks here and abroad on his research on metadata and digital library architecture.

LAWRENCE H. LANDWEBER is the John P. Morgridge Professor of Computer Science at the University of Wisconsin at Madison. He has served as chair of the University of Wisconsin Computer Science Department, as chairman of the board, president, and vice president of education of the Internet Society, as chair of the Internet2 Advisory Committee, and as a member of board of the University Corporation for Advanced Internet Development. He has also been on the board of the Computer Research Association and is a fellow of the Association for Computing Machinery (ACM). For 20 years, Dr. Landweber has contributed to the development of the global Internet. His networking activities included TheoryNet (1977), an early electronic mail system; CSNET (1980-1985), a network for U.S. computer research groups that served as an early test of the Internet concept; the Gigabit Project (1990-1995), a high-speed network testbed for experimenting with new protocols; and projects that helped establish the first Internet gateways between the United States and countries in Europe and Asia in the 1980s. He was an advisor to the National Science Foundation during the development of the NSFNET, the first national Internet backbone. He received a B.S. in mathematics from Brooklyn College and a Ph.D. in computer science from Purdue University.

DAVID M. LEVY is a visiting professor at the University of Washington. Previously, Dr. Levy was a research scientist at the Xerox Palo Alto Research Center (PARC), where he conducted research on document design, use and reuse, structure, systems, and standards, beginning in 1984. During his tenure there, he served as assistant laboratory manager in the Systems Sciences Laboratory and as area manager for the Foundations of Documents Area. Before PARC, Dr. Levy was a software designer and manager at Symantec Corporation and a computer consultant. A graduate of Dartmouth College (1971), he earned his M.S. (1972) and Ph.D. (1979) in computer science at Stanford University and also holds the Diploma in Calligraphy and Bookbinding (1982) from the Roehampton Institute. Dr. Levy's professional activities include service as the conference chair for the Digital Libraries 1995 conference and on the program committee for the past five Digital Libraries conferences. His current book (in preparation) is entitled *Scrolling Forward: Making Sense of Documents in a Digital Age.*

ANN OKERSON has served as an associate university librarian at Yale University since September 1995. She came to Yale with an extensive background in academic library and management experience, especially in collections development and serials. She has also served as senior program officer for the Association of Research Libraries (ARL). There, she was director of the Office of Scientific and Academic Publishing, where her responsibilities included coordinating the association's activities in monitoring scholarly communications and scholarly publishing. Her publications include the synopsis chapter for the Andrew W. Mellon Study of University Libraries and Scholarly Communication (11/92); five editions of the standard Directory of Electronic Journals, Newsletters and Academic Discussion Lists (1991-1995); and four electronic networked publishing symposia organized on behalf of the ARL and the Association of American University Presses (for which she also edited three volumes of proceedings). In 1997, with funding from the Council on Library Resources/Commission on Preservation and Access, Ms. Okerson and other Yale library staff mounted an online educational resource about library licensing of electronic content in a project called Liblicense. Its extensive annotations and links are complemented by Liblicense-l, a moderated online discussion list frequented by over 2,000 librarians, publishers, and attorneys.

DOUG ROWAN has served as chief executive officer of interLane Media, a company providing a new publishing medium to supermarkets and other retail venues, since August 1998. Since June 1997, he has also served as the president and chief executive officer of Imaging Solutions, Inc., a consulting services company. From April 1994 until June 1997, he was the president and chief executive officer of Corbis, a company owned by Bill Gates. At Corbis, Rowan oversaw the acquisition of the Bettmann Archive, established the Corbis brand, and migrated the Corbis business from off-line CD-ROMs to the current Corbis Web site. He also led the building of one of the world's largest and most comprehensive digital libraries. Previously, he held senior management positions at Ungermann-Bass, Ampex, AXS, and MASSCOMP. Rowan started his career in 1962 and spent 22 years at IBM. He earned his undergraduate degree in electrical engineering from Cornell University, where he also received an M.B.A. in business administration.

JEROME H. SALTZER received the degrees of S.B. (1961), S.M. (1963), and Sc.D. (1966) from the Massachusetts Institute of Technology (MIT), all in electrical engineering. Since 1966, he has been a faculty member of the Department of Electrical Engineering and Computer Science at MIT, where he helped formulate the undergraduate curriculum in computer science and developed the core subject on the engineering of computer systems. At the MIT Laboratory for Computer Science, he developed RUNOFF, the ancestor of most typesetting formatters. It, together with the context editor TYPSET, constituted one of the first widely used word-processing systems. He participated in the refinement of the Compatible Time-Sharing System (CTSS) and was involved in all aspects of the design and implementation of the Multiplexed Information and Computing Service (Multics), including the design of the first kernel thread package, the first time-of-century clock, and, in the early 1970s, a project to develop what would today be known as a microkernel. Together with David Clark and David Reed, he articulated the end-to-end argument, a key organizing principle of the Internet. More recently, his research activities have involved designing a token-passing ring local area network, networking personal computers, and designing the electronic library of the future. From 1984 through 1988, he was technical director of MIT's Project Athena, a system for undergraduate education comprising networked engineering workstations and probably the first successful implementation of the network computer. Throughout this work, he has had a particular interest in the impact of computer systems on society, especially on privacy and the risks of depending on fragile technology. In September 1995, Professor Saltzer retired from the full-time faculty. He continues to write and teach about computer systems part-time from his MIT office. Professor Saltzer also dabbles in art history, particularly nineteenth century art of the western United States. He is preparing a catalog of the paintings of Frederick Ferdinand Schafer and is always happy to receive information about either the artist or his paintings. Professor Saltzer is a member of the National Academy of Engineering, a fellow of the Institute of Electrical and Electronics Engineers (IEEE) and the American Association for the Advancement of Science (AAAS), a member of the Association for Computing Machinery (ACM), Sigma Xi, Eta Kappa Nu, and Tau Beta Pi, a former member of the Computer Science and Telecommunications Board of the National Research Council, and a member of the Mayor's Telecommunications Advisory Board for the city of Newton, Massachusetts.

HOWARD TURTLE has extensive experience with information retrieval system design, evaluation, and operation. He is currently the president of CogiTech Group in Jackson, Wyoming, a technical consulting firm that specializes in information retrieval system design and evaluation, technology assessment, and intellectual property protection. From 1990 to 1998, Dr. Turtle was chief scientist and principal research scientist at West Publishing Co., where he conducted and directed research in support of new information retrieval, text management, and text classification technologies and managed the transfer of technology from research into new products. Before that, he was at the Online Computer Library Center (OCLC) for 10 years as a research scientist, senior research scientist, director of technical planning, and, for his last 2 years, chief scientist. Dr. Turtle designed and implemented retrieval software and served as the technical lead of the effort to redesign the entire OCLC system. During this period, he remained active in research in such areas as analyzing user behavior with interactive systems and supporting electronic delivery of full-text journal articles in their original typeset form. Dr. Turtle also represented OCLC in several technical standards groups. Earlier in his career, he was a research scientist at Battelle Columbus Laboratories, where he designed and implemented software for the BASIS information retrieval system. He received his B.A. from the University of Wisconsin in 1971, his M.S. in computer science from the University of Wisconsin in 1975, and his Ph.D. in computer science from the University of Massachusetts in 1991. He is the author of a number of articles on text retrieval and holds several patents on retrieval techniques. He is the vice chair of SIGIR and served as a member of the board of directors of the National Information Standards Organization (under the Platform for Privacy Preferences Initiative).

MARY ELLEN ZURKO is a security software architect at Iris Associates, currently in charge of security for active content. Previously, she was a member of the small team that designed and developed the first freeware reference implementation of the Internet Engineering Task Force (IETF) Public Key Infrastructure X.509 (PKIX) standards, called Jonah. As a senior research fellow at the Open Group Research Institute, she led several innovative security initiatives in authorization policies, languages, and mechanisms that incorporate user-centered design elements. The Authorization for Distributed Applications and Groups (Adage) project produced a modular, distributed, user-centered authorization solution that became a DARPA deployment follow-on project, Pledge. With one other teammate, she designed and developed DCE Web, which provided DCE confidentiality, authentication, and authorization to Web transactions through unmodified Web browsers. Ms. Zurko received her S.B. and S.M. degrees from the Massachusetts Institute of Technology. She has published papers on all her work, including an award-winning paper on an (A1-target) secure virtual machine monitor and influential papers on user-centered security and separation of duty in role-based environments. She is an associate editor of *Cipher* (the electronic newsletter of the Institute of Electrical and Electronics Engineers (IEEE) Computer Society's Technical Committee on Security and Privacy) and a regular contributor. She is a member of the International World Wide Web Conference Committee (IW3C2), which organizes the premier international World Wide Web conference series, and is currently serving as general chair of New Security Paradigms Workshop. She is active in the Agent Systems/Mobile Agents Symposium, the Symposium on Applications and the Internet, and was previously chair of the World Wide Web Consortium (W3C) working group for privacy preferences language under the Platform for Privacy Preferences Initiative.

B

BRIEFERS AT PLENARY MEETINGS AND SITE VISITS

JANUARY 21, 1999

James Billington, Office of the Librarian, Library of Congress
Jo Ann Jenkins, Office of the Librarian, Library of Congress
Donald Scott, Office of the Librarian, Library of Congress
Virginia Sorkin, Office of the Librarian, Library of Congress
Members of the Executive Committee and Senior Management
    Reporting Group

FEBRUARY 18-19, 1999

Herbert S. Becker, Information Technology Services, Library of
    Congress
James Billington, Office of the Librarian, Library of Congress
Michael Burke, U.S. Copyright Office, Library of Congress
Laura Campbell, National Digital Library Program, Library of Congress
Clifford Cohen, Library Services, Library of Congress
Jeffrey Griffith, Congressional Research Service, Library of Congress
Janice Hyde, Law Library, Library of Congress
Jo Ann Jenkins, Office of the Librarian, Library of Congress
Rubens Medina, Law Library, Library of Congress
Louis Mortimer, U.S. Copyright Office, Library of Congress
Daniel P. Mulhollan, Congressional Research Service, Library of
    Congress

Marybeth Peters, U.S. Copyright Office, Library of Congress
Kent Ronhovde, Congressional Research Service, Library of Congress
Donald Scott, Office of the Librarian, Library of Congress
Judy Stork, Information Technology Services, Library of Congress
Winston Tabb, Library Services, Library of Congress
Barbara Tillett, Library Services/Integrated Library System, Library of
     Congress
Margaret Whitlock, Law Library, Library of Congress
Bob Zich, National Digital Library Program, Library of Congress

APRIL 12-13, 1999

Martha Anderson, National Digital Library Program, Library of
     Congress
Ardie Bausenbach, Library Services, Library of Congress
Sam Brylawski, Motion Picture, Broadcasting, and Recorded Sound
     Division, Library of Congress
Michael Burke, U.S. Copyright Office, Library of Congress
Laura Campbell, National Digital Library Program, Library of Congress
David Carson, U.S. Copyright Office, Library of Congress
Rose Marie Clemandot, Law Library, Library of Congress
Martha Dexter, Congressional Research Service, Library of Congress
Robert Gee, Law Library, Library of Congress
Jeffrey Griffith, Congressional Research Service, Library of Congress
Kevin Holland, Congressional Research Service, Library of Congress
Janice Hyde, Law Library, Library of Congress
Mary Isons, Prints and Photographs Division, Library of Congress
Marvin Kranz, Manuscript Division, Library of Congress
Diane Kresh, Preservation Directorate, Library of Congress
Elizabeth Mangan, Geography and Map Division, Library of Congress
Basil Manns, Preservation Directorate, Library of Congress
Sally McCallum, Library Services, Library of Congress
Lyle Minter, Serial and Government Publications Division, Library of
     Congress
Louis Mortimer, U.S. Copyright Office, Library of Congress
Barbara Natanson, Prints and Photographs Division, Library of
     Congress
Nanette Petruzzelli, U.S. Copyright Office, Library of Congress
Dominique Pickett, National Digital Library Program, Library of
     Congress
Jewel Player, U.S. Copyright Office, Library of Congress
Karen Renninger, Serial and Government Publications Division, Library
     of Congress

Gene Roberts, Geography and Map Division, Library of Congress
Kent Ronhovde, Congressional Research Service, Library of Congress
Chandru Shahani, Preservation Directorate, Library of Congress
Mark Sweeney, Serial and Government Publications Division, Library of
    Congress
Winston Tabb, Library Services, Library of Congress
Susan Veccia, National Digital Library Program, Library of Congress
Mary Wolfskill, Manuscript Division, Library of Congress

APRIL 21-22, 1999

David Albee, Office of Human Resources, Library of Congress
Maryle Ashley, Information Technology Services, Library of Congress
Alvert (Al) Banks, Information Technology Services, Library of
    Congress
Herbert S. Becker, Information Technology Services, Library of
    Congress
Dwight Beeson, Information Technology Services, Library of Congress
Ben Benitez, Office of Human Resources, Library of Congress
James Bradford, AFSCME 2477, Library of Congress
Laura Campbell, National Digital Library Program, Library of Congress
Janet Chou, Information Technology Services, Library of Congress
Cliff Cohen, Library Services, Library of Congress
Beth Dulabahn, Library Services, Library of Congress
Mary Ferrarese, AFSCME 2910, Library of Congress
Jeffrey Griffith, Congressional Research Service, Library of Congress
Mike Handy, Information Technology Services, Library of Congress
Dennis Hanratty, Office of Human Resources, Library of Congress
Sue Hayduchok, Automation Planning and Liaison Office, Library of
    Congress
Lafayette Johnson, Information Technology Services, Library of
    Congress
Tom Lambert, Planning, Management, and Evaluation Directorate,
    Library of Congress
Jane Mandelbaum, Information Technology Services, Library of
    Congress
Deanna Marcum, Council on Library and Information Resources
Rubens Medina, Law Library, Library of Congress
Carole Mumford, Information Technology Services, Library of Congress
Marybeth Peters, U.S. Copyright Office, Library of Congress
Lou Pizzoli, Information Technology Services, Library of Congress
Elizabeth Pugh, Office of the General Counsel, Library of Congress

Dennis Roth, Congressional Research Employees Association, Library of
    Congress
Jerry Saunders, Information Technology Services, Library of Congress
Donald Scott, Office of the Librarian, Library of Congress
Robert Stoebe, Planning, Management, and Evaluation Directorate,
    Library of Congress
Judy Stork, Information Technology Services, Library of Congress
Andre Whisenton, Office of Human Resources, Library of Congress

APRIL 22-23, 1999

Maryle Ashley, Information Technology Services, Library of Congress
Alvert (Al) Banks, Information Technology Services, Library of
    Congress
Herbert S. Becker, Information Technology Services, Library of
    Congress
Dwight Beeson, Information Technology Services, Library of Congress
Ann Christy, Information Technology Services, Library of Congress
Shirley Chu, Information Technology Services, Library of Congress
Rich Genter, Information Technology Services, Library of Congress
Mike Handy, Information Technology Services, Library of Congress
Dennis Hanratty, Office of Human Resources, Library of Congress
Sue Hayduchok, Automation Planning and Liaison Office, Library of
    Congress
Kevin Holland, Congressional Research Service, Library of Congress
Tom Littlejohn, Information Technology Services, Library of Congress
Jane Mandelbaum, Information Technology Services, Library of
    Congress
Henry Rossman, Congressional Research Service, Library of Congress
George Sadusk, Information Technology Services, Library of Congress
Judy Stork, Information Technology Services, Library of Congress

APRIL 26, 1999

Martha Dexter, Congressional Research Service, Library of Congress

APRIL 29-30, 1999

Jill Brett, Public Affairs Office, Library of Congress
John Celli, Cataloging in Publication Division, Library of Congress
Kurt Cylke, National Library Service for the Blind and Physically
    Handicapped, Library of Congress
Angela Evans, Congressional Research Service, Library of Congress

Charles Fenly, Cataloging in Publication Division, Library of Congress
Prosser Gifford, Office of Scholarly Programs, Library of Congress
Ron Grim, Geography and Map Division, Library of Congress
Diane Kresh, Preservation Directorate, Library of Congress
Guy Lamolinara, Public Affairs Office, Library of Congress
Sandy Lawson, Photo Duplication Service, Library of Congress
Ellen Lazarus, Congressional Research Service, Library of Congress
Pat Loughney, Motion Picture, Broadcasting and Recorded Sound
    Division, Library of Congress
Bob McDermott, National Library Service for the Blind and Physically
    Handicapped, Library of Congress
Michael Moody, National Library Service for the Blind and Physically
    Handicapped, Library of Congress
Karen Renninger, Serial and Government Publications Division, Library
    of Congress
John Sayers, Public Affairs Office, Library of Congress
Royal Shipp, Congressional Research Service, Library of Congress
Winston Tabb, Library Services, Library of Congress
Barbara Tillett, Library Services/Integrated Library System, Library of
    Congress
Beacher Wiggins, Cataloging Directorate, Library of Congress
David Williamson, Cataloging in Publication Division, Library of
    Congress

MAY 21, 1999

Dan Arbour, ProQuest (formerly Bell and Howell Information and
    Learning Systems or UMI)
Jeffrey Meyer, ProQuest (formerly Bell and Howell Information and
    Learning Systems or UMI)

MAY 26-27, 1999

David Allison, National Museum of American History, Smithsonian
    Institution
William Arms, Corporation for National Research Initiatives
Herbert S. Becker, Information Technology Services, Library of
    Congress
Laura Campbell, National Digital Library Program, Library of Congress
Betsy Humphreys, National Library of Medicine
Joe Hutchins, National Library of Medicine
Mary Levering, U.S. Copyright Office, Library of Congress
Kent Smith, National Library of Medicine

Roy Standing, National Library of Medicine
Judy Stork, Information Technology Services, Library of Congress
Winston Tabb, Library Services, Library of Congress

JULY 23, 1999

Kathryn Mendenhall, Cataloging Distribution Service, Library of
    Congress
Peter Young, Cataloging Distribution Service, Library of Congress

JULY 27-28, 1999

James Bradford, AFSCME 2477, Library of Congress
Nancy Davenport, Acquisitions Directorate, Library of Congress
Natalie Gawdiak, Law Library, Library of Congress
Vern Gehris, Fraternal Order of Police, Library of Congress
LaTanya Hawkins, AFSCME 2477, Library of Congress
Charles Howell, Committee on House Administration
Ed Lombard, House Committee on Appropriations, Subcommittee on
    Legislative Appropriations
Marybeth Peters, U.S. Copyright Office, Library of Congress
David Sale, Law Library, Library of Congress
Margaret Smith, Acquisitions Directorate, Library of Congress
Teresa Smith, Office of Human Resources, Library of Congress
Charles Stanhope, Office of the Librarian, Library of Congress
Fern Underdue, Office of the Librarian, Library of Congress
John Webster, Financial Services, Library of Congress
Kathy Williams, Financial Services, Library of Congress
Grayson Winterling, Rooney Group International
Karen Wood, Office of the Librarian, Library of Congress
Harry Yee, Labor/Management Relations, Library of Congress

JULY 29-30, 1999

Thomas Bland, U.S. Copyright Office, Library of Congress
Michael Burke, U.S. Copyright Office, Library of Congress
Melissa Dadant, U.S. Copyright Office, Library of Congress
Thomas Felt, U.S. Copyright Office, Library of Congress
Natalia Montviloff, Library Services, Library of Congress
Susan Morris, Library Services, Library of Congress
Kim Robinson, U.S. Copyright Office, Library of Congress
Jackie Sansom, Library Services, Library of Congress
Susan Vita, Library Services, Library of Congress

Tom Yee, Library Services, Library of Congress
Stephen Yusko, Library Services, Library of Congress

AUGUST 9-10, 1999

Michael Burke, U.S. Copyright Office, Library of Congress
Victor Holmes, U.S. Copyright Office, Library of Congress
Elmer Klebs, Library Services, Library of Congress
Cynthia Maxwell, U.S. Copyright Office, Library of Congress
Tom Skallerup, U.S. Copyright Office, Library of Congress

SEPTEMBER 15-17, 1999

Elise Darwish, Educational Consultant
Paul Goldstein, Stanford University
Sam Gustman, Survivors of the Shoah Visual History Foundation
Per-Kristian Halvorsen, Xerox PARC
Marlita Kahn, Internet Archive
Michael Keller, Stanford University and Highwire Press
Catherine Marshall, FX Palo Alto Laboratory
James Michalko, Research Libraries Group
Don Muccino, Online Computer Library Center
Pamela Samuelson, University of California at Berkeley
Bob St. Clair, Corbis

OCTOBER 7, 1999

James Billington, Office of the Librarian, Library of Congress
Jo Ann Jenkins, Office of the Librarian, Library of Congress

JANUARY 10, 2000

Michael Albin, Library Services, Library of Congress
Herbert S. Becker, Information Technology Services, Library of
    Congress
Cliff Cohen, Library Services, Library of Congress
Nancy Davenport, Acquisitions Directorate, Library of Congress
Bob Dizard, Congressional Relations Office, Library of Congress
Dennis Hanratty, Office of Human Resources, Library of Congress
Tom Littlejohn, Information Technology Services, Library of Congress
Donald Scott, Office of the Librarian, Library of Congress
Lolita Silva, Library Services, Library of Congress
Teri Smith, Human Resources Services, Library of Congress

Barbara Tillett, Library Services/Integrated Library System, Library of
    Congress
John Webster, Financial Services, Library of Congress
Kathy Williams, Financial Services, Library of Congress
Harry Yee, Labor/Management Relations, Library of Congress

MARCH 15, 2000

Thomas Bryant, Planning, Management, and Evaluation Directorate,
    Library of Congress

MAY 4, 2000

Michael D. Burke, U.S. Copyright Office, Library of Congress
David Ely, NXT Corporation
Robert Kahn, Corporation for National Research Initiatives
Larry Lannom, Corporation for National Research Initiatives

MAY 24, 2000

Michael D. Burke, U.S. Copyright Office, Library of Congress
Mary Levering, U.S. Copyright Office, Library of Congress

JUNE 8, 2000

James Browning, Internal University, Library of Congress
Judith Cannan, Technical Processing and Automation Planning Office,
    Library of Congress
Nila Iwaskiw, Internal University, Library of Congress

C

LIST OF LETTERS RECEIVED

Association of American Publishers,
Patricia Schroeder

Association of American University Presses,
Peter Givler

Association for Research Libraries,
Duane Webster

Congressional Research Employees Association,
Dennis Roth

Council on Library and Information Resources,
Deanna Marcum

D

ACRONYMS

AACR	Anglo-American Cataloging Rules
ACM	Association for Computing Machinery
AHA	American Historical Association
A&LD	Arts and Letters Daily
AMS	American Mathematical Society
ANSI	American National Standards Institute
ARL	Association of Research Libraries
ASCII	American Standard Code for Information Interface
ATM	asynchronous transfer mode
CCF	circulation control facility
CD-ROM	compact disk read-only memory
CDS	Cataloging Distribution Service
CEO	chief executive officer
CIC	Committee on Institutional Cooperation
CIO	chief information officer
CIP	Cataloging in Publication
CLIR	Council on Library and Information Resources
CNRI	Corporation for National Research Initiatives
COINS	Copyright Office In-Process System
COPICS	Copyright Office Publication and Interactive Cataloging System
CORC	Cooperative Online Resource Cataloging project

CORDS   Copyright Office Electronic Registration, Recordation, and
                Deposit System
CPSO   Cataloging Policy and Support Office
CRS   Congressional Research Service
CSDGM   Content Standards for Digital Geospatial Metadata
CSTB   Computer Science and Telecommunications Board

DARPA   Defense Advanced Research Projects Agency
DCES   Dublin Core Element Set
DCMI   Dublin Core Metadata Initiative
DFG   Digital Futures Group
DOE   U.S. Department of Energy
DTD   document type definition

EAD   encoded archival description
ECIP   Electronic Cataloging in Publication
EDI   electronic data interchange

FCC   Federal Communications Commission
FGDC   U.S. Federal Geographic Data Committee
FRBR   functional requirements for bibliographic records
FTE   full-time equivalent
FTP   file transfer protocol

GIF   graphics interchange format
GIS   geographical information system
GLIN   Global Legal Information Network
GPO   U.S. Government Printing Office

HR   human resources
HRS   Human Resources Services (directorate)
HTML   hypertext markup language
HTTP   hypertext transfer protocol

IATH   Institute for Advanced Technology in the Humanities
IFLA   International Federation of Library Associations
ILS   Integrated Library System
IP   intellectual property
IR   information retrieval
ISBN   International Standard Book Number
ISIS   Inquiry Status Information System
ISO   International Organization for Standardization
ISSN   International Standard Serial Number

ITS	Information Technology Services (directorate)
ITVSRP	information technology vision, strategy, research, and planning group
K-12	kindergarten through grade 12
LC	Library of Congress
LHNCBC	Lister Hill National Center for Biomedical Communications
LIS	Legislative Information System
LOCIS	Library of Congress Information System
MARC	machine-readable cataloging
MEDLINE	index of online medical journals and information at the National Library of Medicine
MPAA	Motion Picture Association of America
MUMS	Multiple Use MARC System
NAL	National Agricultural Library
NARA	National Archives and Records Administration
NCBI	National Center for Biotechnology Information
NDL	National Digital Library
NDLP	National Digital Library Program
NEDLIB	Networked European Deposit Library
NEH	National Endowment for the Humanities
NISO	National Information Standards Organization
NIST	U.S. National Institute of Standards and Technology
NLM	National Library of Medicine
NLP	natural language processing
NLSBPH	National Library Service for the Blind and Physically Handicapped
NRC	National Research Council
NSF	National Science Foundation
NTE	not to exceed
NUC	National Union Catalog
OAIS	Open Archival Information System
OCLC	Online Computer Library Center
OD	books on demand
OPAC	online public access catalog
OS	operating system
OSTI	Office of Scientific and Technical Information (in the Department of Energy)

PDF	portable document format
PICS	Platform for Internet Content Selection
PMED	Planning, Management, and Evaluation Directorate
PPBEEES	Planning, Programming, Budgeting, Evaluation, Executing, and Evaluation System
PPLF	Public Policy Literature File
PPOC	Prints and Photographs Online Catalog
R&D	research and development
RDF	resource description framework
RFP	request for proposals
RLG	Research Libraries Group
SCORPIO	Subject Content Oriented Retriever for Processing Information Online
SGML	standard generalized markup language
TAB	technical advisory board
TCP	transmission control protocol
TIFF	tagged image file format
UNIX	Universal Interactive Executive (operating system)
URL	uniform resource locator
URN	universal resource name
W3C	World Wide Web Consortium
XML	extensible markup language
Y2K	year 2000